Ethnic Heritage in North Dakota

Edited with
Introductory Material
by
Francie M. Berg

Published by the Attiyeh Foundation Washington, D.C.

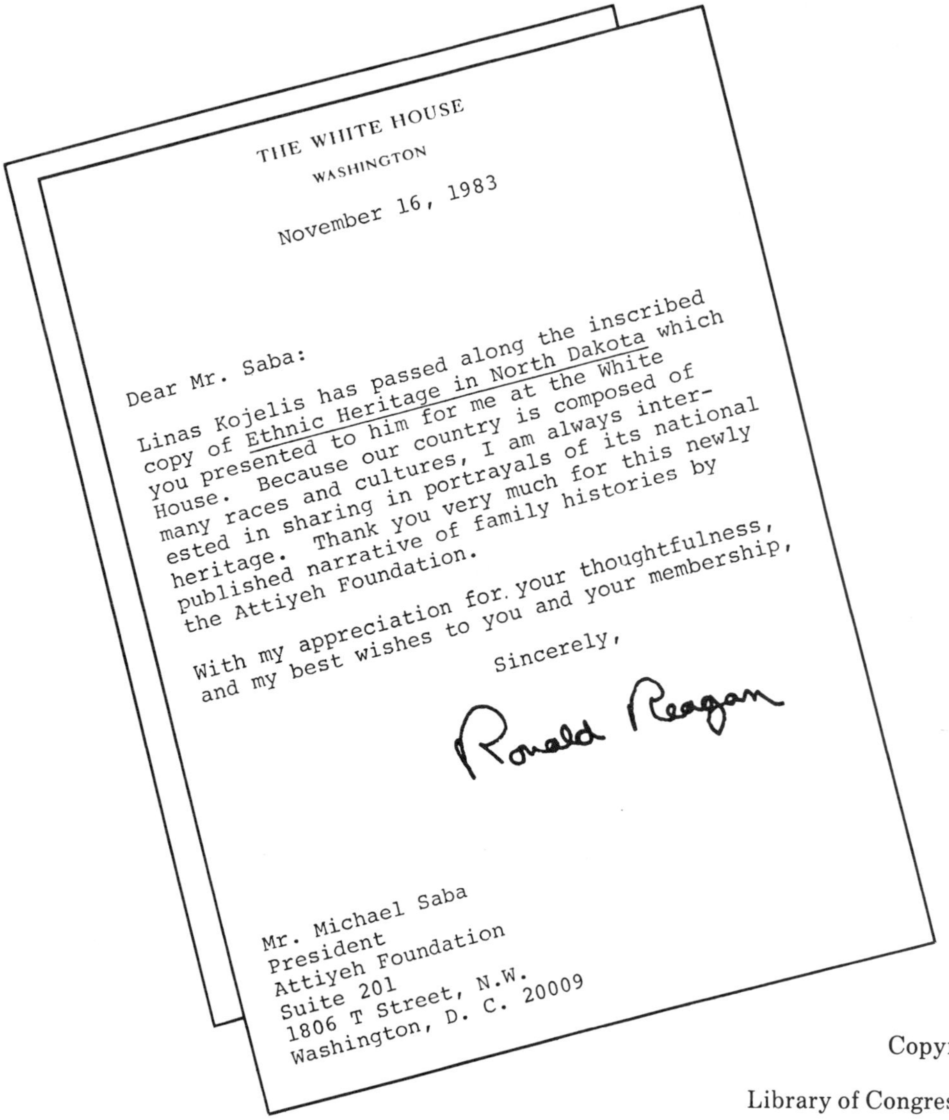

THE WHITE HOUSE
WASHINGTON

November 16, 1983

Dear Mr. Saba:

Linas Kojelis has passed along the inscribed copy of Ethnic Heritage in North Dakota which you presented to him for me at the White House. Because our country is composed of many races and cultures, I am always interested in sharing in portrayals of its national heritage. Thank you very much for this newly published narrative of family histories by the Attiyeh Foundation.

With my appreciation for your thoughtfulness, and my best wishes to you and your membership,

Sincerely,

Ronald Reagan

Mr. Michael Saba
President
Attiyeh Foundation
Suite 201
1806 T Street, N.W.
Washington, D. C. 20009

First printing—1983
Second printing—1984

Library of Congress Catalog Card Number 83-71817
ISBN 0-918532-13-2 hardcover
ISBN 0-918532-14-0 softcover
Published by the Attiyeh Foundation
Washington D.C.
Printed in the United States of America

Distributed by: Flying Diamond Books
Box D301; Hettinger, North Dakota 58639

Children wave American flags at July 4 Attiyeh convention during 1930's.

Introduction

My father, Naif Saba, was twice an immigrant. First, after being born in the Great Plains of the United States, he left North Dakota for Lebanon as a young child to spend the next 15 years in the home of his ancestors. Next, he returned to North Dakota in his early twenties to remake his home on a North Dakota homestead near McClusky.

He taught me pride in Arab American heritage and love for the United States. He shared with me his warm feelings for all the "ethnics" of North Dakota. Whether through his smattering of German or Norwegian and his playful banter with friends in their ancestral languages, or his interest in local Ukrainian dances or Scotch-Irish songs, he passed on to me this love for the mosaic of North Dakota and America.

It is to his memory and to the memory of the heritage of all our grandparents and great-grandparents that we dedicate this book. It was hard work and perseverance that made North Dakota great, but it was our ethnic heritage that gave character to that greatness.

Michael P. Saba
President, Attiyeh Foundation

Kari Sletten of Souris, a native of Norway, spins wool during the Norsk Hostfest in Minot.

Acknowledgment

This book is based on two heritage specials produced by the Bismarck Tribune, "We, the People," published in February 1982, and "North Dakota Indians, A Time of Transition," October 1981. We thank the Bismarck Tribune for permission to reprint from these editions. Special thanks to Sanders Hook, publisher, Charles Walk, editor, George Moore, managing editor, and to the following journalists and photographers from the Tribune: Jack Case, Randy Christianson, Gloria Feickert, Sandra Fettig, Patricia Fix, Marcia Harris, Brooks Hatch, Lucille Hendrickson, Donna Hoffman, Bob Jansen, Larry Johnson, Mark Kinders, Carrie Koski, Rosemary Lynch, Frank Miele, Patrick Miller, Sandy Paraskeva, John Pearson, John Peterson, Ted Quanrud, Vicki Russell, Stan Stelter, Steve Thomas, Greg Turosak, Douglas Van Tassel, Steve Wallick, Kevin Whalen, Abe Winter. We are also grateful to Gus Sorlie of the data processing department and Libby Simes, librarian at the Tribune, for their assistance.

Contents

An ethnic mosaic 7

Cultural traditions 15
- Music 16
- Dancing 24
- Crafts 32
- Food 42
- Celebrations and folklore 52
- Religious institutions 62

Nationalities 77
- American Indian 78
- Norwegian 94
- Swedish 100
- Danish 102
- Finnish 104
- Icelandic 107
- German 110
- German-Hungarian 112
- German-Russian 113
- English/Celtic 120
- French 124
- Dutch 126
- Ukrainian 128
- Czech (Bohemian) 132
- Polish 136
- Arab American 138
- Jewish 142
- Other immigrant groups 143
- Old stock American 144

The immigrant experience 149

Bibliography 169
Credits 171
Index 173

An ethnic mosaic

ıron crosses silhouette against a wide blue sky. A meadowlark, perched atop a tombstone, sings out a liquid melody, and mallards croon and feed together in run-off water at the road's edge. A small white moon lifts high in the afternoon sky forming a halo for the hammered iron angel gaily blowing her Gabriel horn.

German legends on the crosses announce that local folk such as Katharina — geboren im Jahr 1842 and laid to rest "im Gott" in 1907 — walked these wide prairies, fingered winter-cured grasses waving along the fencerow, welcomed other springs of thrusting green grass and mayflower patches, prayed devoutly in this country church, St. Stephens.

The iron crosses are blacksmith-made, pounded out in a fine folk art brought directly here from Catholic Black Sea regions of Russia. They bristle in the graveyards of Czechs, Ukrainians and Germans from Russia and Hungary, and testify to the importance of the church in preserving the ethnic character of this state.

The country church with its graveyard and white spire is a familiar sight across North Dakota. Usually it signals an ethnic community where people of one nationality settled together. It may be the simple white

A country church with its baseball diamond and cemetery marks Norwegian community in midst of rich level farmland.

structure of sturdy Lutheran faith, an eastern-rite Ukrainian style with onion-shaped dome, or an imposing Catholic building. But in every country churchyard, proclaiming whatever culture or faith, a meadowlark is likely singing from a tombstone — the melodious tones carrying clearly through open windows on a Sunday morning — and mallards are rising from the slough.

Immigrants from many countries learned to adapt to what they found here, and put their stamp on the land.

When North Dakota came in as a state in 1889 nearly half the population was foreign born. One-third of these were from Norway. Norwegians have continued to be the dominant nationality in the state, followed by German-Russians, Germans, Canadians and Swedes.

First immigrants were Indian tribes. Modern Indians reach back through dim tribal memory to a time they came here from another place. They pushed and were pushed westward from lake and forest homes as Europeans touched eastern shores. Some came from the south as powerful tribes expanded and populations exploded.

In ancient times other peoples lived here. Ice age hunters killed wooly mammoths and arctic musk oxen with rocks and spears. Through thousands of years plains people came and went with ebb and flow of favorable weather and food supply. Some may have been ancestors of Indian people here today. Or they may have gone off to distant lands in South and Central America.

Mandans were probably first of the modern tribes. They farmed Missouri River bottomlands as early as the 1300s. The Hidatsa and Arikara, also farming tribes, later came to live with them. Forest tribes, Chippewa, Cree and Ojibwa moved across Minnesota and into northeastern Dakota forests. During the 1700s Sioux moved out of Minnesota onto open Dakota plains and took up a nomadic buffalo-hunting way of life.

French trappers and explorers were next to come, in the 1700s, traveling in through Canada, as did English, Scots and other Celtics.

The lure of free land was the catalyst which brought many immigrants to North Dakota. Much homestead land was available here from 1862 through 1910 and later. In addition, more than ten million railroad grant acres were for sale.

Ethnic communities grew up as first comers of one nationality took homesteads together. Relatives and countrymen were encouraged to settle nearby through letters and contacts in American communities of that nationality. Others avoided the locality, knowing they would not be understood. Later as homesteads were proved up, neighbors not of that heritage often sold out to newcomers, sons and cousins of those who were. In this way ethnic communities strengthened and widened their base. Others which began more heterogenously began to readjust and often took on the flavor of one nationality. Again and again in their personal stories, pioneers tell of knowing little of America when they stepped off the boat except the name of one North Dakota town; sometimes the name was pinned to their coats.

Ethnic communities persist today across the state of North Dakota. They have been dipped in the American melting pot, mellowed by intermarriage and modern times. Yet they still show clearly the mosaic pattern which Ole Rolvaag, author of the Norwegian immigrant classic "Giants in the Earth," said was more true of America than was the melting pot theory.

North Dakota ethnic mosaics meld well together, forming brilliant nationality lights at the centers, blending in a less defined way at the edges.

At the shining centers of these mosaics can be identified people from more than 25 nations and culture groups. There are French, Irish, Scotch, Welsh, English, Norwegians, Swedes, Finns, Jews, Polish, Danes, Icelanders, Metis, Sioux, Mandan, Hidatsa, Arikara, Chippewa, Ojibwa, Rumanians, Belgians, Dutch, German-Russians, German-Hungarians, Arab Americans, Germans, Czechs, Canadians, Ukrainians and others including more modern enclaves today of Mexican-Americans, blacks and southeastern Asians.

The North Dakota federal writers project of 1938 gives 42 countries which contributed to the foreign-born population of the state and noted the "patchwork of foreign groups, each still retaining many old world customs of speech, dress and social life."

As late as 1970, 24% of North Dakota's

population was either born on foreign soil or had at least one foreign born parent, compared with a national average of 11%. William Sherman, author of "Prairie Mosaic: An Ethnic Atlas of Rural North Dakota," believes the ethnic makeup of the state will remain much as it is, except perhaps in the larger towns. Towns reflect the nationalities of surrounding communities, he says; land usually stays in the family.

New immigrants still come, on occasion. A nephew from Holland might come to work as hired man, or a niece or third cousin from Norway to help an older couple living alone.

Early bonding for the mosaic was provided by old stock Americans who brought language, laws, educational systems and traditions of independence, democracy and freedom. They gave much of the early leadership which made the state's colorful mosaic work so well.

Canada's influence is and has been significant, too. The Peace Gardens mark 170 years of peace between two countries. They also denote a special bond between Canada

Flags flying over the Peace Gardens symbolize bond between Canada and North Dakota. Friends and relatives settled both sides of the border, now maintain close ties. At left, Chris and Ida Heidt enjoy a cup of coffee with Schnee Balle, a German-Russian favorite of rolled dough, twisted through itself and deep fat fried.

and North Dakota. Many of the state's settlers came from Canada. Immigration went the other way, too, as when a successful promotion by Canada drew away many Dakota families. These people have close friends and relatives on both sides, as do those who farm and ranch the border.

Some nationalities settled above and below the line at the same time. Icelandic settlements in northeastern North Dakota, for example, are bordered by large Icelandic communities in Canada. Belfield Ukrainians regularly attend Ukrainian folk festivals and celebrations in Saskatchewan. Indians traditionally overlook state and national borders and today, as in the past, freely exchange visits with friends and relatives in Canadian reservation communities.

Ethnic communities gave comfort and security to first generation immigrants, caught as they were between the old world and the new. Living among those who spoke the same language, had the same traditions, often came from the same village, meant they could worship as they had before, celebrate the same festivals, get help when they needed it.

Language was invariably difficult. Many, protected by an ethnic community, learned little English in the first generation. Children from these communities often did not speak English when they started school.

Serena Strand in the North Dakota teachers' book, "In Retrospect," recalls teaching in a German-Russian community near Jamestown. "German was the only language in use except when speaking with me," she writes. "The children had had five months in which to forget English and the first school days were difficult for them, for teacher insisted on only English being spoken in school and on the playground." In the same book Matilda Stagel Smith tells of teaching in a community where people spoke their native tongue in the home, church and at all social events. The children didn't like to read as they understood so little, she says, and they couldn't use the dictionary because they couldn't find the words.

Smith says her own parents were proud to have their children speak, read and write Danish, "as no one thought Danish would be replaced by English." In her home church Danish services were held until 1915 when English was used for one Sunday each month, to bring in the younger people. Then it was two Sundays and finally "the switch to English was complete." Many churches continued once-a-month services in the native tongue well after the 1940s.

Churches were probably the single most important factor in maintaining ethnic traditions in North Dakota. Through the church, old traditions continued and ways of celebrating Christmas, Easter, baptisms, funerals and weddings were kept. Even non-religious traditions, such as Norwegian lutefisk suppers, came to be tied to and retained through the church.

Foods eaten in the home also kept their

Ethnic groups are again learning traditional crafts: a United Tribes instructor teaches the art of bone-bead necklaces.

ethnic flavor. Most were economical and therefore essential in a land where for many years frugality was a way of life. The special ethnic dishes eaten today are the ones which are most enjoyed by the family and by outsiders.

Through hard times it was most important to feed the family, hold onto hard-won land, rear children according to the precepts of the church. Other aspects of the heritage, such as handicrafts, music, folk dancing and native dress, seemed less important and interest in these tended to dwindle.

Many people worked hard to shed old-country ways particularly, it has often been said, in the second generation. English was taught children, no longer as a second language but as the first, and frequently the only language. Certain traditions were even forbidden, such as Indian dancing. Drinking customs, so much a part of the Catholic Czech and German-Russian celebrations, were outlawed from the time North Dakota came in as a dry state in 1889 until prohibition was repealed in 1932. During the first world war, speaking German in public, including church, was illegal.

North Dakotans today — whether Polish, Finn, Metis, German, Sioux or Swede — are looking back with pride at the hardiness and courage of their forebears and are reclaiming their heritage.

Indians are traveling the powwow circuit, dancing for weekends in a row, fashioning roaches of porcupine quills and decorating with the prized once-illegal eagle feathers. Ukrainians are teaching egg painting, precise geometric embroidery designs and Ukrainian songs in schools; they are selling psanky at craft stores and demonstrating at art shows; they are reviving old customs such as the all-male Miss Malanka contest and weddings with crowns. Norwegians are spinning, knitting and weaving; they are giving classes in hardanger and rosemaling. A Polish dance group and Polish choir are performing at festivals. Ethnic celebrations are turning into annual events across the state. People are tracing their family trees and studying genealogy charts.

North Dakotans are traveling more freely in foreign countries, discovering relationships which were nearly lost, exchanging letters, gifts and visits, forming new friendships and cementing old blood bonds. They are participating in foreign travel and foreign exchanges of every kind through schools, 4-H, IFYE programs, the Peace Corps, musical productions. Nearly every ethnic group organizes its own two-way exchanges, frequently bringing specialty music and dance performances into the state.

The rise in ethnic interest today may spring from a combination of sources. Several people whose voices are heard on these pages confess to increased interest because of more affluence, an easier life, time for recreation and travel. Others say living in a society increasingly impersonal and homogenized makes them value and find meaning the more in that which is handmade, personal and local. Still others say it is the uncertainties of modern times, a feeling of rootlessness, which impells them backward, searching for who they are, that knowing their background is stabilizing, "a constant in an age of change, something that remains intact."

Perhaps ethnic groups across the state are appreciating each other more today, too. There was a time when children learned by adult example to place people of other nationalities — such as the Swedes to the west, the German-Russians on the south — into convenient categories. Stereotyping was a way of keeping one's own group strong. Religion, too, was a factor in feelings of "us against them."

Lutherans and Catholics in particular viewed each other with deep suspicion; intermarriage caused much pain to families involved.

But time and prosperity have mellowed these attitudes. People no longer believe the old stereotypes; they have plenty of friends who don't fit the patterns. Many have learned that individuals within each nationality usually differ more from each other than they do from people in other nationalities. Today when North Dakotans indulge in a stereotype, it's often with a chuckle and a teasing glint in the eye.

Ethnic pride is frowned upon by some who see it as a means of feeling superior to others. But Tom Katus, director of the Rural Ethnic Institute, calls it an asset. He says those who take pride both in being American and in having another cultural heritage seem to find it easier to relate to people of other cultures. "Learning about these differences makes us all bigger citizens of an increasingly smaller world."

Katus also notes the "highly sophisticated" international awareness of people in this region. Undoubtedly this international viewpoint has been influenced by the richness of ethnic groups here and the warm ties they still feel to other lands. As an example of this closeness, both Polish and Lebanese North Dakotans interviewed in these pages — and their friends and neighbors — are watching recent events in Poland and Lebanon with particular anguish and concern.

Immigrants came here from many countries — to escape poverty, to find freedom, to own land. They came in response to hard-sell railroad promotion and glowing "America letters" passed around in peasant villages. They came in a spirit of adventure and hope.

Not always were they pleased with what they found: rolling prairies, in some places level as far as the eye could see, with a scarcity of wood, scant population and climate that tested the endurance of woman and man.

Norwegians missed their mountains, deep valleys and watery fjords. English missed year-around landscapes of emerald green and the lap of the sea. German-Russians missed their orchards and the warm security of close villages. But they did not miss hovering fogs and constant rain, steep rocky fields hedged in by neighbors, rigid traditions which trampled and buried their dreams.

They adapted, and found a real home in a land with beauty in the prairie, opportunity on vast fertile acres, freedom and friendliness in a light population, fresh dry air with an abundance of sunshine — and a meadowlark singing in the churchyard.

Iron crosses denote community of Catholics from Black Sea regions of Russia.

Ethnic distribution in North Dakota

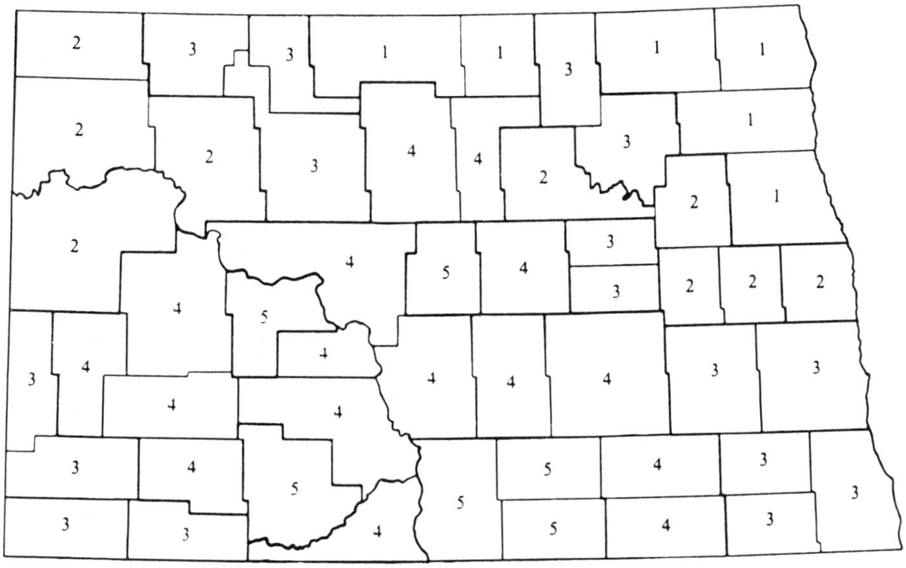

Mapping the distribution of ethnic groups in North Dakota is not easy. What seems a simple task grows quickly more complex as the multiplicity of settlement becomes evident. In many cases the ethnic settlement is very small, overlapping and interspaced with others. Or it may not be a definable community, but rather scattered families of one nationality with an ethnic church as a focal point.

In his study "Mapping Ethnic Multiplicity: A Case Study of North Dakota," Kang-tsung Chang, chairman of the geography department at the University of North Dakota, points out a variety of map styles used, and difficulties of each. Maps which attempt to show many groups in a simple way usually are far from realistic. The area mosaic maps developed by William C. Sherman show the real complexity of ethnic distribution in the state and dispell hopes for an easy solution.

The above map, designed by Dr. Chang, is presented as an alternative to others which are either complex or oversimplified. It shows the five major groups in the 1920 census. (Even here relative percentages will vary, such as the Canadian factor in Region 3 which is high only in northern tier counties.) Region 1 has highest percentages of Canadians. Regions 1, 2 and 3 are all high Norwegian. Regions 4 and 5 are high German-Russian and show clearly the German-Russian triangle through the state.

The reader is encouraged to read "Prairie Mosaic: An Ethnic Atlas of Rural North Dakota," by William C. Sherman, available through the Institute of Regional Studies, North Dakota State University, for a more detailed study of ethnic distribution in the state.

Average percentages of major ethnic groups

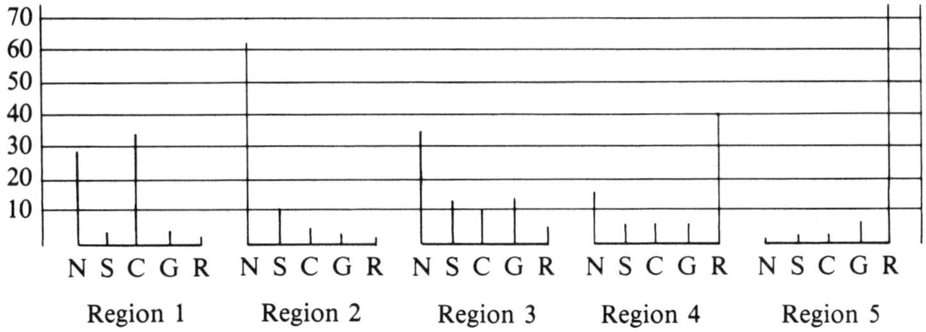

N: Norwegian **S:** Swedish **C:** Canadian **G:** German **R:** German Russian

by Kang-tsung Chang

Foreign-born pop. of North Dakota 1880-1920

	Composition of Foreign Born in %					Foreign—born percent of state
	Canadian	**German**	**Swede**	**Norwegian**	**Russian**	
1880	35	10	a	36	0	49
1890	28	11	7	32	5	44
1900	25	10	7	27	13	35
1910	14	11	8	29	20	27
1920	12	9	8	29	23	20

aCombined with Norwegian at County Level
Source: Federal Censuses

HILLTOP
HOLIDAY

Cultural traditions

North Dakota has inherited rich cultural traditions from many lands.

In the isolation of the past, when little contact existed between communities even in the same country, distinct traditions grew up involving nuances of language, foods people customarily ate, songs they sang and dances they danced, folklore and stories they told, folk wisdom and superstitions they believed or half-believed, religious precepts they taught and practiced.

When immigrants came to America from these close communities, it seemed they would jump into a great melting pot to blend forever these distinctive features of the past.

But in North Dakota new ethnic communities grew up. Often these were very similar to neighborhoods left behind, even to the same families living near each other. For decades, church, language and customs continued much as before.

Today, in spite of the mix of nationalities, the prevalence of mass media and mass culture, many of the same traditions persist and even flourish.

Veselka dancers perform the Hopak for Hilltop Holiday show in Dickinson.

Mike Dosch of Strasburg plays his accordian.

Songs not fancy, but you feel darned good

Oom-pa-pa, oom-pa-pa.

You're in Czechoslovakian orchard country.

Oom-pa-pa, oom-pa-pa.

Prunes as big as your fist are falling off the trees.

Oom-pa-pa, oom-pa-pa.

Now the prunes are rolling down the street.

Oom-pa-pa, oom-pa-pa.

Actually, you may just be at the Eagles Club in Dickinson, or at a wedding dance at the Terra Cotta Ballroom in Pisek.

A Bohemian band is playing "The Prune Song," and as the accordions and vocalists carry the Czech-language melody, the tuba oom-pas the beat.

It doesn't matter if you don't understand the words. Soon you're tapping your foot; you feel good and, darned if you don't feel like dancing.

Old-time Bohemian dance bands will do that to you.

They don't bother with unusual names like Black Oak Arkansas or Kiss. The musicians don't paint their faces with weird makeup or wear outlandish costumes.

And "we don't sing the same lines over and over, like some of the modern bands do," says Gabe Kinzel, a New Hradec Bohemian.

"There's nothing classy or flashy about the bands here. They just play down-to-earth music," says Kinzel, leader of a three-piece band called the Jolly Czechs.

Old-time music, combined with good company and perhaps a beer or two, is a sure cure for the blues, as folks of any nationality will attest. Bohemian musicians, who usually make their living farming or at other occupations unrelated to music, say it's fun as a hobby to lift people's spirits with song.

For Kinzel, 50, a farmer and rancher, starting the Jolly Czechs group 12 years ago at New Hradec was the culmination of a lifetime dream as well.

"It's something I always yearned for — to get on the stage someday and make people happy," he says.

Kinzel, like the musicians and vocalists of many old-time bands, has never had a music lesson. He plays by ear.

When you've been playing together a few years, you don't even have to practice, says Myron Pecka of the Myron Pecka Orchestra at Lawton, a small town in Bohemian country northwest of Grand Forks.

Chuck Kadrmas of the Chuck Kadrmas Orchestra, Dickinson, says Bohemian music is helping to preserve history.

"That's the only thing that keeps the Bohemian heritage going, besides the food," says Kadrmas, who was a member of the Bohemian Melody Boys in the '40s and the Bohemian Band in the '50s before forming his own group.

"Most of the older Czech people really do appreciate the Czech music," he notes, "probably because it brings back some ties they have with their ancestors."

Yet no generation is too young to enjoy and dance to Czech music.

"The Prune Song" is a favorite waltz. Also popular are "The Deer Waltz," "The Little Vagabond Waltz," "The Gypsy Polka," "The Red Beer Polka" and "The Barnswallow Polka." Modern numbers, including Top 40 and country and western music, are also played by some of the old-time bands.

A big hit at wedding dances is the butterfly, where groups of three march elbow-in-elbow to slow, waltz-like cadences, then swing their partners in cyclonic fashion when the tune suddenly becomes polka-fast.

"Later on in the night, when the crowd gets going," says Kinzel, "they like polkas best."

Czech songs are not easily translated into English, says Myron Pecka, because words that rhyme in Czech don't rhyme in English. However, English words have been adapted to familiar Czech melodies, giving them a completely different — sometimes silly — meaning.

And "The Blue Skirt Waltz," a love song in English about a blue-eyed, blue-skirted woman, was originally "Cervena Sukinka," or "The Red Skirt Waltz," in Czech. It was about a little girl with a red skirt.

Somewhere along the line someone transformed "The Prune Song," which in Czech is about bountiful prune orchards, into "We Left Our Wives at Home," Pecka says.

Bohemians musicians smile a lot. They relate to their dancers.

"The crowd is what makes the music," says Kinzel. "If you get a good dancing bunch on the floor, it's so much more fun to play."

Patricia Fix

Frank Nadvornik's band of New Hradec specialized in Czech music for wedding dances.

Modern folks still like the old songs

"The emigrant may lose everything — love of fatherland and the use of his mother tongue, but the songs of his homeland survive the longest." — Translated from the writings of 19th century German dramatist and novelist Gustav Freytag.

"Dakota voices are good and clear, the climate probably having something to do with it."

So said Wasyl Halich, a North Dakota Ukrainian, in a 1951 issue of North Dakota History.

He was describing music heard in the state's Ukrainian Catholic churches but his comment might just as easily apply to other ethnic-related music and instruments in use today in North Dakota.

Icelandic

Mrs. Alvin Melstad of Edinburg, whose husband is of Icelandic descent, says, "During the Icelandic centennial held in 1978 in Mountain, a chorus of about 20 local men from the Gardar area sang traditional Icelandic songs. They have been talking about reactivating the chorus, which was called Kalakour (Icelandic for men's chorus)."

During its fairly brief life, the men's chorus sang at church services and at Gardar Community Club meetings. The Melstads live about three miles from Gardar, a town with Icelandic roots.

At Christmas Eve services in Gardar Lutheran Church, the congregation still sings one chorus of "Silent Night" in Icelandic. The words are printed in the church bulletin to help those who do not fluently speak the language.

Icelandic music is heard at some funerals, when Esther Jonasson of Mountain sings. Her town, about eight miles north of Gardar, has the oldest Icelandic church in North America.

Swedish

Swedish music is often performed in the Fargo area, says Yvonne Anderson. She is a member of the Red River Valley Swedish Heritage Society of Fargo-Moorhead and works at Concordia College, Moorhead, Minn. The college's Swedish Folk Ensemble includes a half dozen or so students who play such instruments as violins and clarinets.

In Bismarck, a Swedish language choir has been organized by Dr. Marlin Johnson, a member of the Missouri Valley Swedish-American Association of Bismarck-Mandan. The choir, which is directed by Johnson, sang at the Swedish Julota service held Christmas morning at Bismarck's First Lutheran Church.

German-Russian

The state's large population of Germans from Russia appears to be continuing its music heritage, both instrumental and vocal.

Dorothy Preabt, office manager for the Germans from Russia Heritage Society headquarters in Bismarck, says, "For $85 each, the society sells a slide/cassette combination concerning the history of Germans from Russia in North Dakota, with musical accompaniment. We also rent these out, but you'd be surprised how many people buy them."

Music by the Tibor Brothers band of Hebron is not strictly ethnic, but the band does play many German tunes.

Their "Lieder von Wandern" record and cassette tape is a big seller at the Germans from Russia Heritage Society office, as are records of German music sung by the Ashley Lutheran Church Quartet and by Rocky and His Happy Valley Gang.

On weekends, Rocky (accordionist L.J. Rambousek, Glen Ullin) and his band members provide live entertainment at Rocky's Bar and Lounge in Glen Ullin, which Rambousek owns.

An example of groups continuing the German-Russian music traditions is the Young German Singers of the Napoleon, Linton, Kintyre, Wishek and Tappen areas.

John J. Gross of Napoleon, one of the organizers of the singers, says, "This group does a lot of singing of tunes that our German-Russian people sing anyway. Most of us were part of a group of people who used to go out snowmobiling, but since there was not much snow last year, we spent more time singing, and the group really got going then."

Carol Vetter of Kintyre was one of the principal organizers of the group of 22 singers, who range in age from the early 30s to mid-50s.

Formed about two years ago, Young German Singers performs at nursing homes in Wishek, Strasburg, Napoleon and Bismarck, and at housing for the elderly in Linton. August Vetter, who farms between Linton, Wishek and Napoleon, directs the singers.

All but one person in the group

have totally German-Russian backgrounds. "And that one has a mother who was German-Russian," says Gross.

Folk songs and some church songs are part of the singers' repertoire, and 95 percent of the songs are sung in German. Some of the song titles are "Strasburg to Strasburg," "Nice is the Youth," "There Would be No Greater Friendship," "The German Waltz," "When the Soldiers Come Marching Through the Town" and "The Sailer."

"Most of the German songs we sing are very old, and we sing many of them in the low-German dialect of the Germans from Russia. The songs were brought along with our ancestors from Germany when they went to Russia as long as 200 years ago."

Gross continues, "Our kinsmen did a lot of singing when they traveled by oxen for five months from southern Germany to southern Russia, near the Black Sea. They not only cried, they sang much to keep from going into despair, and to help keep their spirits up. So it was in Russia and in the early pioneer days here in America."

Musicians who perform with Young German Singers are organist John Vetter of Kintyre, Anton Wangler of Tappen, who plays electric organ or piano, and Carol Vetter, who plays the accordion.

John M. Gross of Napoleon, who is John J.'s father, was a church organist for 30 years, and he now plays piano occasionally to accompany the German songs sung at the Golden Age Club in Napoleon.

Notes for several songs in the "Folksongs of Our Forefathers" songbook were written by him.

Some hymns still are sung in German at churches throughout the state, including St. Boniface Catholic Church 12 miles southwest of Napoleon.

And German music is played by bands at numerous wedding dances in areas of the state where descendants of the Germans from Russia live.

A quartet of Napoleon men sings German songs. They are Leo Gross, Andy Weigel, Andrew Johs and Aloyius Gross. "The quartet has no name, they just sing when they are asked to do so," Gross says.

Gross says that German singing is done all over North Dakota by groups from Dickinson and Jamestown, to name only two. "Mr. and Mrs. Julius Miller of New England sing in German, and up at Harvey, there is a German band, and they also play German tunes."

Young German Singers performed in Bismarck at the opening ceremonies for the North Dakota Heritage Center, at a Germans from Russia convention at Kirkwood Motor Inn, Bismarck, and at the South Central North Dakota Germans from Russia convention in Wishek.

"We've talked about practicing more, making tapes, and traveling to such German-Russian areas as Alberta and Saskatoon in Canada," Gross says. "Every time we have singing practice, each family throws $2 in the 'kitty' for our travel fund."

"Our kinsmen did a lot of singing traveling by oxen from Germany to southern Russia."

"The accordion is definitely *the* German-Russian instrument. You can carry it with you wherever you go, and it is used for polkas and waltzes. In the early days, almost every German-Russian family had either a pedal organ or an accordion in the house," says Gross.

Mike Dosch of Strasburg and Joey Schmidt, son of Mr. and Mrs. Ray Schmidt of Napoleon, are two well-known North Dakota accordionists.

Schmidt now lives in California, where he performs on the television show of another musician whose early career was as an accordionist — North Dakota native Lawrence Welk.

Dosch grew up on a Strasburg farm two miles from Welk, his boyhood friend, and later played the accordion on numerous national and Bismarck radio and television programs.

"Sixty or 70 percent of the homes here in Strasburg have an accordion," says Dosch. "People often stay home and furnish their own entertainment — like playing cards — and playing music for singing, waltzes, fox trots and polkas."

Welk, as most people know, is a Strasburg farm boy who "made good" with his "Champagne Music." Welk's father, who was a farmer and a musician, came to the United States in 1870 from Alsace-Lorraine. He and his wife settled on a farm near Strasburg in Emmons County and were the parents of five girls and four boys.

The second youngest of the boys is Lawrence, who took an intense interest in his father's accordion. Until he was 13, Lawrence Welk never had taken a music lesson, but he was furnishing music for community dances. By 1927, he was leader of a band called the Biggest Little Band in America.

Julius and Rose Boespflug Miller are members of the German Folk Singers from the Dickinson area. The Millers, Joey Schmidt and German singer Tony Schaaf of Glen Ullin are featured on the Tibor Brothers' "Lieder von Wandern" album.

The album is one of many that have been recorded and mixed at the Tibors' JoMar Record Studio in Hebron.

The studio is named after the brothers' parents, Joseph Tibor and the former Margaret Hecker, whose father, Leonard Hecker, was born in Russia, came to the United States and began a band in Dickinson in the 1920s. Margaret played piano in the band.

Her sons' first album recorded at JoMar was entitled "A Special Old-time Tribute to Our Grandfather," and it featured the nine Tibor brothers who sing and play such instruments as accordion, drums, banjo, guitar and bass.

Currently, the Tibors' music includes traditional polkas, waltzes, country tunes, hits from the 1950s and many of their own compositions.

In Beulah, a group called German-Russian Singers includes members of the Beulah Germans from Russia Society. It and three other German singing groups were organized during the past 10 years by Rose Schulz of Beulah.

One of the ethnic singing groups Schulz organized includes older women singers, all of whom were born in Russia. Eva Scheid, who now lives at the Joachim Nursing Home in Beulah, is in her 80s and was one of the group's lead singers. The black skirt and black blouse with ruffled waist she performed in were garments that came from Russia.

The other singing groups Schulz formed are the German-Russian Dakota Singers, a group of younger people; a children's chorus; and an adult chorus, the Nondenominational German Singers.

She and her two sisters are members of the latter group, which sings locally at anniversaries, parties and Beulah Germans from Russia Society events. The singers are accompanied by an accordionist.

Songbooks of traditional German tunes help disseminate the German-Russian music tradition. "Folksongs of Our Forefathers," compiled by the late Joseph Height of Illinois and published in 1977, and "Songs We Love to Sing," compiled by the Germans from Russia Heritage Soci-

Sig and Margie Peterson, Almont, play piano and eight-stringed Hardanger fiddle and sing Norwegian folk songs.

ety and published in 1977, are two songbooks popular with the German-speaking residents of North Dakota, as well as the rest of the society's members.

Polish

Some Polish musical traditions are maintained at St. Stanislaus Catholic Church, Warsaw. The church was built in 1900 and is called the "Cathedral of the Prairie."

The Rev. Stanislaus Duda of the church says the church's choir sings at least one or two hymns in Polish each Sunday.

The choir members of all ages sing from a loft in the back of the church before a huge pipe organ. It is the state's only Polish-singing church choir.

Duda says there are only a few dance bands in the Warsaw area that play Polish polkas and waltzes.

"Church music by our choir is more important in this town of 120 people. We will soon begin an all-Polish Mass at the church the first Sunday of each month. At Christmastime, our choir sang Polish carols and hymns at St. Michael's Catholic Church in Grand Forks, where choir director Al Gratz of Grand Forks is also introducing a few Polish hymns into his choir's repertoire."

In addition to such hymns as "A Lullaby to Jesus," the St. Stanislaus choir sings Polish folk, drinking and military songs. "I play the clarinet and saxophone and have a little music background, so I teach them the songs," says Duda.

He says interest and participation in many Polish traditions, including music, is declining in the Warsaw area. "When they closed the school here in 1970, that also put the skids to a lot of the Polish culture we had."

Why does Duda think it is important to carry on the Polish music traditions? His answer reflects an opinion shared by most musicians who play or sing ethnic music:

"We have something to contribute to this state by passing down the Polish songs. When you get right down to it, the United States doesn't have many traditions that haven't been brought to it by immigrants."

Some ethnic music and traditions have diminished in occurrence as the state's early settlers have died.

"People used to live on 20 or 30 acres of land. Farms got bigger, more impersonal, more mechanized — everything got to be more 'Americanized.' Even as late as 25 years ago, everything around Warsaw used to be in Polish. Even plays were done in Polish then," Duda recalls.

Duda is attempting to preserve Polish music and traditions by teaching the church's children to sing in Polish. "I'm translating into English versions of some Polish hymns, and I've been trying to introduce the children and the adults to Polish customs."

Daughters of two of his parishioners sing in Polish at weddings and funerals, and one of them sings with a Polish music band in Minnesota.

Czech

A relatively new ethnic music tradition — "polka Masses" — are held several times a year in the Czechoslovakian areas of Lankin and Bechyne, according to John T. Kosobud of Adams.

"When you think of polka, you think of red vests."

The polka Masses' popularity spread from Czechoslovakian communities of New Prague and Gibbon, Minn., to North Dakota several years ago, and the Masses now are held at St. Joseph's Church in Lankin, St. Catherine's Church in Lomice and the Catholic Workmen's Hall across the road from Saints Peter and Paul Church in Bechyne.

At a polka Mass, a three- or four-piece band of musical instruments like saxophone, accordion and bass tuba will provide accompaniment as the congregation sings words of the liturgy to the tunes of such old standards as "Blue Eyes Crying in the Rain" and "Let the Sun Shine In."

"These polka masses attract tremendous crowds — even people from Protestant churches," says Duda. "But instead of the choir and organ, we have the polka band and local singers, usually dressed in costumes that have red vests. When you think of the polka, you think of red vests or red jackets," Duda continues.

"The polka Mass tunes are played and sung in waltz or polka tempo, or in the manner of a slow country western number," he says.

Norwegian

Norwegian music still fills the North Dakota air at churches and Sons of Norway lodge meetings.

For example, the Smaa Fjell Mixed Chorus of the Sons of Norway lodge of southwestern North Dakota is composed of six men. The lodge serves a 50-mile area around Reeder.

The men's wives are just getting started with singing in the chorus, too, according to Dora Johnson of Reeder. Her husband, Marvin, is one of the singers.

The chorus sings Norwegian folk songs at the lodge functions and does some entertaining at Norwegian couples' anniversaries.

Other examples of Norwegian singers are Inga Kelnar of Scranton, who may be heard singing in Norwegian at weddings and funerals, and Gerhard Christianson of Hettinger, who performs Norwegian tunes and even translates them for his audiences.

Playing the traditional Norwegian Hardanger violin and singing Norwegian folk tunes is the musical specialty of Osmund Vallevik, who lives at Spring Brook, near Williston.

In addition to performing at social functions and Norwegian "lags" (gatherings) around North Dakota, he has recorded at the Norwegian Folk Museum in Decorah, Iowa.

The eight-string Hardanger violin Vallevik plays was one of 28 such violins hand-crafted by his father.

"When someone gets wind of one of these, they go to great lengths to get one. The violins are inlaid with pearl and have eight strings rather than the four of the normal violin. The Hardanger violins are specially made for each individual," Vallevik explains.

Vallevik's sadness at the diminished supply of Hardanger violinists is similar to a lament voiced by Ted Pedeliski, an associate professor of political science at the University of North Dakota in Grand Forks.

Ukrainian

Concerning the Ukrainian musical heritage in North Dakota, Pedeliski says, "One problem that's put a dent in musical expression is a lack of violinists and dulcimer players. They died off in the 1950s and 1960s and the ones they have now don't have such an extensive repertoire of music as the old ones."

Members of the Ukrainian Cultural Institute of Dickinson are trying to preserve old-time Ukrainian music.

According to society spokesman Agnes Palanuk of Dickinson, three-musician groups (violin, dulcimer and accordion) play Ukrainian music for weddings, private parties, anniversaries and the like.

One such group includes Laudie Burian of Manning and William Namyniuk and August Anheluk, both of Belfield. They have accompanied Ukrainian folk dancers from the Belfield area.

"There are specific folk songs for specific Ukrainian rituals," according to Palanuk.

Indians sing to drumbeat at early powwow on Standing Rock reservation at Fort Yates. Photo by Frank Fiske.

"At a wedding anniversary, for instance, the musicians' part in the proceedings occurs mostly at the door and at the receiving line," she says.

In the past, the most common instrumental combination was the violin and the dulcimer. "In later years, the accordion has been added for emphasis," Palanuk says.

Burian, Anheluk and Namyniuk usually perform in southwestern North Dakota, but sometimes they are asked to perform in the Wilton area, where there is another Ukrainian settlement.

Dulcimer player Namyniuk has played the instrument for 30-some years and makes and tunes dulcimers.

Another Belfield area music group is the Ukrainian Folk Orchestra.

Accordionist Ernest Klem, drummer William Cerkoney and guitarist Al Roller are members of another three-man Ukrainian music group.

They play Ukrainian dance music at such events as a New Year's Eve party at the Ukrainian Cultural Institute in Dickinson. The three often sing, too, Palanuk said, and they specialize in contemporary arrangements of Ukrainian music.

"Some of the instruments that the Ukrainian immigrants brought with them to North Dakota have died out," Palanuk says. "The sopilka, a wind instrument similar to a flute, is now extinct in North Dakota. I have talked to people older than I who remember it, though. When people are no longer interested in playing the old instruments, their usage dies out."

Another instrument indigenous to Ukrainians is the bandura, a string instrument similar to the dulcimer, but with slight variations. "In Saskatoon, there are people who play it, but nobody I know in the Dickinson-Belfield area does," Palanuk says.

Dulcimers in use by Ukrainians in the state usually are handmade, Palanuk said. They resemble harps, but are much smaller and are held horizontally, on the knees. On top of a dulcimer are 12 or more groups of four strings. The instrument has a range of two or three octaves, depending on its size.

The dulcimer is an ancient instrument, mentioned even in the Bible.

Folk songs are sung at Ukrainian weddings in western North Dakota. One well-known tune is "Dark Eyes." It is about two lovers who ask, "When are we going to get married, and where are we going to live? We will live in the meadow 'til we build our own house."

The Ukrainian musical heritage contains many Cossack songs. "These vibrant marching songs were very popular in the 16th and 17th centuries, and people still sing them today," says Palanuk.

She is a member of a group of about 10 Ukrainians who sing in the Dickinson area. "When we sing with our Ukrainian folk dancers, we sing so they can get a few minutes of rest. We call ourselves the Ukrainian Folk Singers," she says. The singers have performed in Washington.

"North Dakota Ukrainians' strongest music area is our church music, in which songs are always sung a capella," according to Palanuk. "It just has not been part of the Ukrainian way to have instruments in the church music."

St. Demetrius Ukrainian Catholic Church north of Belfield and St. John's Ukrainian Catholic Chruch in Belfield both have choirs that sing divine liturgy and religious songs in Ukrainian.

In Wilton, ancient Ukrainian Christmas carols are sung at Saints Peter and Paul Ukrainian Catholic Church.

Indian

Traditional native American instruments and ceremonial and secular songs continue to be heard in North Dakota, although the sacred songs are not performed much anymore except in connection with the sun dance of the plains Indians.

At powwows, Indian young people stand by the circles of singers and drummers to record the music on cassette tapes. In part, this is how the music is being handed down to the next generation these days.

While some Indians criticize the commercialism of some powwows, in which dancing and singing contest winners receive cash prizes, they also consider powwows to be forces in preserving their heritage, according to Wallace "Butch" Thunderhawk. He heads the Four Winds Culture Center at United Tribes Educational Technical Center, Bismarck, and oversees powwows held at the center.

Various percussion instruments (like drums and rattles) and recorder-type flutes constitute the majority of musical instruments used by Indians in North Dakota. The Turtle Mountain Dancers, a metis singing and dancing group from the Belcourt, Rolla and St. John area, performs not only in North Dakota, but was featured at a folk festival held in St. Louis in 1976. In addition, it has performed at the National Folk Festival and appeared on Walter Cronkite's U.S. bicentennial television special.

Edward Johnson, Belcourt, facilities manager and a public relations worker for Turtle Mountain Community College in Belcourt, is coordinator and leader of the group. He plays traditional French fiddle tunes and other members dance the Red River Jig. The music shows the influence of French settlers and trappers, while the Red River Jig shows the influence of dances the French learned from Irish soldiers and settlers.

Vicki Russell

Folk songs evoke memories

Folk songs from the homeland were sung throughout North Dakota in early years. The songs evoked deep memories of other times and other places, of longing for loved ones left behind. Many songs expressed a love for mountains and fjords of Norway, for lush green moors of England, for closely-built stone villages of France and Germany.

The following Hungarian folk song "Farewell, Beloved Homeland," sung in western North Dakota, touches this familiar feeling of loneliness for a far off land.

O farewell, beloved homeland,
Sad I leave my Magyar homeland.
Oft in my dreams...I see your hills.
Mem'ries of their beauty haunt me.
Oft in my dreams...I see your hills.
Mem'ries of their beauty haunt me.

Scotch ballads were sung in homes and at Scotch gatherings in Towner County, says a depression-era federal writer, E.S. Oderkirk. Favorites were "There is a Wee Bit of Land Across the Sea," "Wee Banks and Braes," "Bonnie Doon" and "Annie Laurie." "Auld Lang Syne" was, writes Oderkirk, "always sung before the gathering is broken up and departure for their homes."

French Canadians near Rollette expressed a double loyalty, notes another federal writer. They would sing "Le Canadian" and "Au Canada," then go to a spirited French song such as "The Duke of Malborough Goes to War." But their favorite was the haunting "Au Clair de la Lune" ("By Moonlight").

Au Clair de la Lune
Mon ami Pierrot
Pretemoe ta Plume
Pour ecrire un mot.

Czechs sang their national hymn "Kde domov Muy."

Kde domov muy, kde domov muy?
Voda huci po lucinach
Bory sumi po skalinach
Vsade stkvi se jara kvet,
Zemsky raj to na pohled.
A to je ta krasna zeme,
Zeme ceska domov muy.

Where is my home, where is my home?
Where brooks rumble through the meadow
Pines murmur in the moutain side
All the orchards are in bloom,
What an earthly paradise in view.
This is the beautiful land,
The land of Czechs, that's my home.

But when people gathered to celebrate former national holidays they also forged loyalties to the new land. They sang old songs in the mother tongue and sometimes new lyrics to old tunes as in the German-Russian "Dakotaland":

Dort in Dakotaland, da leigt mein Heimatort,
Es ist gar lang schon her, dasz ich von dort bin fort.

Doch die Erinnerung, die bleibt mir stats gewisz,
Dasz ich Dakotaland gar nie vergisz.
'S'war in Dakotaland, wo meine Wiege stand
in sonnigen Dakotaland
Es war im Prairieland, wo meine Wiege stand,
im schon' Dakotaland.

Many old songs recalled the haunting threat of war, so familiar to European immigrants. One is this German-Russian child's song:

Maikafer, flieg!
Der Vater ist im Krieg,
Die Mutter ist im Pommerland,
Pommerland ist abgebrannt.
Maikafer, flieg!

Lady bug, fly!
Father's gone to war,
Mother's in Pommerania,
Pommerania has burned down.
Lady bug, fly!

Polish army songs such as the two that follow, with their hint of bravado and sadness, were familiar to Polish communities and are sung today with their many verses by the St. Stanislaus choir.

A Nasza Kompanja
(Our Company)

Nasza kompanja tam wokopach stoi,
Tam wokopach stoi, tam wokopach stoi.
I pisze do cara ze go sie nie boi,
Ze go sie nie boi, Hupaj siup.
Hupaj siupaj, Hupaj siupaj, Hupaj siupaj dana!
Hupaj siupaj dana, Hupag siupaj dana!
Wczoraj spalem na podlodze,
Dzis na wiazce siana, do sanego rana.
Hupaj siup!

Our company is now standing in the ramparts,
Standing in the ramparts, standing in the ramparts.
They write the czar that there is no fear in their hearts,
There's no fear in their hearts, Hupaj siup (Hoop-aye-shoop).
Hupaj siupaj, Hupaj siupaj, Hupaj suipaj dana!
Hupaj siupaj dana, Hupaj siupaj dana!
Last night I slept on the bare floor,

Violin music was much loved, as played here by Icelandic immigrant.

Now I sleep on soft hay till the dawning of day.
Hupaj siup!

Rolis, Rolis

Rolis, rolis, rolis kochana,
Rolis, rolis, rolis kochana.
Ktozcie bedzie rolis oral
Jak ja bede maszerowal?

Furrow, furrow, furrow straight and true,
Furrow, furrow, furrow straight and true.
Who will turn the furrows long
Guide the plow with muscles strong?

Meadow, meadow, meadow green and wide,
Meadow, meadow, meadow green and wide.
Who will mow the hay so tall,
When I'm marching in the fall?
Meadow, meadow, meadow green and wide.

Marys, Marys, Marys my own love,
Marys, Marys, Marys my own love.
Who will love you, who will love you
When the foe I will pursue?

Marys, Marys, Marys my own love.

"Ist das nicht eine Schnitzelbank?" sing Germans from Russia at Minot convention.

Songs helped to speed long days spent in monotonous chores. Thorstina Walters, an Icelandic writer from Akra, treasures the memory of her mother and grandmother singing old Icelandic lyrics while spinning and knitting. Translated, their "Spinning Song" begins:

My spinning wheel in motion
Creates a thrill of glad emotion.
With joy and pure devotion
The silken yarn is deftly wound.

Mothers and fathers sang the old songs to entertain children and soothe them to sleep. Typical is the Ukrainian children's song "The Mosquito's Wedding."

Ой що ж то за шум
Учинився, гей,
Що Комар та й на Мусі
Оженився.

He selected such a bride,
Just a teeny-weeny fly,
She can't cook, she can't sew,
And she doesn't care to try.

All bugs, beetles and mosquitoes
Gathered there to celebrate,
As they sang and they danced
Such delicious food they ate.

When the feasting was all done
The mosquito wanted more,
"Make some borshch," he yelled out
As he entered through the door.

She got down on her knees,
First she pleaded then she cried.
"I can't cook, weave nor sew
And I've never even tried!"

Lena Gulutsan
Kazka Productions

Lighthearted songs and songs of fun such as "Schnitzelbank" helped people look at their situations with humor. This song through 12 and more verses, asks the question "Is this not a sawhorse?" ("Good sausage...great thirst?") The question is answered — in a single breath if possible — with a rollicking shout that adds each new term to a long string of other items, "Yah, this is a Schnitzelbank!"

Ei du schoene, Ei du schoene, Ei du schoene Schnitzelbank.
Ist das nicht eine Schnitzelbank?
Ja das ist eine Schnitzelbank.
Ist das nicht ein Kurz und Lang?
Ja das ist ein Kurz und Lang.
Kurz und Lang un-er Schnitzelbank.

Ei du schoene, Ei du schoene, Ei du schoene Schnitzelbank.
Ist das nicht eine Gute Wurst?
Ja das ist eine Gute Wurst.
Ist das nicht ein Grosser Durst?
Ja das ist ein Grosser Durst.
Grosser Durst, Gute Wurst,
Reifenrock, Geisenbock, Grosse Eier,
Judenmeier, Schoenes Ding,
Goldener Ring, Wagenrad, Krum und
Grad, Lichtputzscheer, Hin und Her,
Kurz und Lang, un-er Schnitzelbank.

Freytag has said that the songs of the homeland survive the longest in an uprooted people. It was through songs such as these, filled with nostalgia, humor, love and strength, that an immigrant people held onto their roots and eased into a new kind of living.

F.B.

Warsaw area dancers perform in typical Polish costume.

Whirling dancers rekindle old pride

Perhaps the most colorful and tangible way to recapture the spirit and attitudes of a people is through its dance.

A flash of electricity, a rekindling of cultural awareness can unite an audience through deep-seated and perhaps long-dormant pride as they watch a parade of colorful dancers whirl through lovingly executed choreography and music that is saved for special occasions.

Ethnic dance in North Dakota evokes those images routinely in audiences around the state. And perhaps those who guard that part of a heritage are admired all the more by their people because such dance groups are not commonplace in North Dakota.

Through its history, North Dakota has seen the rise and fall of many ethnic dance groups. Nearly all towns of one predominant ethnic population can claim that they had a dance group at one time.

Among whites, most dance groups ceased to exist decades ago. They usually were groups composed of adults and children — immigrants or the children of recent immigrants. Now the immigrants are dead or too old to dance. Their children have grown up and moved away.

The groups that remain are composed mostly of third-generation descendants of the early settlers and may have had to turn to resources outside their communities in order to continue the traditional dances.

Still remaining as dancers are the Ukrainians, through the children's Veselka (Rainbow) Dancers in Belfield, and the Poles at Warsaw, through the Polish National Alliance Lodge 3043 Dancing Youth Group and adult PNA Dance Group. And the Sons of Norway Lodge in Bismarck recently formed a folk dance group.

There also are Indian dance groups: the Turtle Mountain Dancers in Belcourt, the Cross Culture Group and Activities Inc. in Bismarck-Mandan, the Eagle Feather Indian Club at New Town High School, the Williston Indian Cultural Club, the Wahpeton Indian School Indian club, the Ojibwa Indian Mission in Belcourt, the Fort Yates High School dance club, and the University of North Dakota Indian Cultural Center club.

Rainbow Dancers

The Ukrainian group, Veselka (Rainbow) Dancers, is centered in Belfield and draws its dancers from that town and Dickinson. The group is composed of 23 dancers in two groups: children 8 years and older and children 11 years and older who are good enough to make the older age bracket, according to Lana Procive, 21, the dance group coordinator.

The group has been in existence about two years, according to Procive. It filled a three-year void left after a similar dance group disbanded. That group reached a level of expertise that brought an invitation to bicentennial festivities at the Smithsonian Institution in Washington. Once that goal was reached, though, it disbanded because many of the dancers had graduated from high school and were too old for the group, Procive said.

Veselka was formed by Carol Palaniuk, who was a younger member of the previous dance group. Palaniuk, 17, is a junior at Belfield High School and serves as dance instructor.

"We didn't want it (dance) to die. If we younger people don't do it, no one else would," Procive explains.

"We just like to do it so much, and the people really like it. They come up to you after the performances and hug you and tell you you're great. We eat it up, and it really gives you a swollen head," she says.

Since there were not enough cultural resources available within Dickinson and Belfield, the present group of dancers, with the financial help of the Ukrainian Cultural Institute, sought outside help. For the past two summers two professional dancers with the Yevshan Ukrainian Folk Ballet Ensemble of Saskatoon, Saskatchewan, have conducted dance seminars.

The Veselka dancers practice twice a month, Procive says. There are few traditional Ukrainian musicians in the community so the group relies on recorded music for practices and performances, Procive says.

The dances performed are the privritz, a welcome dance by two girls that always opens the festivities; a sword dance by the boys; and challenge dances by the boys to match each other's steps. The challenge dance centers on matching the difficulty of kicks executed from a squatting position.

Couples also participate in courting dances, where the boy proves successful as the couple runs off together at the conclusion. A performance ends with a traditional hopak dance by couples.

The organization is relatively new, so most performances have been limited to western North Dakota. As an immediate goal, the group wants to expand its dance repertoire in time for the diamond jubilee celebration of St. Demetrius Ukrainian Catholic Church in Belfield later this year.

Children's dance group

There are 18 dancers in the children's dance group in Warsaw, according to Kathy Gudajtes, a rural Warsaw housewife who serves as dance instructor to the group.

Gudajtes says the group was formed in 1975 to coincide with the diamond jubilee of the local church, and because PNA lodges traditionally have dance groups. Then, too, "We're pretty proud of our Polish heritage around here and we decided it would be nice if we could perform the dances."

When the group formed, one member, Mary Kosmotka Woods, then a teen-ager, was sent by the lodge to PNA national college in Cambridge, Mass., to be instructed in several dances.

She returned and taught them to several adults and children. When Woods graduated from school the next year and left, Gudajtes, now 34, took over the group.

Since its inception, the group has traveled widely through North Dakota and Minnesota performing at fairs, artistic gatherings and other events.

Currently, the youngsters, who range in age from 6 to 16, specialize in two dances. One is the golobiek, which comes from the city of Opole in the region of Silesia in south central Poland. It is danced by four to 12 couples to a traditional song entitled "Ma Szklanej Gorze."

The dancers had been accompanied by a teen-age accordionist, who graduated from high school and has left. The group is seeking another musician and is relying on tape recordings in the interim.

The group will be expanding its dance repertoire in anticipation of the University of North Dakota centennial celebration next year at Grand Forks. To expand its dance selections, the group will send a dancer to Cambridge this summer to learn another half-dozen dances and the traditions behind them.

Gudajtes explains, "We'd like to be able to perform quite a few more. We've made many appearances and a lot of people have already seen what we do now. So we want to expand more in our dances. And as an instructor, I know that for myself and my kids, that in order to broaden ourselves we should do more dances and know more about them."

Gudajtes says the dancing cannot be categorized as polkas or schottische. There is some of each in the style, but there "is also a lot of hopping, hand-holding and clapping, with a lot of twirling and intricate foot movements."

Gudajtes says the adult dance group is composed of 12 couples from Warsaw, Minto and Grand Forks. They do not appear as frequently as the youngsters do because many of them are farmers with limited time.

Their speciality is the krakowiak, from the city of Krakow in the region of Galicia in southeast Poland.

Costumes, according to Gudajtes, are based on illustrations sent to the group by the PNA college and shirts and dolls brought back from Poland as souvenirs.

Folk dancers

The Bismarck Sons of Norway Lodge recently formed a folk dance group, according to Helen Storlie, lodge cultural director, who will coordinate the dancers.

According to Storlie, the group, composed of six adult couples, was formed to present folk dances as part of Norwegian Independence Day festivities at the North Dakota Heritage Center.

Storlie says the group plans to learn four dances and will dress in traditional black, red and white costumes.

She said the lodge once had another folk dance group, but it disbanded because its members were spread in too large an area surrounding Bismarck and found it difficult to practice and perform.

The Indian dance groups range across a spectrum of goals and abilities. The Turtle Mountain Dancers perform a blend of Indian dance and Irish jig and are composed entirely of adults.

The Bismarck/Mandan group is recently formed and includes dancers and singers from more than six tribes. It also has opened its doors to whites who are interested in learning the Indian cultural aspects of dance and song.

At New Town, the Hidatsas formed a dance club at the high school for junior and senior high students and hope to continue to expand the membership of the club.

At the Wahpeton Indian School, 30 students representing more than six tribes operate the club on their own. They range in age from 7 to 15 years. The school was founded in 1908 and the club well may be that old.

The UND group, composed of faculty and students, has laid the groundwork for expanding into a dance group that would not be aligned with the university. It would be aimed at Indian and non-Indian students in the Grand Forks school system. In April, some university students will dance for 750 fourth-grade students who could be prospective members.

Turtle Mountain Dancers

The Turtle Mountain Dancers are atypical of other Indian dance groups because they are of metis or mixed-blood ancestry, in this case a blend of Chippewa, Cree, Irish and French.

In the 10-member dance group are a fiddle player, guitar player, square dancers, jiggers and callers. French singing also accompanies the music.

The dance tradition the group practices evolved in the late 1800s when the Catholic church dubbed traditional Indian dances as "pagan." Eventually the Cree and Chippewa bands mixed parts of their dances with the reels, quadrilles, jigs and double jigs they learned from French and Irish trappers who intermarried with them.

Traditionally, metis dances were performed at all social functions.

But there also was a colorful spontaneity involved: historians note that the Cree and Chippewa in the Turtle Mountains practiced what were known as "bush" dances.

A bush dance dance started quite simply when the head of a household took up his fiddle and started to play. His family would join in and as other nearby families heard the music, they would come to the party. Such dances often lasted until daylight.

Weekend dances and bush dances are still common, and that's how the dance group stays in form, according to Eddie Johnson, its fiddler.

Johnson has worried in the past that the tradition may be dying because of the intricacy involved in the dance steps, and the sheer work for the fiddler, who must keep the dance rhythm through his feet while playing the fiddle.

In 1975 and 1976, the group was brought to Washington by the Smithsonian Institution to perform at the Festival of American Folklife. In 1976, it was billed as the top group and was called back by the audience for numerous encores. It also has appeared at the French Folk Festival in St. Louis.

The dancers are Edward, Brian and Mae Johnson, Alex Moris, Leon and Agnes Poitra, George and Georgaline Longie and Farrell and Sandy Gourneau.

There are two differences between whites and Indians in their approaches to dance. Foremost, in the Indian culture dancers are inseparable from singers. Were it not for singers, there would not be dancers, according to those associated with the groups.

Hidatsa dance club

Secondly, Indian dancers learn their art from their parents, grandparents or other family members. Because of their culture, and perhaps because they did not break their ties with a nation on the other side of an ocean, more of the traditions and etiquette are known.

Don Rush, a parent associated with the Hidatsa dance club at New Town High School, notes that "the drum is center to everything; the dancers dance around the drum."

Agreeing strongly with Rush is Earl Bullhead, a Hunkpapa at Fort Yates who is a former dancer and now, at 33, is a singer with the Bismarck/Mandan cross-cultural group.

"Dance and song are interrelated," Bullhead says. "Some kids will dance to records and tapes. But after a while they always end up with singers because there is a unity there; it doesn't seem right to dance to a record.

"One can't go without the other. To see the music and dance together will explain it far better than I can. The motion and continuity between them is something; it is beautiful by itself."

Many of the dances and songs are thousands of years old, according to Rush and Bullhead.

Typically, they are the "traditional" dance in which the men dance out stories of battle. The regalia is Indian clothing and feathered headgear without bustles.

In "fancy" dancing, the purpose is to prepare for a confrontation or war. In modern times, the garb is fancy in color and two bustles are worn. The garb is more contemporary, according to Rush, who says that dancers add items to their outfits that will leave the impression of speed.

There also is the "grass" dance, performed in traditional garb. According to Bullhead, that dance is performed at celebrations. Bullhead says it derives its name from the tradition "of the dancers coming to a certain area and singing certain songs and performing certain dances and laying all the grass down. The object of the dance was to flatten the grass down with their feet, but they cannot destroy it. They would dance until the grass is bent, but not broken and turned brown. When it would break and dry out they had to stop; it was done that way so that no one would know that you were there."

In recent decades the traditions and etiquette have not changed, but there has been an expansion of how they are applied.

For example, a recent addition at powwows has been social dancing, "kahomanie," where members of all tribes participate.

Bullhead, whose Indian name is Nicha Ole, "Looking for Something," notes that new songs may be written these days, but that those who write them must have stature within the tribe. Likewise, there is an etiquette of who is allowed to sing certain songs and when those songs can be sung.

A typical performance of song and dance begins with a flag song, during which the flags of the nations present are introduced. Bullhead relates, "The song varies between the tribes; each has a different song that is sung in the native tongue. Years ago the tribes used to have a beckoning song to tell the people they're to come because there is something for them." The flag song serves the same purpose today.

It is followed by a combination of dances and songs related to the purpose for the gathering. For example, on Veterans Day, there would be songs and dances relating to each of the branches of the armed forces that men served in, Bullhead says.

Mark Kinders

Powwows are family affairs

The setting — a dusty gymnasium — seemed incongruous with the event.

Under the basketball hoop, raised for the occasion, the wide, squatty drum was placed. In the center of the floor the dancers performed. Most were dressed in "fancy" style, decked out in colorful feathers and beaded garments.

It was a weekend powwow in celebration of the latest graduating class from Standing Rock Community College.

When non-Indians think of powwows, the image usually is of the large, outdoor gatherings during summer months.

However, powwows are held throughout the year and range from the very large and commercial to small gatherings in reservation communities.

For the Indian people, powwows have a variety of meanings.

To some, they are among the few remnants of traditional culture.

To others, they are a commercialization — even a "bastardization" — of their original heritage.

Indian dances feature colorful costume and dance tradition: hoop dance, battle scene in leaf-shaded outdoor arena, a dancer pounds his feet to the drumbeat.

Bob Wilson, a Lakota Sioux who considers himself a spiritual leader, compares the commercialized powwow to a circus. Traditionally, "dancing is a form of prayer. ... very sacred, supposed to be treated as such." He is particularly disturbed that the powwows have been made into monetary contests for dancers.

Wilson says he tries to remain traditional and believes "money is what is destroying our traditions." In a few communities, such as Wakapala and Bullhead on the Standing Rock Sioux Reservation, traditional powwows are held, he said.

Wallace "Butch" Thunderhawk, who oversees the United Tribes Educational Technical Center's powwows in south Bismarck, believes the events are a little of both.

At some powwows, the dances are now contests, with judges awarding prize money to the best dancers. Vendors set up food stands and arts and crafts booths around the powwow grounds.

During the summer, a softball tournament may be scheduled along with the dance and singing contests.

But, each culture has to adapt to change, either from internal or external forces.

Thunderhawk pointed out that the eagle feather was once passed down from generation to generation as a religious symbol.

Now, an Indian must apply through the Bureau of Indian Affairs to obtain an eagle feather, he said. And, because federal law protects the eagle, it wasn't until five or six years ago that the government made provisions allowing Indians to legally obtain eagle feathers.

"Before, it was a part of their life to sing and dance," Thunderhawk said. Certain ceremonies were prescribed for specific events, such as a name-giving, preparing for a hunt, or for a war party, he said. And powwows still are held for particular events, such as the graduation in Fort Yates.

However, many powwows have gone "big time," attracting hundreds of dancers from tribes all over the country.

And "it takes a lot of money to operate a big powwow," Thunderhawk said, from paying advertising costs, to prize monies and crews to clean up the grounds afterward.

While some Indians criticize the commercialism, they also regard the powwow as a force in preserving their heritage.

Gordon Runs After, 25, has been dancing at powwows for four years. A Lakota Sioux from the Cheyenne River Reservation in South Dakota, Runs After sees a powwow as "a good place to meet different people ... to become associated with other types of customs."

Runs After said "powwowing" is a family affair for him. His elaborate costume was designed and made by his mother and sisters, and the family usually attends powwows as a group.

Runs After thinks "most dancing families are really traditional, and they express this through their dancing."

Besides, he said, powwowing is just "very fun."

Rosemary Lynch

Ukrainian dance features dainty footwork, dazzling acrobatic leaps. Dickinson-Belfield youth are seen here in practice and full-dress performance.

Learning the Ukrainian dance

Welcome to the Ukrainian dance! With smiles and graceful hand movements the girls skim across the stage with dainty, complex footwork and tiny, quick turns ending in a beautiful pose as still as a picture. Powerful jumps, large turns, and floorwork with dazzling acrobatic feats bring on the boys. The audience watches fascinated and thrilled, feeling the beat of the Ukrainian music and wishing they could join in. And you can!

Stand tall — good posture gives you the proud look so characteristic of Ukrainian dancers.

Starting with your rib cage, lift up gently, front, side and back. Think of gently pulling the ribs as far away from the legs as possible. Pull in the tummy. Back is straight. Keep centered over front part of both feet. Keep arms at side but lift elbows slightly for a rounded effect. Don't touch body; think of the arms framing the body.

Hands — oh how difficult it is to have soft hand movements! And how much professionalism hands add to our dance. Girls should hold the fingers slightly rounded. Try to keep the hand relaxed. Boys, hold the hand with fingers close and thumbs in, as if you are going to shake someone's hand.

Keep your head high, look proud of your dance. Your expression should say you enjoy doing your dance.

Now you are ready for warmups. Place heels together, toes slightly out. Place your hands on hips, fingers forward, thumb to the back. Bend knees gently down, over the toes, keeping heels pressed firmly to the floor. Rib area lifted, back straight, tummy in. Count 1-2 down. Press the knees up very straight, counting 3-4. Do this slowly and carefully eight times.

Take a step to the right with the right foot. Heels are about 18 inches apart, toes slightly turned out. This is the second position. Gently bend knees over toes, using the same counts as before. Stretch up before you begin and close the feet back to the first position when you have finished.

Marja Venscha
UCI newsletter

Halling dance: a 'dance of death'

The most fantastic of the Norwegian dances is the Halling Dance still seen on special occasions. It is reputedly the survival of a 'dance of death' from the days when the knife was the means of avenging jealousies among the young men of Halling Valley in Norway. When a man began the intricate acrobatic steps of the Halling Dance, the other dancers knew he had seen an enemy or rival in the crowd, and unobtrusively withdrew to the edge of the dance floor, leaving the enemy, often unsuspecting, in the clear. Then, in a great whirl, the Halling dancer would send his knife spinning through the air with its message of death. The dance today is an acrobatic performance which requires great skill. It includes handsprings, the Halling-kast — a whirling and kicking step — and the krukeng, a jiglike step done in a half-sitting posture with the dancer moving about the floor.

North Dakota Federal
Writers' Project, 1938

Stephanie Arendt helps Christina Mulikin straighten her cap before Minot dance group performs Norwegian folk dance.

Arab dance responds to beat of the drum

Mike Saba (right) and son Jesse dance the Dubke in Bismarck.

My earliest memories of growing up as an Arab American were of dancing and singing and eating the food. Of waking up in the morning when my father was singing Arabic songs in the bathroom, words I didn't understand, but whose rhythms and sounds I knew.

I remember when I was three or four, and I have these visions of Derbaka, the Arabic drum, playing sounds I can hear. I can see my grandfather, my great uncles and all my older relatives responding to the beat of that drum, by jumping up from a couch or from a chair, and putting their hands above their heads and dancing to the beat. This is a very vivid memory. And I remember the joy, the tremendous feelings, that were generated amongst all the people watching this.

My recollections were stimulated about five years ago when we were at a convention of my family, an annual affair.

The drum beat started and many people got out on the dance floor and started to do this wonderful line dance, with everyone joining hands in the front, and the dancer putting his hands above his head, bouncing up and down, dancing to the beat of the music.

Well, my son Jesse, about three or four years old, was watching on the side, I said to him, "Jesse, come on, let's go dance."

He looked at everyone out there, with a shy look, and kind of reluctantly looked at me and said, "No, I don't want to go right now."

I said, "Well, let's try it."

So he took my hand, but said, "Lift me up and hold me, because I don't know how to do the dance."

I said, "No, it's best for you to just try."

And he said, "No, no, I want to get in your arms while you're doing this dance and get the feel of it."

So I put him in my left arm and got at the end of the line, grabbed hands with the person in front of me and started to dance, to move to the rhythm of the drum.

I could feel his little body begin to move to the beat and then all of a sudden he looked at me and said, "You can put me down now. I've got the feel."

And I put him down. He grabbed my hand and started dancing to the beat like the rest of the people. At that moment I looked over to the side of the dance floor and saw my father, and the look on his face as he saw his grandson getting the "feel" of being an Arab American was more than words can describe.

Mike Saba.

Strasburg's old Blue Room still draws crowd

It started as a poolroom just after the turn of the century in the small, south central North Dakota community of Strasburg.

But as time passed, that poolroom evolved into the Blue Room and Lounge — a famous wedding and dance spot, attracting bands of national renown and drawing folks from many parts of the Peace Garden State.

Even today, the lounge and dance hall play host to wedding dances just about every weekend between May and September, as well as a few now and then during the colder months.

The name has been altered a bit — it now is known as Horner's Lounge and Blue Room — but little else has changed during the past 35 years or so in the Blue Room, located in this bustling town of 660 residents.

Virgil Horner has owned the place for about seven years now. He says the hall, with its walls covered by murals that could have been backdrops from the movie, "Casablanca," still draws the wedding dance crowds.

Donna Vander Vorst and Ed Schnabel swing to the lively Liechtensteiner polka at Bismarck Oktoberfest.

But it didn't start out that way.

Pius Kraft, a Strasburg resident since 1907, says what is now the Blue Room was built as a pool hall in 1908 and 1909. Only the front part of the current building existed then, says Kraft.

According to a book celebrating the golden jubilee of Saints Peter and Paul Catholic parish in Strasburg, the pool hall was built by Gregory Bichler, who ran the establishment for many years.

Sometime later, the building was remodeled and served as a liquor store.

Kraft, now 86, remembers when the building was used for a time as a bowling alley, but that was many, many years ago.

"We'd set a game," recalls Pius, who was 12 or 13 back then. "For that we used to get a bottle of pop."

Then, there were the regular public dances, which attracted young and old alike from Strasburg and neighboring towns.

Current owner Horner said he can recall attending the dances as a kid growing up in Strasburg.

His most vivid memory of the hall while he was a youth was one month when about 25 weddings were held — "and I didn't miss one, that's why I remember."

A former owner, Leo Mattern, now of Bismarck, also remembers the dances.

He said the crowds generally were well-behaved, although minors were served liquor.

But the facility did not realize its fame as a wedding dance hall until Mattern, his father, Fred, and his brother, Elmer, bought the bar, then known as the Matt-Ray, in 1946 and dubbed it Mattern's Lounge and Blue Room.

They decided to purchase the building after Leo returned to the area following World War II, and Fred was unable to buy any more farmland.

The Matterns are just a few in a long line of owners of the building, so many that even Pius could not recall them.

Elmer bailed out of the partnership in 1947 — "He didn't like the bar business," Leo said — and the two remaining Matterns operated the Blue Room until 1968, when Fred sold out to his son. Leo continued with it until upcoming surgery forced him to sell in 1970, he said.

Because they owned the place for such a long time, they made many of the hall's major changes and operated it during its heyday.

The Matterns started using the hall, which then was about half its current size, for wedding dances a year after they purchased it, although at the time the Blue Room was without running water and sewage facilities.

Water had to be hauled in, cooking was done on kerosene stoves and people had to make use of outhouses.

In those days, Mattern said, weddings were all-day affairs, and the Blue Room attracted wedding parties not only from Strasburg but from many surrounding communities.

The wedding ceremony was held in the morning, followed by a soup dinner in the Blue Room, he said. Of course, the spirits flowed all afternoon and the dancing continued the whole time..

"Those days, everybody danced," Mattern said. "It was a little different than today — completely different."

After an evening dinner, everyone retired to the lounge, where more refreshments were served.

That style of wedding celebration, Mattern said, went out in the '50s when rock 'n' roll became popular, but the Blue Room continued.

What was it that drew people there to celebrate?

"I don't know why it was so popular," Mattern said. "Maybe it was convenient." Convenient, he said, because its downtown location meant the town's four other bars were within a minute's shuffle.

That was not the situation in Linton, for example, where people wanting to try another watering hole had to hop into their vehicles and drive.

While the weddings were the biggest attraction for the Blue Room, they were by no means the only activities held there.

Public dances were held Fridays, and they drew large crowds, Mattern said.

"Oh, they went over big," he said. "It's hard to believe."

Those public dances featured such famous bands as the Six Fat Dutchmen, Whoopee John and Don Shaw, as well as a number of Bismarck-area bands.

"It was pretty well-known all over the United States," Mattern said.

The hall also played host to basketball, community gatherings, movies and, from 1946 to 1949, Saturday roller-skating.

Mathern said roller-skating wasn't very popular, but it was "something for the kids to do."

The bar and dance hall took on a different look under the Matterns, and their changes and remodeling included adding 40 feet to the dance area, putting in a kitchen and installing plumbing in 1949.

The roller-skating wore out the Blue Room's wooden floor and a plastic mat — a relatively new idea at the time — was laid in 1949.

"A guy came in and said he's got plastic and said he'd guarantee it," Mattern recalled. "So we put her in and by God she did the job.

"It's still there."

The front of the building also was remodeled.

The murals that still decorate the walls of both the lounge and Blue Room also were done under Mattern ownership.

Mattern said the mural work was done by a family friend from South Dakota.

"He looked at the place and said, 'Gawd, that's a big job.' "

"Weddings were all-day affairs —everyone danced."

But he completed it all for about $700, Mattern recalled.

The mural in the lounge is a wilderness scene that could have come from northern Minnesota, with lakes surrounded by trees and rolling hills, complete with wildlife.

The Blue Room conveys an atmosphere that would be welcome to Humphrey Bogart and Ingrid Bergman, what with the palm tree murals and gently-rotating ceiling fans and all.

"He figured it would be the nicest scenery," Mattern said.

But not everything has changed. Much of the woodwork around the bar, for example, is original equipment.

There is one thing the place did not experience, however, and that is the sound of Lawrence Welk, Strasburg's hometown hero.

According to Mattern, Welk and his band never played the Blue Room, neither before nor during the Mattern reign.

"He came back but never played there," Mattern said, adding that when Welk did play, it was at the local school gymnasium.

So put that old rumor out of mind. Lawrence Welk did not play in the Blue Room.

Maybe it was his loss.

Kevin Whalen

Prairie Arts Guild of Bismarck area displays needlework heritage from many countries.

Old world crafts regaining favor

The pioneer home was the center for entertainment and learning.

Families would visit each other and organize card parties, play chess and checkers or while away the time with stories and news of the area. If the home had a piano or reed organ, neighbors gathered to sing hymns. Getting together with neighbors helped to overcome the loneliness.

The women brightened their home environment with handmade art, which often served a functional purpose. Much traditional folk art of the various ethnic groups has been passed down through generations.

Recognizing the beauty in some of the old folk art, today's public has asked that classes be taught so they can participate.

Marge Underdahl of Hebron has studied rosemaling, a type of Norwegian freehand painting on wood, in classes offered by the Morton County extension agent's office. Rosemaling was at its peak in Norway between 1750 and 1850, she says.

Paper Cutting

Judith Kuczynski of Bismarck has been working with the Polish art of paper cutting called wycinanki (pronounced "visheenankee") for six years.

Every section of Poland has its own design and style, she says, but the use of birds, animals and people in scenes is common, with the dove being a more modern symbol. One region may have a medallion form and another region may use one color mounted on another color, she continues.

Angels and hearts by themselves also are favorites of the Poles. The angel has a traditional heart for a mouth, a crown on its head and a star in one or both hands. A decorated heart is a typical Christmas tree ornament, says Kuczynski.

One common characteristic of wycinanki is that the paper is folded and cut to get a symmetrical type of art.

The art started in Poland in the 1800s, and the tips of sheep shears were used to cut the paper figures, she says. Every spring, walls of the homes were whitewashed and new designs of cut-paper art were put on them.

Although Kuczynski works mostly with solid-colored paper for her pictures, she may use some patterned paper.

Ukrainian eggs

The colors and decorations of Ukrainian Easter eggs and the egg itself all have symbolic meanings, according to Ukrainian Betty Sprynczynatyk of Bismarck.

Since taking up the Ukrainian art seven years ago, Sprynczynatyk has painted more than 100 eggs.

The egg symbolizes the rebirth of man. The colors have various meanings: red for love, black for remembrance, pink for success, green for money and orange for attraction.

The wheat decoration symbolizes the bread of life. A continuous line shows eternal life. Crosses and fish represent Christ and triangles symbolize the fishermen's nets.

Sprynczynatyk uses an electrically heated stylus to draw a design with wax on the egg, one step at a time. Special dyes are used to color the eggs, starting with the lightest color and working through to the darkest. When all of the colors have been put on, the egg is held over a candle to melt off the wax. A high-gloss finishing coat is applied as the last step. It takes about three hours to complete one egg. Sprynczynatyk is teaching her daughters the art.

Sioux beadwork

Lillian Swift Horse of Cannon Ball on the Standing Rock Reservation is one of the older Indian women who have helped to teach younger generations the art of beadwork.

Beadwork, according to her, began when the Indian people got trade beads. The beadwork designs, she explains, have meanings such as the circle of life, the four points that represent the four winds and seasons, and the triangle for the tepee.

Beadwork takes patience, says Swift Horse. You have to want to learn. Four years ago she spent some time as a crafts instructor at Northern Michigan University in Marquette.

Quiltmaking is not an Indian craft, but many women on the state's reservations have become skilled at it. A star quilt is a prized gift.

Chippewa basketry

Francis and Rose Cree of Dunseith are well-known for their practice of the traditional Chippewa craft of weaving willow baskets. This intricate art form one was widely practiced by Chippewa women, but now is limited to a very small number of people in North Dakota.

Though the basketmaking traditionallly was done by women, Francis assists Rose by constructing the ash frames for the baskets. Rose learned the skill from her mother, Pearl Machipinas (Hunting Thunder) in 1936 when Rose was 15 years old. Pearl learned basketmaking from her mother, Little Shell. Pearl also made grass baskets, a skill that Rose says she is sorry she didn't learn.

The Chippewa name for the baskets is "aneepiu maka," which

Muriel Schwartz, Mandan, works on hardanger embroidery.

means "willow box." The round basket is the oldest form. Ash is used for the frame and willow branches called the "weavers" fill the skeleton. Sinew once used to used to tie the ribs of the skeleton together has been replaced by string and wire.

The materials are gathered from all over the prairie. Willow is found along rivers, streams and sloughs. The ash comes from bush areas like those surrounding the Turtle Mountains. A pocketknife and pliers are the tools.

When Rose was young, the baskets were made to sell or trade locally and for everyday use, such as picking berries and corn, for sewing items and for laundry. Now they frequently are found in gift shops.

According to Francis, the baskets will last 40 years with proper care.

Their children and grandchildren help gather the materials for the baskets, and the Crees save the first willow baskets made by each grandchild.

Tole painting

Tole painting actually means painting on tin, which is what the early colonial women did, buying tin and paint from peddlers.

Toleware is tinware. But today, tole painting is more properly called tole and decorative painting, because it is done on other surfaces such as wood, plastic and glass, too, according to Judy Rockenback of Bismarck, who has been teaching the art for three years.

Tole is a combination of all kinds of folk art from different countries, leaning toward the Pennsylvania Dutch, whose cultural traditions go back to the German migrations of the 18th century.

It is method painting, a technique rather than a talent, and it can be learned by anyone with a sincere desire to paint, says Rockenback.

"You don't have to design or draw in order to do tole and decorative painting because you work from patterns from a tole book, a coloring book, wallpaper and even a decoupage print. Tole is very realistic; our strawberries look like strawberries," Rockenback says.

Fruits and flowers are popular patterns. Rockenback uses mostly oil paints, but is beginning to use acrylic also.

She learned the art at tole painting classes in Bismarck and has attended several seminars that enabled her to become a certified instructor for Priscilla Hauser Technique, Tulsa, Okla.

Rockenback is a past president of a 30-member Paintin' Folk Tole Club which meets monthly in Bismarck.

Chippewa willow baskets made by Frances and Rose Cree of Dunseith. A beaded Sioux pendant.

Polish krakowiak dolls dressed by women of Warsaw parish. A Standing Rock Sioux star quilt.

After soaking wheat stalks in long tub, Connie Sprynczynatyk weaves them into medieval English designs.

Geometric designs on bags denote Sioux, Mandan, Hidatsa and Arikara style of beading. Floral designs of Chippewa, lower left, show French influence.

In top photo Judith Kuczynski, Bismarck, shows Polish paper cutting. Plates with Scandinavian rosemaling are sold at the Heritage Center.

Hardanger embroidery

Hardanger embroidery, a form of counted-thread embroidery originated in the Hardanger region of Norway hundreds of years ago, gradually spread to other parts of Europe and then to the United States with the Scandinavian immigrants.

It must be worked on an even-weave fabric. Traditionally the work was done with white thread on white linen, but the fabric most commonly used today is an even-weave cotton with 22 threads per inch.

The fabric, appropriately known as Hardanger fabric, can be found in a variety of colors and is both imported from Scandinavian countries and produced in this country.

Hardanger embroidery often is featured in blouse detailing, on a skirt or across the front of an apron. The delicate threadwork is also found in tablecloths and doilies.

Muriel Schwartz of Mandan, who does various kinds of needlework, started taking lessons in Hardanger embroidery when they were offered in Mandan in 1969.

She bought Hardanger fabric while visiting relatives in Norway. Her relatives also made a beautiful beaded chest plate, which she wears with her Norwegian native dress to Sons of Norway functions, along with handmade silver pin and earrings. Schwartz's Hardanger embroidery is featured throughout the costume's blouse and apron.

Wheat weaving

One craft that is growing in popularity is wheat weaving.

Centuries ago when farmers began cultivating grains in England, they also began to work decorations symbolic of their thanks for a successful harvest. All grains were called "corn" and early farmers believed there was a spirit world of idols responsible for harvests. Therefore, these traditional decorations became known as "corn dollies." The form the dollies took was limited only by the imagination of the weaver, and the same is true today.

In feudal times, a suitor would use wheat to weave a rope 2 or 3 feet long and would take it to the lady of his choice. If she tied the rope into a knot, his proposal was accepted. Thus, the origin of "tying the knot."

The first farmer to finish his harvest would weave a sceptor-type rod of wheat called a "knack" and hang it in his home. He was the only one allowed this privilege. And so the saying "I've got the knack."

Wheat woven into two-headed snakes was a symbol for good health. The caduceus of the American Medical Association is said to have had its origin in this custom.

A heart-shaped symbol called a "mordiford" represents good health and sometimes love. If it is tied with a red ribbon, it has been made with spring wheat. Those made with winter wheat are tied with green ribbon.

Interest in wheat weaving was revived in Kansas in the mid-1970s and has spread rapidly.

Connie Sprynczynatyk of Bismarck saw a demonstration in wheat weaving, took several classes in it and three years later at the age of 25 left the teaching profession when wheat weaving became a full-time business for her.

Between supplying gift shops, museums and galleries and giving demonstrations, she doesn't have time to select and prepare her own wheat so she orders it from Wheat Craft supply house in Alamo.

In harvesting a supply of wheat for weaving, the most desirable is bearded wheat with short heads and long stems. The stems are cut close to the ground while the wheat is in the "dough" stage, about a week before harvest. The wheat should have just turned from green to gold and the heads should be straight with compact beards. Small bundles tied together must be hung to dry and stored in a cool, dry, rodent-free place.

Before weaving or plaiting, the wheat is soaked for 30 to 45 minutes in lukewarm or cool water and wrapped in a damp towel until used. Hot water will take the sheen from the wheat, Sprynczynatyk says.

She has designed many patterns so there isn't a duplication in the finished woven piece. Her wall hangings varying in size from a few inches to several feet.

Spinning wool

Spinning wool into thread isn't an art one can see every day. So Valborg Fisher of Mandan draws quite a crowd when she gets into her colorful Norwegian dress and brings out her spinnng wheel to demonstrate the art.

She was especially busy giving programs during the nation's bicentennial year and still is much in demand in the schools.

Daughter of Norwegian immigrants who came to this country in 1898, Fisher sent for her mother's spinning wheel in Norway in 1951, after she learned that the spinning wheel was available. She paid $30 for the spinning wheel and $60 air freight.

In 1978 she ordered a new spinning wheel from a company in Oslo, Norway, enclosing a detailed drawing of the spinning wheel she wanted. It cost her $300 plus $100 air freight and $30 at customs.

"But now I have a Cadillac spinning wheel. Why drive around in a broken-down car if you don't have to," was her explanation.

Fisher, who began to play a pump organ in the Lutheran Church at Sims at the age of 10, says pedaling the spinning wheel is like playing the pump organ in waltz time.

She has dyed her own wool, but usually purchases wool that is washed, dyed, carded and ready to spin.

Gloria Feickert

At annual Ethnic Festival in Dickinson Elsie Huether displays items from German booth; Lois Teske, in lower photo, shows Scandinavian crafts.

"Tole is realistic— our strawberries look like strawberries."

Ukrainian pysanky glisten like jewels

"I saw the pysanky when only the show case lights were on, and they glistened like jewels," said one visitor to the annual pysanky show and sale held during the Easter season each year at Dickinson State College.

The Ukrainian pysanky are known as the jewels of Easter eggs. Colors and decorations used and the egg itself all have symbolic meanings that reach back into a history of both pagen and Christian beliefs. Devout Ukrainian women begin decorating their eggs with a prayer that the symbols will be meaningful to all who see them.

Ancient Ukrainian legend from pagen times has it that the more of these decorated eggs on earth, the harder it will be for evil spirits to take over. Evil is seen in the guise of a vicious monster chained to a high cliff. According to legend, "Each year many of the monster's servants circle the globe, keeping record of the number of pysanky made. When there are few the monster's chains loosen and evil flows through the world. When they are many, the monster's chains hold taut, allowing love to conquer evil."

A Ukrainian egg, given in love and friendship, is believed to expand the power of love. The pysanky with their beautifully intricate patterns and sparkling sheen last indefinitely, or "forever" according to tradition.

Norwegian items displayed include needlework wall hanging, hardanger lace, lidded hand-carved mug, troll, beer server inscribed "Gunnild Thoresdatter, Hilde den yngre 1845" and an 1879 immigrant chest.

Blacksmith displays ancient art of working iron using forge and anvil at Minot Hostfest.

Scandinavian wooden food container with lid has old style rosemaling decor, is dated 1874. Lefse rolling pin is grooved for lighter lefse.

Hand carved Scandinavian dairy utensils are shown in top photo: two styles butter molds and a wooden bowl for setting milk to skim. A closer look at square mold shows its intricate carved sides and top, each of a different design. It's held together with wood pegs.

Hand knit socks, sweaters and Icelandic items fill this old immigrant chest. Note slanted handles so chest would rest flat against sides of sturdy little Icelandic ponies in traveling.

Janelle and Darlene Johnson of Gardar wear sweaters from Iceland. A continuing exchange of visits brings to North Dakota hand knit and sheepskin articles as well as this rough-textured lava pottery.

Spinning, knitting, weaving are ancient arts

Spinning and knitting were everyday "spare time" tasks for Scandinavian and German women and girls in early North Dakota, as well as many other nationalities.

Nina Farley Wishek who taught in German-Russian communities writes of her pleasure in watching the women deftly spinning, making the work appear easy but showing their skill by the fine even yarns they spun.

In "Along the Trails of Yesterday," Wishek tells of the women washing wool after shearing, carding it into white piles, spinning the white skeins into yarn ready for dying.

The method of dying was an ancient and primitive art, she explains. For this a ten-gallon crock was heated in a manure pile. Horse manure was considered ideal. The crock was filled with warm water and nested into the pile with manure heaped close around. The manure was lit and burned for a day and a night until the water was boiling. Then purchased lump dye was pulverized in a cloth, added and dissolved. The white yarn was then added and cooked in the dye bath for two days and a night. "The colors were almost indelible," notes Wishek.

She also describes the fine wool "tuechles," fringed black scarves worn by the women, and the "blachtes," or shawls which often had vivid stripes and borders. Although they'd been used for 50 years or more, she says, they were as heavy and strong as the day they were woven, with colors practically unfaded.

Scandinavians from Iceland, Sweden, Norway, Denmark and Finland also kept their flocks of sheep and depended on the warmth of wool through long cold winters. They spun their own yarn, wove blankets and knit socks, underwear and sweaters. Such important home items were kept darned and useable for years.

Ole Abelseth of Hettinger, one of the few survivors of the Titanic who was actually in the ice-filled water, credits his survival to the warm homespun underwear his mother made him in Norway for the trip back to his Dakota homestead. F.B

Wearing Hardanger lace and beadwork, Valborg Fisher of Mandan spins wool into thread on her imported Norwegian wheel. She weaves this into cloth on looms in her home.

German-Russian women wore tuechles, fringed black shawls of fine wool, as shown at left with the hand-beaded baby caps. Above, a black sheep in the flock was highly prized for color variety in weaving and knitting.

Ethnic foods are common fare

Recently I sat at a table in a restaurant in this area with friends from the eastern part of the state. As they studied the menu, two unfamiliar words caught their eye. "Fleischkeukle and knifle soup — what in the world are they?" they asked, stumbling over the pronunciation.

As I described to them the meat pies and the tiny dumplings, I wondered if perhaps we in this state take too much for granted our access to such a fine selection of ethnic foods.

I was a very small girl when I was first introduced to what is now known as "ethnic cooking." My brother used to accompany me on periodic trips across the street in the small McLean County town where we lived to visit "Grandpa and Grandma" Lillehaugen, an elderly Norwegian couple whose home was a tidy little shingled bungalow. Chief among the attractions of these visits was the afternoon lunch we knew we would be invited to share, and which was served with a certain amount of ceremony.

Never allowed to have coffee at home, we felt very grownup when Grandma filled our cups half-full of the forbidden beverage, added an equal amount of rich milk from their own cow and set it before us all at the oilcoth-covered kitchen table. Grandpa showed us how to suck the coffee through a sugar cube held tightly between our teeth. An even greater treat than the coffee, however, was the brown-flecked "lefse" that Grandma offered us on a thin china plate covered with roses. She always cut the big rounds, made from potatoes and flour and baked on the top of her immaculate coal range, into triangles that she buttered and sprinkled with sugar, or sometimes spread with honey. Then she rolled the triangles, point first, into small cylinders, and stacked them on the plate.

She also served "flatbrod," a thin, brittle bread that was baked in the oven in flat sheets, but this we did not care for, though we remembered our manners and never told her so.

The lefse was very different from anything we ate at home, for our parents were both from Indiana, where their families had lived for several generations. As a result, our mother's excellent cooking was strictly "Mid-American," with a leaning toward cornmeal mush, cornbread, boiled and baked beans, fried pork, baking powder biscuits, and stewed chicken with noodles or dumplings.

When I was ten years old we moved away from that small town, and it was a long, long time before I again ate lefse. Still later, I learned how to make it, to please my Norwegian husband; now that I am alone I no longer bother, but thoughtful friends often remember me with some when they prepare it. Grandma Lillehaugen has been dead for many years, but she lives in my memory every time I butter a piece of what some people irreverently have dubbed "fried dishrags."

In the next little town (in Oliver County) where we lived where my father was the only teacher in the local school, I was introduced to another fine example of ethnic cooking. A good friend, who lived in the country, often stayed in town with her grandparents, and after school she sometimes asked me to walk with her to their home on the outskirts of the prairie village. It was there that I first tasted "kolaches," and became an instant devotee of the luscious, fruitfilled buns. The grandmother had a "light hand" with dough, and the kolaches were so tender and airy that I learned the truth of the phrase "it melts in the mouth." The filling of spices ad cooked, dried prunes or apricots that centered each roll was a contrast in taste and texture that emphasized the goodness of the bread. I still consider kolaches to be the best of treats.

When I taught a country school in the west-river country in the 1930s, I lived with a German-Russian family; in that home I ate many dishes that were new to me, but that I greatly enjoyed. Among them were little watermelons, pickled whole with dill in wooden barrels, and green and red peppers fried with onions in oil. I had never before eaten meat prepared with garlic, but I learned to like very much the sausages and roasts seasoned with the pungent root. Here, too, for the first time I ate "halupsi" (or "halubsy"), the meat-stuffed cabbage rolls cooked in tomato sauce or beef broth that we now call "pigs in blankets."

It was at another boarding place in the same area that I was first served German potato dumplings cooked with ham; I thought them heavy after my mother's feathery ones, but in time I acquired a real taste for them. I also ate "knifle" soup — tiny dumplings simmered in meat broth or creamy potato or vegetable soup. Again, the knifle were like and yet different from the large, light dumplings that accompanied my mother's boiled chicken. I was learning that there are many basic foods, but that each group or nationality adds its own special touch to the method of preparation. It is discovering these differences (and also the similarties) that make the eating of ethnic foods an exercise in anticipation and enjoyment.

My German friends also served "kuchen," the delicious coffee cake with the sugary crust and the creamy custard that covers a layer of whatever fruit the cook has on hand; one tasty variety incorporated dry cottage cheese instead of fruit into the custard.

It was also while I was teaching that I ate my first "fleischkeukle," the meat-filled pies tht are much like Cornish "pasties" except that they are fried instead of baked. They have since become a staple at many community events where Homemakers Clubs or other groups will operate a "fleischkeukle" stand. They also appear on the menus of regional eating places, and sometimes threaten to displace hamburgers as the first choice of local patrons.

After I was married, I was fortunate to live next door to a woman who was born in Norway, and who made not only lefse, but also "fattigmand," "rosettes" and "krum kaka," those crisp, delicate cookies that always call for "just one more"!

It was at the annual smorgasboard of a local 4-H club that I first tasted "sot suppe" or "sweet soup," so loved by Swedish homesteaders. Made of mixed dried fruits stewed and thickened with cornstarch or tapioca, it was a traditional gift taken to a new mother or to a home where sickness had struck. Swedish meat balls, lightly flavored with nutmeg, and Swedish rye bread are still featured at the traditional buffet dinner, both dishes a legacy of the Swedes who settled in the area in the 1870s.

It was not until I began writing for the Wilton News that I became acquainted with Ukrainian cooking, and added "pirohi" (there are many English versions of the spelling) little filled dumplings served swimming in butter, to my list of all-time favorite dishes. It makes no differ-

Mrs. Gus Belohlavek, Mandan, holds a plate of her Bohemian kolaches. Top center, Bohemian poppyseed candy. Good German food, upper right, is specialty of the Mosbrucker sisters of Bowman-Scranton: Frances, Josie, Jennie, Madeline and Roszella. Traditional Ukrainian kolach is topped with candle. Swedish meatballs are served with rich brown gravy rather than a tomato sauce.

ence whether the small morsels of dough contain sauerkraut, mashed potatoes, or cottage cheese — all are delicious. Wheat and bread play an important role in Ukrainian religious and secular festivals, so it is not surprising that their cooks are justly famous for their dough products. "Baba," the saffron-flavored Easter bread baked in round, tall tins is a notable example.

We are fortunate that many different nationalities settled here, making it possible for everyone to share a variety of cultures — and not the least important part of any country's culture is its foods. In larger cities there are Scandinavian and German and Ukrainian restaurants that specialize in dishes that we can enjoy at any church supper or potluck dinner, but for which they charge astronomical prices; ethnic foods command these prices because they are out of the ordinary and special. We should not allow familiarity to lessen our appreciation for our gastronomic heritage.

Incidentally, my friends ordered both the fleischkeukle and the knife soup (a more than satisfying meal) and were delighted with both.

Frances Wold
Prairie Scrapbook

Good food transcends differences

The names may vary with the ethnic groups and people within those groups may use different spellings, but when all the ingredients are measured and the stirring, rolling, kneading, dropping, cutting, folding, pressing, baking, frying and cooking is done — don't be surprised if the results are variations of basically the same foods.

In a "sampling" of foods throughout the state for this story, the frequent duplication was evident, and choosing which recipe to use for publication was an almost "indigestible" task.

But it is a common trait of people, from whatever background, that they enjoy good food. Through years of population shifts on other continents, in the United States and finally in North Dakota, groups of people have borrowed recipes from each other, revised and improvised.

The process still is going on in North Dakota, and perhaps the strongest remaining evidence of North Dakota's mixture of ethnic heritage is the diversity of foods prepared in homes across the state.

The growing popularity of ethnic-food cookbooks that have been compiled by several communities and societies in North Dakota indicates that the people of today's generation enjoy broadening their culinary taste by giving "foreign" foods a try.

German

Raphael and Susie Mosbrucker, Germans from Russia, arrived in New York City in 1899 and homesteaded in Bowman County in 1902. After their death, their five daughters and two sons who live in the Bowman and Scranton areas cooked and served two German dinners for the public and cleared $1,000 toward a new church in Bowman in memory of their parents. Decorating the dinner tables were their mother's flatirons, kerosene lanterns, a sausage stuffer, meat grinder and old crocks. They also gathered family recipes for a cookbook called "From Her Kitchen to Ours."

The daughters are Roszzella Blees, Madeline Lutz, Genevieve Volk and Josephine Andrews, all of Bowman, and Frances Hedman of Scranton.

Geraldine Dittus, Almont, folds strudel with a flip of the tablecloth. For Swedish tea ring, or bullar, cardamom is the secret ingredient. At right, Rita Nassif of Bismarck prepares Lebanese baklava; in pot are stuffed grape leaves.

The two sons are Pete and Nick Mosbrucker, both of Bowman.

When the Bowman County homemakers clubs staged a "Fling Thing" last fall, Josephine demonstrated how to make kase-nipfula (cheese buttons) and gave out at least 500 samples. She has been the chief cook for banquets at a nightclub in Bowman for 12 years and her sister, Genevieve, operated Jenny's Drive-Inn there for 18 years.

Their recipe for Borscht:

Place a good soup bone in a kettle and cover well with water, bring to boil, reduce heat and let simmer until meat is tender. Peel and cut up 3 medium potatoes and dice 2 medium carrots and 1/4 cup onion. Cut up and add small head or about 2 cups of cabbage, 1 cup of celery, 2 medium beets including most of the tops. Add 1 cup of peas and 1 cup of corn. Simmer slowly until vegetables are tender, then add 1 can chopped tomatoes. The older the soup, the better. For variety you can add cream just before serving or put in some pearl barley.

Fleischkuechle: Combine 1 cup milk, 1 cup evaporated milk, 1/4 pound butter, 1 teaspoon salt, 1 teaspoon sugar, 1/2 teaspoon baking powder, 3 cups flour; mix and set aside for 1 hour. Filling: Combine 1 pound ground pork, 1 pound ground beef, 1 onion chopped fine, 1 1/2 teaspoons salt, pepper to taste, 1/2 cup water; mix and let rest 1 hour. Roll dough in circles the size of a saucer. Spoon some meat mixture on one half of each dough circle, fold other half over it and seal well around the edges. Fry in deep fat until golden brown.

Kase-nipfula: Combine 2 cups cottage cheese, 1 egg, pinch of salt, dash of pepper, 1 teaspoon sugar; mix and set aside. For dough, combine 5 cups of flour, 2 eggs, 1 1/2 cups milk. Mix together, turn out on board and knead to a stiff dough, adding about 1/2 cup more flour. Roll out to 1/8-inch thickness. Cut into 2 1/2- to 3-inch squares. Place 1 teaspoon cheese mixture on each square. Take one corner and fold over to the opposite corner to make a triangle. Pinch edges together. Cook in boiling, salted water for 15 to 20 minutes. Brown 1 cup bread crumbs in butter and pour over buttons after they have been drained.

A cookie recipe for Springerli has been in the family of Freda Redding from Cathay for more than 100 years, having been brought from Germany. It's a pretty cookie because of the designs in the board that is pressed into the dough, she explained. The ingredients: 2 cups fine granulated sugar, 4 eggs, 4 1/2 cups pastry flour and 1 teaspoon oil of anise. Beat whole eggs until thick. Add sugar gradually, beating well between each addition until all is combined. Then beat for 15 minutes. This makes the finished cookies fine-grained and light. Add anise oil and blend. Fold in flour lightly. Roll out all of the dough about 1/2 inch thick. Flour the springerli board and press firmly into the dough. Cut cookies along the lines of imprint. Place on greased cookie sheets. Flour springerli board or rolling pin each time it's used. Leave cookies in cool place overnight to dry. In the morning, place first into preheated 375-degree oven to set the shape. Reduce heat immediately to about 300 degrees. Bake until light brown. Do not overbake. When baked, cookies should be light in color with the appearance of having been iced. Store in tight can for 2 or 3 weeks to develop flavor. Redding places half an apple in the can to help soften them.

Another familiar German cookie is Pfeffernusse. The ingredients: 1 cup sugar, 3 eggs, 2 sticks of margarine or butter, 1 pint honey, 1/2 cup sour milk, 1 cup chopped almonds, 1/2 cup chopped walnuts, 7 cups flour, 4 teaspoons soda, 1 1/2 teaspoons salt, 2 teaspoons cinnamon, 1 teaspoon allspice, 1 teaspoon cloves, 1 pound mixed glace fruit and 1 teaspoon oil of anise. Cream margarine or butter, add sugar and honey, then well-beaten eggs. Add sifted dry ingredients with sour milk. Fold in nuts and fruits. Makes a very stiff dough. Chill for several hours. Roll into balls. Place on greased baking sheets and bake at 375 degrees until nicely brown (about 10-12 minutes). Roll in powdered sugar and store in airtight containers.

Geraldine Dittus of Almont is known for her German Strudel recipe. Take 3 cups flour and a dash of salt, add 1 1/2 cups warm water a little at a time to make a soft dough. Knead well and let set about half an hour, then knead again. Roll out dough on a well-floured surface to about 18 inches round. Then put a large tablecloth on your table, flour it well. Lay the rolled-out dough in the center of this. Spread hot melted lard on dough. Then carefully stretch dough into a thin rectangle about the size of the table. Be careful as it will tear easily.

Spread with about 14 medium-sized sliced apples, 2 cups sugar and cinnamon. Dot with sour cream. The more apples, the better. After all these ingredients have been put on, lift the tablecloth, rolling up the dough in jelly roll fashion from one of the long sides. Put in a 9-by-13-inch greased cake pan. Probably will fill two pans. Bake at 350 degrees about 45 minutes until nice and brown. You may use dry curd cottage cheese or shredded pumpkin instead of apples.

English

Ann Miller came to the United States from England in 1962 and was a nanny to the children of a Minnesota family in the Wayzata area. Having a nanny seemed to be the "in thing" at that time, she explained. Three years later she came to Mandan and married Mel Miller.

The following Christmas Plum Pudding is a recipe shared by her and Gwen Jensen: 1/2 cup flour, 1/2 teaspoon baking powder, 1/2 teaspoon nutmeg, 1/4 teaspoon salt, 1 teaspoon allspice, 1/2 cup sugar, 3 cups mixed dried fruit, 1 1/2 cups soft bread crumbs, 1 cup grated suet or / cup margarine, 1 tablespoon marmalade, 1 tablespoon grated carrots, 2 eggs, 2 tablespoons milk and 3/4 cup rum or brandy.

Grease well a 1 1/2-quart pudding

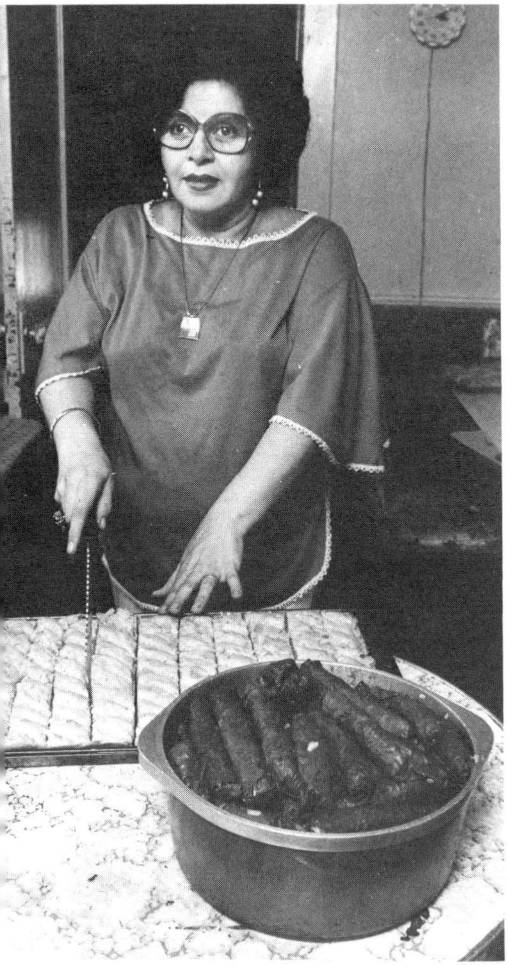

dish (oven-safe mixing bowl) and place waxed paper in the bottom of the bowl. Wash and dry fruit. Sift dry ingredients into large bowl, add spices, fruit, suet, bread crumbs, marmalade, carrots and sugar. Mix well. Stir in well-beaten eggs, milk and brandy. Stir thoroughly and make a wish while you stir. Put into pudding dish and smooth the surface. Cover with greased aluminum foil, making a center fold in the foil to allow for expansion. Tuck securely under rim. Place in the top of a steamer and steam for 4 hours. Cover top with fresh foil and store in cool place. Steam again for two hours before serving. The longer it sets, the better. Keep in cool place. Need not be frozen.

Dutch

Anna Zandstra of Strasburg tells us more than 300 people attended a Dutch supper that her couples club put on last fall at the Hope Reformed Church at Westfield. She says that her Dutch family always had a raisin bread for Easter and her mother made a good pea soup. She also made Balcon Bray for breakfast from the following recipe: 2 quarts of water, 3 cups of cracklings, 1 teaspoon of ginger; boil and thicken with buckwheat pancake flour. Let it get cold. Fry it in slices and eat with syrup.

Dorothy Huizenga of Hull, who is Dutch, has been a cook with the hot lunch program at the Bakker School in Strasburg for several years. She also cooks at her daughter's cafe in Pollock, S.D. Her Buttermilk Pop recipe, which can be used as a dessert, is: thicken sour buttermilk with oatmeal or flour and sprinkle brown sugar on top.

She also makes a drop doughnut called Olie Ballen: 3 eggs, 1½ cups milk, ¼ cup oil, 1½ cups sugar, 4 cups flour, 1½ teaspoonsbaking powder, ½ teaspoon baking soda, ½ teaspoon salt, 1 teaspoon vanilla, 1 cup raisins and 1 chopped apple. Mix well and drop a teaspoon of dough in hot fat. When golden brown, remove and roll in sugar.

Swedish

Sand Bakkelse (sand tarts) is a Swedish pastry made by Esther Asplund of Bismarck. The recipe calls for 3 cups powdered sugar, 1 cup butter, 1 cup lard, 1 teaspoon vanilla or cardamom seed and 3 eggs. Cream butter, lard and sugar. Drop in unbeaten eggs and vanilla or cardamom seed. Mix well. Gradually stir in enough flour to make dough almost as stiff as for cookies. Mold into ungreased sand bakkelse tins with fingers. Bake in moderate oven until light brown.

Danish

Erling Schacht of Bismarck came to this country from Denmark when he was in his 20s and furnishes this recipe for Danish Apple Cake: 2 cups thick applesauce, 1½ cups zwieback crumbs or Holland rusk, ¼ cup butter, 2 tablespoons sugar. Brown the crumbs with sugar and butter over low heat (do not burn) and cool. Make applesauce by cutting apples in half, removing cores and cooking with peeling on for color. Squeeze through a colander and sweeten to taste. Alternate layers of applesauce and crumbs. Set in refrigerator to cool and serve with whipped cream as a topping.

He also makes a Danish Brown Cookie using 1 cup butter, 1 cup sugar, ½ cup molasses, 1 tablespoon grated orange rind, ½ teaspoon ginger, ¼ teaspoon cloves, 4 cups sifted flour and 1 teaspoon baking soda. Cream butter and sugar, add rest of ingredients, knead well. Make into 2 long rolls. Wrap in waxed paper and refrigerate. Slice with a sharp knife, put half an almond on top of each cookie and bake 8 to 10 minutes at 325 degrees.

Norwegian

Norwegian Sweet Soup is a recipe Mrs. Ralph Mangnall of Oakes got from her grandmother. The ingredients: 2 quarts water, 1 cup sugar, 1½ cups prunes, ¾ cup raisins, 1 cup pearl tapioca, ½ teaspoon salt, juice of 1 orange, juice of 1 lemon, 3 apples cut fine, 1 stick cinnamon.

Crisp rolled krumkaka is baked on heavy waffle-like iron heated over burner, then rolled on wood form while hot. At left, Ida Heidt makes kase-nipfula, or cheese buttons. North Dakota kuchen takes two forms: the "Catholic" type made thin with sugar-cinnamon filling as in center photo with Schnee Balle, and the thicker dough-like crust with fruit filling, shown at right by Delores Green.

Soak tapioca overnight in water, then discard water. Put all ingredients in a heavy kettle and boil slowly until tapioca is transparent.

She also shares her Swedish Meatballs recipe. Mix thoroughly 1 pound ground beef, 1/2 pound ground pork, 1/2 cup minced onion, 3/4 cup fine dry bread crumbs, 1 tablespoon minced parsley, 1 1/2 teaspoons salt, 1/8 teaspoon pepper, 1 teaspoon worcestershire sauce, 1 egg, 1/2 cup milk.

Shape in walnut-sized balls, brown in 1/4 cup hot fat or salad oil. Remove meat and stir into fat 1/4 cup flour, 1 teaspoon paprika, 1/2 teaspoon salt and 1/8 teaspoon pepper. Stir in 2 cups boiling water and 3/4 cup sweet or cultured sour cream. Return meat to gravy and cook about 30 minutes.

Theresa Netzer at Hazen has been making Lefse for sale for three years so more than just her family and relatives can enjoy the thin potato pancakes. Most people, she says, like to eat them spread with butter and sprinkled with sugar. Her recipe requires 7 cups of boiled, mashed potatoes, 1/4 cup cream, 1 stick butter, 1 tablespoon salt and 2 cups flour.

Mix the ingredients and refrigerate until mixing in the flour just before rolling. Keeping the dough cold is one of the tricks, she says. If it's warm it'll get sticky and you can't handle it. Roll into large-size pancakes and fry on an electric griddle. It is easier to control the heat in an electric griddle than in a pan on top of the stove, she says. The recipe makes about 20 lefse.

Finnish

A recipe for Finnish Tarts comes from Jane Glander at Grafton. The prune filling: boil 1 pound of pitted prunes and add 1/4 cup sugar, 1 teaspoon flour, 1/4 teaspoon cinnamon, 1/4 teaspoon cloves and 1/4 teaspoon allspice. Set aside. The crust: 5 cups sifted flour, 4 teaspoons baking powder, 1 teaspoon salt, 1/2 teaspoon nutmeg, 1 1/2 cups sugar, 1 1/2 cups lard and butter (half and half), 2 beaten eggs, 1 1/4 to 1 1/2 cups of milk and 1 teaspoon vanilla. Mix dry ingredients together and work lard and butter in as for pie crust. Mix milk, eggs and vanilla together and pour over dry mixture. Mix to rolling consistency as for pie crust.

Roll dough quite thin, cut in 3 1/2- to 4-inch squares and make a diagonal cut into each corner about half way to the center. Place a small amount of prune filling in the center of each cookie and fold alternating corners into the center over the filling to make a pinwheel. Bake at 350 degrees until light brown.

Several Icelandic recipes have been offered to this section from a cookbook prepared by the Borg Memorial Home Auxiliary at Mountain. The cookbook project was chaired by Marcella Melsted of Edinburg.

Icelandic

Icelandic Cake "Vinarterta," a recipe from Emma Johnson of Mountain requires 2 cups sugar, 1 cup butter, 1/2 cup shortening, 4 eggs, 1/2 cup milk, 1 teaspoon salt, 5 cups flour, 3 teaspoons baking powder and 2 teaspoons ground cardamom seed. Cream butter, shortening and sugar. Add eggs, beat thoroughly. Add milk and dry ingredients. Put dough on large plate and cover with plastic wrap. Refrigerate overnight. In morning, divide into 3 rolls, then divide each of those rolls into six. Turn out on lightly floured board. Roll like cookies, using an 8 1/2-inch plate to cut around. Bake in 400 degree oven until light brown. Cool. This makes 3 cakes, each with six layers. Filling: soak 2 packages (32-ounce size) prunes overnight. Cook until tender in water to cover. Mash prunes and add 3 cups sugar. Bring to boil. Cool. Remove pits. Spread between layers of three cakes. Top with icing sugar frosting and decorative candy if desired.

Icelandic Kleinur is a recipe from Gudrun Geston of Gardar. The ingredients: 4 eggs, 4 cups sugar, 1 cup milk, 1/2 cup sour cream (not very thick), 1 teaspoon soda, 2 teaspoons ground cardamom seed, 1 1/2 teaspoons salt and flour (about 10 cups). Beat eggs until light. Add sugar, milk, sour cream with soda added, cardamom seed and salt. Add enough flour to roll. Roll 1/4-inch thick, cut in strips 3 inches long and 1 1/2 inches wide, using kleinur cutter (like pastry cutter with scalloped edge). Cut lengthwise slit in center and pull one end through slit. Fry like doughnuts in hot lard.

Rullupylsa is a cured pressed meat shared by many ethnic groups and eaten on rye or brown bread. Bjorn Olgeirson of Mountain shares her recipe. Combine and mix well 1 1/8 cups curing salt, 2 tablespoons pepper, 2 tablespoons onion powder, 1 teaspoon cloves and 1 teaspoon allspice. Remove tough, heavy membrane from beef or lamb flank with sharp knife, Pull and slice flank apart at membrane layers, 3/4- to 1-inch thick. Keep membranes intact for outside covers. Cut out thick or hard fat, leaving a thin layer of fat. Cut a cover piece. Sprinkle generously with spice mixture. Fill in the layers of meat to make a shapely roll. Sprinkle with spice mix and roll. Tie in everal places to hold roll together.

Tuck in ends and pin with skewers. Sew edges or tie firmly over ends and then around, or insert the roll in mesh tubing, tying the ends. Remove skewers. Brine for 2 days (if sprinkled generously with spice mixture, brine for up to 4 days) or you can apply curing salt on the outside of the roll and place in a plastic bag in the refrigerator for several days, turning daily.

Smoke if desired. Boil 3 1/2 hours. Press while cooling. Remove all string. Slice thickly and enjoy on bread. Save any leftover spice mix in a glass jar with a tight cover.

Polish

Although Judith Kuczynski of Bismarck is Italian, her husband, Ken, is Polish and the majority of the foods served in their home follow the Polish trend. Her Polish Potato Pancakes recipe calls for 2 cups grated

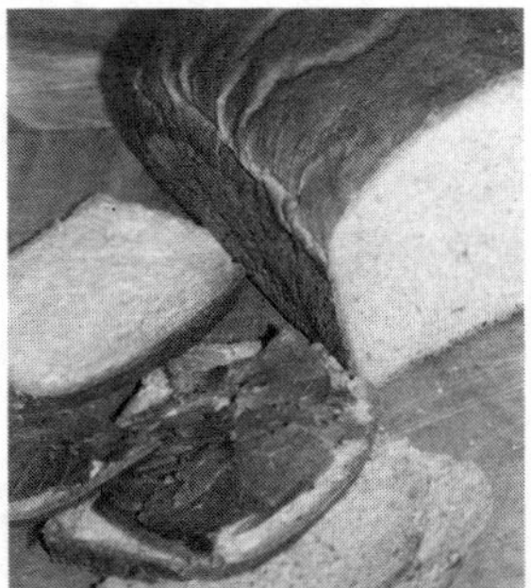

Afternoon coffee in Scandinavian homes might feature Icelandic vinarterta and twisted kleinur with loaf sugar for coffee, at left: brown bread with slices of rullupylsa or smoked mutton, center; or Norwegian lefse and krumkaka as enjoyed by Violet Olson and daughter Donna of Hettinger, at right.

raw potatoes (these are best if pureed in blender or food processor), 2 tablespoons flour, 2 well-beaten eggs, 1 teaspoon salt and 1 teaspoon sugar. If the potatoes are hand-grated, pour off any dark water that accumulates. If a blender or food processor is used, the puree will not separate so there will be no water to pour off. Mix all ingredients and beat well. With a spoon, drop the mixture onto a hot, lightly greased griddle or pan. Spread the mixture as thin as possible. Fry on both sides. Serve with a generous helping of sour cream and applesauce if desired.

Another Polish recipe is Cabbage Rolls or golabki: 1 pound ground beef, 1/2 pound ground pork or veal, 1/2 cup uncooked rice, 1 egg, 1 head of cabbage, 1 onion chopped fine, 1 tablespoon butter, salt and pepper. Optional ingredients are tomato puree, bacon and sour cream.

Remove core from whole head of cabbage with a sharp knife. Scald the cabbage and remove the outer leaves one at a time as they wilt. Cool before using. Wash rice in cold water and stir into 2 quarts of rapidly boiling salted water. Boil 10 minutes and strain. Run cold water through rice in strainer. This rice is only half-cooked now.

Saute onion in butter only until it becomes transparent; don't let it turn yellow. Combine with meat, egg, rice and seasoning and mix well. Spread each cabbage leaf wth meat, about 1/2 inch thick. Roll the leaf, fold in the ends and secure with a toothpick.

To cook, place the rolls in a baking dish, cover with 5 slices of bacon and roast uncovered for 2 hours at 300 degrees. Baste from time to time. If using tomato puree, pour tomato puree 1 1/2 inches deep over the rolls in pan, cover and bake at 300 degrees for 2 hours, adding water as necessary.

The cabbage rolls may be served with mushroom sauce, tomato sauce or sour cream. Kuczynski says they are even more delicious reheated and served the next day.

Bohemian

A Bohemian Poppy Seed Candy has been a favorite among relatives of Mrs. Charles Grantier, Mandan. The recipe is: 1 pound poppy seed, 2 cups honey and 2 cups mixed nuts. Boil honey about 10 minutes, add poppy seed, keep stirring, add nuts and boil until it turns light brown, then add 2 teaspoons of vanilla. Pour on buttered cookie sheet, pat flat with spoon, cool, then cut in diamond shapes.

Mrs. Gus Belohlavek of Mandan said she's failed many times with Bohemian recipes during her 46 years of marriage. Her husband taught her how to prepare the various dishes and he learned from his mother who was handicapped and sat by the table giving him the instructions. Here is her recipe for the popular Kolache. Ingredients: 3 packages of dry yeast, 1/2 cup lukewarm water, 1/2 cup sugar, 4 beaten eggs, 1 cup sour cream, 1/2 cup melted shortening and 4 1/2 to 5 cups of flour.

Disolve yeast in water in a large bowl, add sugar to dissolved yeast, add eggs, sour cream and melted butter and mix well. Add 3 cups of flour and mix well, gradually adding remaining flour. Dough should be soft and rather sticky. Turn dough onto floured pastry cloth and knead about 3 minutes until smooth. Grease bowl and place dough inside, turing to grease top. Cover with clean cloth. Place in a warm, draft-free place and let rise until doubled, then shape dough into small balls and place about 1 inch apart on greased cookie sheets. Let rise until light and then push down center with index finger and fill with prune filling. Makes 4 dozen small kolache.

Prune filling: 2 cups ground cooked prunes, 1/2 cup sugar, 1 teaspoon cinnamon, 1/2 teaspoon nutmeg, 1/2 grated lemon, 1 teaspoon vanilla and 1/8 teaspoon salt. Combine all ingredients. Add prune juice for desired thickening.

Instead of potatoes, they often prefer Bohemian Dumplings. Combine 2 cups flour, 2 eggs, 1 teaspoon salt, 1 teaspoon baking powder, add milk as needed. Drop into kettle of boiling water and cook until done. Remove dumplings and add fat from chicken or turkey and pour liquid over dumplings to roast in the oven for a short time. Serves large family.

Lebanese

Rita Nassif of Bismarck shares her Lebanese foods with people at local nursing homes, schools and hospitals, as well as with other people. Among her unusual dishes are Stuffed Grape Leaves, which require 2 pounds of course ground pork, beef or lamb, 2 cups uncooked rice, 2 tablespoons salt, 1 tablespoon pepper and 100 fresh or canned grape leaves.

Soak rice in boiling water for 30 minutes, then rinse thoroughly. Mix meat, salt and pepper thoroughly by hand. Run hot water on grape leaves for 60 seconds. Combine meat mixture and rice and put a tablespoon of mixture in the center of each grape leaf, roll from the top and boil them for 30 minutes in enough water to cover the stuffed leaves, using a high fire. Combine 8 ounces tomato sauce or 4 ounces tomato paste, 1 tablespoon salt, 1 tablespoon pepper, 3 crushed garlic cloves or 1/2 teaspoon garlic powder and 4 cups of water. Pour over stuffed grape leaves that have been placed in a pan and bake for 40 minutes at 400 degrees.

Baklava is on the order of a rich-tasting bar. To purify the butter used in the recipe, melt 1 1/2 pounds butter in a heavy saucepan. Bring butter to a full boil, reduce heat and simmer 20 minutes. Remove from heat. Drain butter into a clean pan and discard the cloudy butter residue. The filling recipe for this pastry is: 2 pounds of any ground nut meats, 1 cup granulated sugar, 1 tablespoon grated fresh lemon or orange rind. Mix together all ingredients for filling and set aside.

Pour one-third of the butter on the bottom of a 17-by-11-inch pan. Lay half of a 1-pound package of phyllo dough over the butter, allowing dough to hang over the edges of the pan. Take the overhanging dough and fold it to the middle. Pour another one-third of the butter over the dough. Pour all of the filling over the layer of phyllo dough and spread evenly. Take the remaining dough and place it over the layer of filling. Take the overhanging dough and fold it to the middle. Use a very sharp knife and cut the baklava into diamond or bar shapes. Spread the remaining butter over the dough. Bake in a 330 degree oven for 30-35 minutes until light brown. While baklava is baking, prepare the syrup.

The syrup recipe is: 1 cup water, 2 cups granulated sugar, 1 tablespoon lemon juice, 1 teaspoon grated freshlemon or orange rind and 1 1/2 cups honey. Combine water and sugar in a heavy saucepan on high heat. Stir constantly to dissolve sugar. Bring mixture to a boil and boil hard for 15 minutes. Then add the lemon juice and rind. Remove from heat and stir in the honey.

When the baklava comes out of the oven, immediately pour the syrup over the entire panful. Tip the pan slightly on one side to collect the excess syrup. Save and refrigerate the excess syrup, which can be used on pancakes and waffles.

Jewish

Marcia Harris of Bismarck considers her Aunt Lillian's Jewish Noodle Kugel among her favorite dishes. It requires 1 pound flat noodles, 4 eggs, 1 stick melted butter, 1/2 cup sugar, 1/2 cup raisins, 3 apples and a dash of cinnammon. Peel and slice apples, add part of the sugar and cinnamon, set aside. Cook and drain noodles. Beat eggs, add melted butter, remaining sugar and raisins. Add this mixture to noodles. Add apple slices. Heat a well-greased baking pan. Heating the pan before adding the mixture will make the bottom and sides crusty. Pour in mixture and bake at 350 degrees for about an hour. Cut in squares and serve warm.

She also shares a recipe for the well-known Matzoh Balls for chicken soup, using 2 eggs, 4 tablespoons fat, 1/2 cup matzoh meal and a pinch

Lutefisk keeps Norski traditions

Lutefisk might be called the food that has a personality all its own.

The very mention of lutefisk — that delicacy notorious for gracing the dinner tables of those of Scandinavian descent during the holiday season — seems to conjure up visions in people's minds.

A lutefisk hater may refer to the dish as rotten, stinking fish soaked in lye.

A lutefisk lover, on the other hand, will probably talk about beautiful, steaming hot, flaky, white cod fillets drenched with melted butter.

Who is right? And just what is this lutefisk, the butt of many jokes, the subject of songs and poems, the main attraction at annual church dinners to which thousands flock?

Dick Juel of Lyon Food Products Inc. and William Andresen, president of a company called Olfisco, helped answer these questions. Both companies are located in Minneapolis and both are manufacturers and wholesalers of lutefisk.

Although Juel said that the translation of lutefisk is "lyed fish," lye no longer is used in the lutefisk-making process as it once was.

Lutefisk starts out as dried cod fillets. Both Olfisco and Lyon Food Products get their dried cod from the Lofoten Islands off the northern coast of Norway.

Juel explained that the Lofoten Islands are a particularly good source of cod because the climate there is perfect for drying the fish in the open air. It's cool enough that there are no insects to bother the fish, but warm enough that the fish don't freeze.

When the dried cod reaches the United States, it is packed in 100-pound bundles that somewhat resemble shingles in texture and appearance.

At Olfisco, Andresen said the dried cod is first soaked in "caustic chemicals" for four or five days, then in fresh water for several more days. The company soaks up to 1,300 pounds of cod at a time in stock tanks.

The goal of all this soaking is to get the fish to look the way it did before it was dried. "What we're doing is putting the water back in it," Juel said. "If everything goes well, you end up with a beautiful, flaky white fish."

Around November, lutefisk starts showing up in the meat markets of local grocery stores. Juel says North Dakotans may consume more lutefisk per capita than residents of any other state.

Meat market managers from the Red Owl and Super Valu stores in Bismarck say that once lutefisk season starts, they generally have no problem selling whatever amount they can get. Last holiday season, one Super Valu store sold between 500 and 600 pounds of lutefisk.

Rolland Reinke, meat market manager of the Red Owl Family Center in Bismarck, seems to have the ideal job for someone with an appetite for lutefisk. He says he buys some extra lutefisk every year to take home and freeze.

"That way I can have lutefisk on the Fourth of July," he laughs. "I'm just a Norwegian boy who loves that Norwegian turkey."

No one seems to know for sure just how or when lutefisk came into being. Juel says it was a Viking accident, which seems reasonable.

He said the Vikings dried cod in order to take it with them on their long excursions at sea. As a food, dried cod traveled well, but getting it back to tasting or looking anything like fresh cod was a problem.

All this changed, Juel says, when some poor Viking accidentally dumped some ashes into a container of dried cod that was soaking in water. This error wasn't discovered for some time, and by the time it was, the ashes had turned to lye.

For some unknown reason, Juel continued, someone noticed that this accident had nearly restored the cod to its original, undried condition. Thus, the Vikings found that they could haul around their dried cod, then transform it into something more edible whenever they desired.

A more humorous theory about the origin of lutefisk is told in a story that comes from the Bismarck Sons of Norway chapter. This tale claims that centuries ago, there were many Norwegians living in Ireland during a famine.

Potatoes and fish were the only foods available. The Norwegians were snatching up all the potatoes for their lefse. Then they started going after the fish, which made the Irish very angry.

Well, as the story goes, the Irish decided to get rid of the Norwegians by rotting all the fish. The Norwegians ate it just the same. The Irish then resorted to dumping lye on the fish. That action resulted in the delicacy the Norwegians called lutefisk.

Eventually, the story goes, St. Patrick came to the rescue and drove the Norwegians out of Ireland, just as he did the snakes.

Tei-Tei Markley, chancellor at the Norwegian Consulate in Minneapolis and a native of Oslo, Norway, says lutefisk is a traditional holiday food in Sweden and Norway, just as it is in this country. It may not be eaten as much as it once was, but it is still eaten, she says.

"Some of the traditions are changing," Markley explained. "Norwegians are actually starting to eat more turkey."

She said she had eaten lutefisk only once before coming to the United States. Now she eats it about once every two years.

How does American lutefisk compare with Norwegian lutefisk? Markley thinks the American stuff tastes better.

Learning to like lutefisk may be a lot like learning to like beer, coffee or Lawrence Welk music.

"It's an aquired taste," Juel says.

Sig Peterson, who helps organize the town of Almont's annual lutefisk dinner, is a little more blunt: "It can take four or five years to get used to it."

According to die-hard lutefisk eaters, the secret to enjoying lutefisk is to have plenty of melted butter on hand. Also, overcooking lutefisk is to be avoided at all costs. Otherwise, it turns into fish mush.

There are two primary methods of cooking lutefisk — baking and boiling.

Mrs. Norman Hanson, who has been supervising the cooking of about 800 pounds of lutefisk at Almont's annual dinner for more than 20 years, says she prefers the boiling method.

She cuts the fish into strips 3 inches wide and ties three or four strips in a cheesecloth bag. The bundles containing the fish then are dropped into boiling water for five to

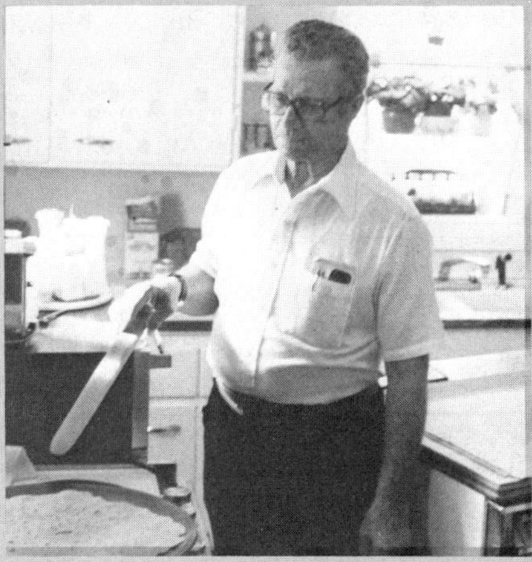

Lutefisk supper at Trinity Lutheran Church of Bismarck is served by Olga Ericson in Norwegian garb and enjoyed by the T-shirted pastor, Rev. John Nicolai. At center, Reynold Olson flips lefse with special stick; lefse is a staple at lutefisk suppers.

10 minutes. The bundles are periodically poked with a fork to test the lutefisk for firmness.

The Almont dinner usually attracts around 900 people. For those who haven't acquired a taste for lutefisk, but get dragged along to the dinner anyway, there are Swedish meatballs. Having the meatballs available for lutefisk haters is a standard lutefisk dinner tactic.

Shjeflo, who along with her husband, Jelmer, helps oversee the cooking of 850 pounds of lutefisk for the annual Sons of Norway dinner at Trinity Lutheran Church in Bismarck, prefers to bake the fish.

She recommends wrapping several pieces of lutefisk in aluminum foil, placing it on a cookie sheet, then baking it at 400 degrees for half an hour. This method, she says, has the advantage of keeping to tolerable standards the smell for which lutefisk is well-known.

That raises one point on which lutefisk lovers and haters seem to agree: Lutefisk really smells when it's being cooked. How badly it smells may be open for debate.

One can get some idea of the smell of cooking lutefisk by reading a few selected passages from a poem by Don Freeburg titled "Lutefisk Lament":

From out in the kitchen an odor came stealing
That fairly set my senses to reeling
The smell of Lutefisk creeped down the hall
That wilted a plant, in a pot, on the wall
...The scent skipped off the ceiling and bounced off the door
And the bird in the Cuckoo Clock fell on the floor.

This poem, obviously written by a lutefisk hater, is a good example of the poems, songs and jokes that give lutefisk a bad image. One would think that lutefisk lovers would be outraged by such propaganda.

On the contrary, they commonly sing songs like "Oh Lutefisk" (sung to the tune of "Oh Christmas Tree") at their annual dinners. Here is a portion of that song:

Oh lutefisk, oh lutefisk
You put me in a coma
You smell so strong
You look like glue
You taste yust like an overshoe
But lutefisk come Saturday
I tink I'll eat you anyway.

The taste of lutefisk is something that even longtime lutefisk lovers have a hard time describing. It seems the quality of a meal of lutefisk has a lot to do with how the lutefisk is served.

Norwegians have a preference for drowning their lutefisk in drawn butter with liberal doses of salt and pepper. Swedes prefer a thick, gravy-like cream sauce. The lutefisk may be spooned over boiled potatoes or lefse. Some like to eat it with mashed potatoes. Others like to eat their lefse separately with lots of brown sugar.

Patrick Miller

of salt. Beat the eggs, add salt and the fat (can be butter, chicken fat or a combination), gently fold in matzoh meal. Refrigerate at least two hours. Wet hands and form mixture into balls. Add to boiling chicken soup. Cook about 15 minutes. Makes about 1 dozen small matzoh balls.

And now for the Chicken Soup, which she calls "Jewish Penicillin." Ingredients: whole chicken, 3 carrots, 3 stalks of celery with some leaves left on, whole onion, salt and pepper, pickling spices and matzoh balls. Cover whole chicken with water in large pot, bring to a boil and skim the top. Lower heat to simmer, add onion, salt, pepper and spices. Let simmer, covered, about $1^1/_2$ hours. Add cut-up vegetables, season to taste, cook another hour or until vegetables are soft and chicken is falling off the bones. Remove chicken, debone and put meat back in the pot. Bring to boil again and add matzoh balls. Serves many.

Indian

Louis Gipp of Fort Yates, who was a tribal judge there for many years, likes to make Indian soup from a recipe used by his Sioux Indian mother. Because it calls mostly for dried foods, you need to prepare them when they are available in summer and then cook up the soup on the first nippy fall day. The recipe calls for salt pork, dried meat, corn and wild turnips.

The turnips, said the judge, are important for flavor. They grow on North Dakota hillsides and are best picked in July. Dried and properly stored, they will keep for several years, he said. The plant has a gray, fuzzy stalk and grows about 6 inches tall. It looks like a little tree and the flower is blue. Wild turnips are about golf-ball size and have a leathery brown outer layer. Peel down to the snow white flesh, put in a cheesecloth bag and hang in a high, dry place. Indian people used to hang their drying foods on the tepee ridge log because warm but dry air is best. Gipp uses a tall pole.

The soup calls for about $1^1/_2$ pounds of meat. In place of the buffalo used by his forefathers, Gipp uses round steak. Slice it about $^1/_8$-inch thick and hang it up in a high, dry place for four or five days. It will turn brittle and blackish in color but won't spoil as long as the humidity is low.

To dry corn, take sweet corn that has reached the roasting ears stage and boil until tender. Let it cool, then use a spoon to remove the kernels one row at a time. Spread the kernels out to dry. Then store the corn in a cool, dry place. The kernels will expand again when put into the soup broth.

Now you're ready to make the soup. Soak a cup of dried corn overnight. Parboil 1 pound of sliced, lean salt pork a few minutes to render out some of the fat and salt. Discard the liquid. Put about four turnips in a pot, cover with water and boil until tender, maybe an hour. Add the corn and meat, broken into bite-sized pieces. Simmer until all ingredients are tender, about half an hour. Don't overcook, the judge cautioned.

Gloria Feickert

Doughty German soup regains favor

Renae Hornbacher dishes up knoepfle soup at a Bismarck restaurant.

Dough is German-Russian soul food.

"It seemed that everybody made a dough dish for dinner," according to Wilhelmina "Minnie" Geiger of rural Mandan, who teaches an adult education course in German cooking through the Mandan public schools.

Of Germans who immigrated to this area from Russia, Geiger said, "They were poor people and they had to make things with what they had."

Almost all had eggs and flour, the two absolute necessities for dough, she said. "I think they were really inventive people. Instead of sitting around eating flour and bread, they learned to invent all these dishes."

"Most of it was just dough," she added.

But therein lies the appeal of knoepfle soup.

Knoepfle, also known as noeffle, nueffla, noefle, niffle, knoefle, knepfla, knipf and by other spellings, but most often pronounced "nifla," is the name given to the very basic noodles or dumplings that have been a staple of the diet of many Germans from Russia since, at the very least, the middle of the 1800s.

Knoepfle soup at its most basic is just these dumplings cooked with a hearty vegetable or chicken broth.

According to Geiger, knoepfle soup was especially important during winters on the farm or ranch, when it provided both nutrition and quick, lasting warmth.

While it was never in any immediate danger of extinction, knoepfle soup began to appear more rarely on the dinner table as times changed.

"I think they were tired of them (knoepfles)," Geiger said. "As they became more affluent, they would go into more potatoes and meat."

But it's apparent to any cafe-hopper that knoepfle is making a big comeback in the Bismarck-Mandan area and throughout the German and Germans-from-Russia strongholds in the state.

Whereas for most of the 1970s it was featured at — as far as could be determined — only two restaurants in the Bismarck-Mandan area, it now is on the menu of more than a dozen, either daily or as one of several "soups du jour."

The majority of area restaurants that have added knoepfle soup did so since last fall. There is no apparent reason why it has so suddenly burst upon the culinary scene, though it seems every new restaurant to add the soup to its menu contributed to a chain reaction of interest.

"It seems like everybody likes it," Geiger said. Newcomers, like a British friend of hers, have found "it grows on you."

Geiger said that potatoes and chicken, either as a base for the broth or as meat, are a common addition. Some people also flavor the soup with onions, dill weed, bay leaf or parsley.

And those who find the soup is too thin or too bland or too low in calories may well add sweet or sour cream to the broth.

"Everybody's been more interested in going the old way," Geiger said, by way of explaining the craze over knoepfle soup.

Young people who did no have knoepfle soup in the past like it because it's different and because circumstances don't force them to consume it almost daily, she said.

And, she said, of those who grew up with it and had almost forgotten it, "They remember, 'Hey, that wasn't bad at all.'"

Randy Christianson

Sausage recipe calls for 3 steers, 2 hogs

Homemade sausage is a specialty of German and German-Russian communities. In pre-freezer days, when preserving meat was important to livelihood, families would get together every fall for sausage-making. Some still do.

The daughter and two sons of Albert and Opal Friez traditionally come home to Bentley with their families for Thanksgiving and stay on for the two or three days it takes to butcher and make sausage. Gary and Earleen Friez live in Hettinger, Bev and Terry Klein in Bismarck. Opal Friez has been a widow three years and now lives in Bismarck. Her son Wayne and Reva, his wife, farm the home place where the butchering is done.

It takes three beef steers, two hogs and a deer or two to begin the Friez sausage-making operation, according to Earleen Friez. Meat is cut into steaks, chops and roasts and wrapped for the freezer. Hamburger is ground in an electric grinder and packaged.

Scrap pieces go into two tubs, one for beef, one for pork, with vension chunks in a third tub — all for sausage. Nothing is wasted. Pork heads are boiled for sausage, as are tongue, heart and liver. Lard is ground and rendered in the oven, then poured in jars and sealed. This home-rendered lard is especially good for deep fat frying, pie crust and ginger cookies, says Earleen.

The basic Friez recipe for sausage combines 65 pounds of ground pork and 28 pounds of ground beef with one and a half cups of Tender Quick and three-fourths cup each of salt and pepper. Garlic, mixed in the blender with water, is added to taste. This involves mixing, frying a small patty and passing around tastes for a family opinion.

Much of the sausage is pressed into long casings, twisted at intervals so it can be hung in the smokehouse. For variety, some remains unsmoked, some is frozen, some canned. Canned sausage keeps longer with better flavor, according to Friez.

Liver sausage for lunch meat is made from ground cooked liver mixed with ground boiled beef, seasoned with mustard seed and other spices and sealed in small jars. *F.B.*

Making sausage takes a sure hand at the stuffing machine, in filling hamburger bags, and in canning and freezing. The jars hold, from left to right, liver sausage, pork sausage —without casing, canned unsmoked in casing, canned smoked in casing. On plate is smoked sausage in casing as taken from the freezer.

Earleen and Nancy Friez enjoy canned pork sausage on bun halves.

Crowning of Miss Malanka and an auction climax Ukrainian New Year's Eve celebrations in Belfield. According to legend, Malanka dressed as a woman and went about the country seeking liquor and stealing items which he sold on New Year's Eve.

Christmas was simple in early times

Christmas was the white man's "big medicine day," according to North Dakota Indians, but some of the first whites to explore the territory had a miserable Christmas.

French explorer Pierre de la Verendrye spent the Yule holiday of 1738 sick in bed at an Indian village on the Mouse River.

Christmas Eve of 1797 in North Dakota wasn't much better for geographer David Thompson and his party of explorers. Hiding from an Indian raiding party near Butte, they had to camp in snowdrifts because they could find no shelter. The temperature dropped to 17 below that night and Thompson's fingers froze.

But Christmas celebrations were a little better at the first trading posts. Alexander Henry of Northwest Co., who established a post at the junction of the Park and Red rivers, wrote that, for his first Christmas in 1800, he treated his employees to "high wine, flour and sugar."

On New Year's Day, he added, they fired volleys into the air to usher in the new year. That surprised a band of Indians living nearby, who immediately grabbed their guns and rushed into the fort. The Indians, who had never seen the white man celebrate the New Year, according to Henry, thought that the gunfire meant danger nearby.

At Fort Mandan in McLean County in 1804, the Lewis and Clark expedition danced and fired guns to celebrate Christmas Day, the completion of the fort and the first official hoisting of the American flag in Dakota territory.

Prince Philip Maximilian of Germany, who spent the winter of 1833 in North Dakota, wrote about similar Christmas activities at the Knife River Indian villages. Highlights of the day, wrote Maximilian, were the arrival of couriers from Fort Union, who brought mail and the latest gossip, and a special meat ration for fur company employees, who had been on a diet of boiled corn for some time.

These are just a few accounts of yule celebrations on the Dakota frontier in "How Christmas Came to North Dakota," a book published in 1929 by Clell Gannon of Bismarck.

Celebrations of Christmas in North Dakota became more formal and refined as settlers moved in, starting about 1870.

With improvements in mail, transportation and retail services, North Dakotans were able to obtain more easily the store-bought items needed for yuletide celebrating. These included manufactured candles, tree ornaments and specialties such as "Oplatki" (special Christmas wafers for Polish Catholic church services).

The immigrants from European countries each had their own Christmas traditions, some of which have been preserved.

Gute Stube

"Weihnacht" was what the Germans called Christmas Eve, according to the late Arthur Leno of Bismarck, who researched Christmas traditions.

North Dakota Germans may remember the "Gute Stube" (Christmas room), a separate room or corner off limits to the children, where an ornamented tree and things for the eve mysteriously gathered.

The room was guarded by a rough character named "Belz-A-Nickel," according to legend. Like Santa Claus, he had the power to monitor behavior all year long and the authority to deny all but a piece of coal or wood to children who didn't measure up.

On Christmas Eve, the Christmas tree would be brought forth and decorated with ornaments, often homemade.

The Christmas Eve meal would be simple, sometimes with fish the main course. Afterward, the "Gabenbringer" would bring out the gifts, to be opened after church services. Some families would take time to sing some carols.

Then would come the "Bescherung," or bell-ringing, signaling a welcome to midnight church services. During the services, the children would recite and sing in programs for which they had spent many hours in rehearsal. Everyone would sing in German such favorites as "Silent Night."

Often, a sack of nuts would be distributed among members of the congregation at the close of the service.

Favorite German Christmas foods were "Der Kunterbunde Niklaustell-er," a Christmas plate decorated with pine twigs and cones and loaded with confections and baked goods. Goose, carp and hot drinks mixed with wine, rum, sugar, spices and fruits were favorites. So was marzipan, a confection of ground almonds, powdered sugar, egg whites and rosewater.

According to Mrs. Freda Redding, Cathay, her "Redding clan" still gathers at her home — her parents' homestead — for Christmas Eve. They sing German carols, drink German refreshments and her grandchildren "say their pieces."

Smoked mutton

According to author Thorstina Walters, a North Dakota native of Icelandic descent who studied the culture and customs, Icelandic settlers gradually have abandoned their native yuletide traditions. Fairly early in their history in North Dakota, they adopted most American Christmas customs. Among the few Icelandic Christmas traditions preserved in many families, she wrote, are Christmas dishes such as smoked mutton and the piece de resistance — the Vinarterta (Vienna tart). Between the six layers of thin cookie dough are chopped prunes, flavored with spices and sweets.

According to Mrs. Alvin Melstad, Edinburg, Icelandic customs are still part of Christmas Eve services at the Gardar Lutheran Church in northeastern North Dakota. A couple of Christmas carols are sung in Icelandic and apples and bags of candy are distributed to everyone in attendance.

They serve favorite Icelandic dishes including Vinarterta and lamb served hot as a meat course with potatoes or cold with dark bread as sandwich meat. They also make Jola Kaka, which is similar to the Norwegian Jule Kake — a white bread with candied fruit peel and raisins.

On Christmas Eve, Melstad's family eats lutefisk and lefse for dinner in the early afternoon. Then they go to church for a 7:30 p.m. service, where they sing "Silent Night" in Icelandic and English and an Icelandic song in the native tongue.

Around the tree

Gerda Farr, Mandan, recalls that her family would dance around the Christmas tree, holding hands and singing Norwegian carols. They would learn pieces for the Lutheran Church children's program to be held later that evening, which they would sometimes repeat in front of the tree when they returned home.

Christmas Eve supper consisted of lutefisk, lefse, boiled potatoes, spareribs and pork links. They would hurry to get the supper dishes done so they could open their gifts.

Caroling

Some Ukrainians in the Belfield-Dickinson region say they still practice numerous Christmas and New Year's Eve traditions.

For instance, they start out with the "Koliada," or caroling, just before Christmas Eve. Carolers go through neighborhoods, singing traditional Ukrainian Christmas carols. As they come to each house, the "Koliadnyki" (carol singers) announce their arrival by ringing a small bell. After singing some carols, they then sing "plyas" — verses on why they should be allowed inside for food and drink.

The Ukrainians celebrate Christmas Eve with a "Sviata Vechera" (holy supper), which cannot begin until the North Star appears in the evening sky. As the family gathers around the dinner table, a chair is left empty out of respect for deceased relatives. The supper consists of pirohi, molaches, kutia and breads.

Burning candle

According to Jane M. Glander of Grafton, whose uncle was a pastor in Finland, one of the most beautiful Finnish customs was to place a burning candle in a glass container on the graves of the family members and friends. He recalled it was beautiful to see all the candles burning in a graveyard at night.

"If we did not eat all day we were told we'd see the golden pig."

One of the Polish Christmas customs is "Oplatek."

The Polish community at St. Stanislaus Catholic Church, Warsaw, still "shares the wafer" in church and at organization meetings during Christmas, according to the Rev. Stanislaus Duda, the minister of the 99-year-old parish.

Oplatek means "something flat," according to Duda.

The tradition of the Oplatek goes back to at least the 10th century, when the Catholic Church of Rome made a white, liturgical wafer with a religious motif engraved on one side.

According to Duda, the Poles call Christmas Eve dinner "Wigilia." The wafer is shared in a ceremony before they eat and also later that evening at church services.

At the dinner, the father presents his wafer and mother and children each break off a piece. Then each member of the family takes turns presenting the wafer to others, from the mother on down to the youngest. Each person must offer the others forgiveness for transgressions before he or she can eat. The wafer represents the Lord, Duda said, adding, "The spirit (is) to share it with everyone to get rid of any animosity between people."

There are at least seven courses in the dinner and the number must be uneven. Some Poles set an extra plate at the Christmas Eve supper table for an unexpected guest or Jesus Christ. Each person must eat a mouthful of each course and a little of each leftover will be thrown later to the animals.

The early Czechoslovakian settlers in the New Hradec area kept up a number of traditions at Christmas, according to Albert and Lillian Ficek.

Albert says the Czechoslovakian, or Bohemian, Christmas season was a very special, solemn occasion. It started Nov. 25 with the beginning of Advent and the feast day of St. Catherine.

"The saying was 'Katerina zavira muzinkanti do chleva' — Catherine locks the musicians in the barn," Ficek says.

Tradition allowed no dances, weddings or music during this period.

A golden pig

Czechoslovakians fasted the day before Christmas. They could eat only one meal, at supper, and no meat. During the fast, children were encouraged to be especially kind to one another. "We were told that if we did not eat all day we would see a golden pig," he says. The temptation to taste the goodies was great, he recalls, and he never saw a golden pig.

According to Lillian, the Czech tradition didn't allow meat to be served at the Christmas Eve meal, so fish usually was the main course. The fish bones would be saved and thrown into the fields afterward to ensure that next year's crops would be bountiful.

The door of the living room was locked early Christmas Day. The mother, in addition to preparing the feast, would enter the living room to get it ready, dress the tree and stack presents.

Just before supper, there would be the cutting of an apple cross-wise. The person whose core showed a cross instead of a star was supposed to die or have misfortune during the coming year. To offset any fears, later on in the evening another apple was sliced into as many pieces as there were persons present, and each person had to eat his slice to keep the family together for the coming year.

After this was done, then everybody would enter the living room to open presents.

Christmas celebrations continued on Christmas Day and the two days afterward, the days of St. Steven and St. John. The men would play cards or other games.

The Czechoslovakians would celebrate the Feast of the Three Kings on Jan. 6. Three men would dress like kings and go from farm to farm with appropriate sayings.

John Pearson

Belfield couple keeps tradition

Edward and Lana Procive are crowned with regal wedding crowns during traditional Ukrainian ceremony.

Edward and Lana Procive started a tradition by returning to a tradition.

In July 1980 they were married in a Ukrainian ceremony at St. Demetrius Ukrainian Catholic Church in Belfield. Since their wedding, several other couples have followed in their footsteps, Lana says.

The return to a traditional wedding was the result of Edward and Lana's desire to participate in a ceremony that goes back to their roots, with strong encouragement from the Rev. Tom Glynn, pastor of St. Demetrius.

"It was both our ideas, Father Tom's and mine," Lana says. "He was tired of everyone fighting him to do things differently during the ceremony. He said it (the marriage) should occur the way it was meant to. I wasn't going to fight him; I didn't want to."

Some of the traditions are a throwback to when matchmaking was the province of fathers in the Ukraine, Lana says. There is a bit of superstition and traditional religious rites, as well.

The wedding ceremonies actually began at the home of Lana's parents when Edward arrived and Lana's father gave her away to him.

A Ukrainian band that had been waiting at the door was welcomed into the house by Lana's father, who informed the musicians that a wedding was going to take place and they would be needed for the celebration.

First, the bridegroom was brought into the home by his parents and introduced to the bride's parents. Then the bride was brought into the room.

As part of the festivities, bread with a cup of hardened salt — signifying a wish for prosperity — was placed on both their heads. Then a sprig of myrtle was placed in Lana's hair to signify purity.

Then the couple was blessed in turn by both sets of parents and grandparents.

From there, Lana and Edward, accompanied by the wedding party, went to St. Demetrius. Lana and Edward headed the wedding party as it lined up in the vestibule of the church behind a closed door.

The wedding began as Glynn walked down from the altar to the church doors, bearing two candles that he presented to Lana and Edward. He then introduced the couple to each other and led them to the altar.

The ceremony was of the Byzantine Catholic rite, including a Mass.

During the ceremony, both Lana and Edward drank altar wine from the same chalice, which is called the "cup of joy and sorrow."

Finally, two wedding crowns were placed above their heads and switched back and forth three times, signifying the three figures of the trinity. A couple is not considered married until the placing of the crowns, Lana says.

From the church, the wedding party proceeded to a banquet reception. At the start of the festivities, a master of ceremonies clutched a white handkerchief and handed one end to Lana. Lana then held hands with Edward, and members of the wedding party also held hands in a line alternating between men and women.

Then the master of ceremonies led the party at a run around the head table three times, which again signified the trinity.

Lana, with a merry laugh, summed up her feelings about her marriage ceremony in three words: "It was great!"

Mark Kinders

Czech wedding celebrated with drama, humor

A Czech wedding, as celebrated in the New Hradek community north of Dickinson, began with the delivery of spoken invitations by two groomsmen who dashed up on horseback, according to Lillian and Albert Ficek of New Hradek.

These young friends of the groom would gallop into the yard, shoot blanks from their pistols in the air, and deliver a poetic invitation. Then they offered drinks all around and rode off to the next place.

Meanwhile at the bride's home much baking went on. Both families, especially the groom's, stood ready to provide barrels of wine and gallons of whiskey, often homemade. It was considered important for everyone to be happy and generously provided with food and drink at the wedding.

A master of ceremonies was selected — an uncle or neighbor with a flair for speaking in a dramatic and humorous way. On the wedding morning he came with the groom and parents to the home of the bride. He gave a formal speech in rhyme informing the family they would lose their daughter and must tell her farewell and he asks their blessing on the marriage. The scene was appropriately touching with "lots of crying," say the Ficeks.

In this bridal photo of Joe and Mary Zimbrick, best man Joe Kudrna demonstrates Czech custom of announcing weddings by shooting blanks into the air. Ribbons are worn by groom, and waxed-flower wreaths in hair of bride and bridesmaid.

They then went together in buggies to the morning wedding ceremony at the church, with horses decorated with ribbons and keeping a lively pace. Afterwards all returned to the bride's home. There both mothers, who arrived first, greeted the bridal couple at the door with a plate of kolache (rolls with fruit filling).

Guests were welcomed by the master of ceremonies and invited to sit at long tables set for the wedding dinner. Homes might be small, but the Ficeks remember there always seemed to be room for everyone. A mealtime prayer was given by the master of ceremonies — the end of his serious duties — and he said, "Now my dear guests, eat heartily, and you musicians play merrily." From this time he was full of jesting and humor, continuing however to speak in rhyming phrases. (The Ficeks note that not always do the Czech phrases translate well into English rhymes.)

The unmarried girls wore wreaths in their hair and sat with the bride and groom. Boys and young men were waiters, serving first the bridal table, then other guests. The menu began with rich soup, followed by fried or baked chicken, mashed potatoes, kolache and many heaping bowls of homemade buttered noodles.

Each dish, as it was brought from the kitchen, was presented by the master of cermonies. In his book "My Experiences" Frank Nadvornik of Dickinson recalls the master of ceremonies at his sister's wedding shouting as he brought the soup, "Please give me room, I have something for the bride and groom." Whereupon he deliberately tripped and spilled the soup. He apologized elaborately to the bride, saying he had handled oxen for the last ten years and repaired shoes when he was manager of "Dlouhe Lhoty" — a town of low esteem — so he should be well fit for this task. Then he brought a second bowl of soup with another short verse.

After eating, guests remained seated while the best man went to each in turn with a plate and glass of liquor requesting money for the crib of the firstborn and a wish for good luck. He began with the maidens, and as each dropped in a coin she took a sip. This could last for an hour or two, Albert Ficek recalls, and might be repeated several times during the next day's celebrating.

Guests visited during the afternoon and then sat for another formal meal. This was the last sit-down meal; afterward anyone hungry went to the kitchen where huge amounts of food were always available.

Dancing began in the evening. In the early days this was in the bride's home, or perhaps in a granery or barn. Wedding dances were later held in the town hall. A band played throughout the night, paid for by the groom; a collection was also taken among the single men.

Until midnight the bride wore her wedding dress and veil. Then her veil and wreath were removed. A silk dust cap was placed on her head and she was told, in song, that she was no longer a girl, but a woman.

Dancing, drinking and eating continued the next day and often on the third, with bride and groom staying throughout. Some men would go home for chores and others napped on the floor. Practical jokes were played and occasionally fights broke out. "It's no wonder fights developed, when so much liquor was consumed," says Nadvornik. "But the people didn't mind. It was something to talk about." *F.B.*

Brauche: a healing gift

Among the community of Germans from Russia in North Dakota are those who are said to have a special gift of healing called "brauche."

It has deep roots in those people's history. It is still being carried on today in North Dakota. Some say the practice is dying out, while others say its use is gaining in some areas.

It has been credited with sometimes miraculous cures, but critics say its power is mostly in the mind of patients — people seeking simple cures to complex maladies. It is akin to the modern versions of faith healing, the critics contend.

Further clouding the mysterious practice is its confusion with "hexe," or witchcraft, and magic, thus giving it an anti-religious identity.

Brauchers — those who practice the prayer healing — and others are adamant that brauche involves no witchcraft or magic. Brauche actually has "strong religious connotations, but critics want to make it anything but," says Tim Kloberdanz, assistant professor of sociology at North Dakota State University. Many brauchers say, for instance, that Jesus was a braucher himself, according to Kloberdanz.

He says that, historically, the practice of brauche falls into the category of folk religion as contrasted with official religion. He also notes that in pre-Reformation times, priests practiced healing.

There also were village shamans, or medicine men, who claimed healing powers. Some were branded as witches and persecuted, underwriting the historical confusion between witchcraft and brauche.

Brauche was brought to North Dakota by those Germans who had left their homeland to seek a better life in Russia. Isolated in that strange land, they continued many traditions, including the practice of brauche, according to Kloberdanz.

Brauche served as an answer to a practical problem: the transplanted Germans found themselves short of doctors and other medical help. Villagers relied on some talented residents who, according to one historian, were "old women (who) picked the herbs and made the remedies."

Intermingled with brauche are folk remedies and some formal training, perhaps midwifery or massage therapy, which some Germans, mostly women, received.

With the German-Russian immigration to the United States, brauche was continued in North Dakota as the new settlers again found themselves in similar circumstances — isolated and lacking formal medical help.

Today the greatest concentration of brauchers reportedly can be found in the south central section of the state because of the high concentration of German-Russian settlement there.

There are no figures on how many brauchers there are, but Kloberdanz says that, contrary to popular notions, the practice continues to be strong in some parts of the state.

In simple terms, brauche involves the use of prayers or incantations, combined with folk medicine and home remedies, to heal.

The word brauche is a euphemistic adaptation of the German verb "brauchen," which means to use or need, notes Kloberdanz. However, brauche has come to mean — at least to those who believe in it — "helping" or "healing."

Brauchers are firm believers and they claim no special powers themselves, saying that God has given them a special talent to use their knowledge.

Says one braucher, according to Schock: "I don't have any more power than you, except I believe Jesus helps us, and that's all."

When a patient visits for the first time, the braucher's usual procedure is simply to question the person on the circumstances surrounding the illness, find the area of the body that may be in pain and then make a diagnosis, based on experience or training.

Some sort of curing substance is usually used and prescribed, ranging from salves, ointments, herbs and teas to salt and cabbage leaves.

A prayer is recited in German, usually in tones so low that even the patient can't hear it clearly. A common denominator in those prayers is calling upon the Holy Trinity — the Father, Son and Holy Ghost — to heal. The incantations usually are said three times.

Brauche is a positive part of the culture, says Karen Retzlaff of Aneta, state president of the Germans from Russia Heritage Society. She notes that because of circumstances, people came to rely on those who were said to have the healing gift.

The healers' approach also is akin to the holistic method now becoming popular, she says.

Kloberdanz agrees, saying there is growing support for treating the body as a whole, rather than as a machine.

Stan Stelter

Icelandic sagas kept history alive

"It is 50 years ago since I left Iceland," said a speaker at the 50th anniversary celebration of Icelandic settlement in North Dakota, held in Mountain in 1928. "But thanks to my early training, Iceland and its lore became a living reality at an early age. The Icelandic sagas were familiar to me before I knew any English, and the heroes of Iceland's golden era were clearly pictured in my mind."

Icelandic tradition of telling stories, often 9th and 10th century sagas, was kept very much alive in North Dakota homes. In her book "Modern Sagas," Thorstina Walters recalls her grandfather's stories. He told her of the dangers of ocean fishing in small rowboats, of the great geysers of Iceland, of the lava fields and the mountains, "sometimes gleaming and inviting, sometimes dark," and fearful tales of trolls, ghosts and other mystic beings. Walters recalls his tale of the mysterious mountain Holmafjall, the home of a mighty giant who, it was said, kidnapped the most beautiful maiden in the land. When the midnight sun lighted the landscape on a summer night a mournful singing, the lament of this lovely girl forced to be wife to the giant troll, could be heard from the depths of the mountain.

Walters writes she never tired of hearing of the strange shaped lava rocks and folklore explanations: they were trolls of the night, turned to stone when caught outside after daybreak.

Juleboks still roam North Dakota countryside at Christmas seeking treats as here at Rolf Berg home near Maddock.

Juleboks invade festive homes

The Julebok custom stems from a Scandinavian legend that at Christmas the trolls — or other malevolent spirits — come down from the mountains and invade people's homes. If given food or wine, they go away without harming anyone.

In some Norwegian communities in North Dakota the Julebok tradition continues today. In the Viking community near Maddock, old eyes sparkle with pleasure, and the very young with apprehension, as there comes a great pounding and shouting at the door. Without waiting for the door to open, the Juleboks burst in — a strange-looking group in red flannels, ragged coats, or grandmother's dress with padding fore and aft. All are masked in painted flour sacks, decorated paper bags or stockings. They shriek and jest with their hosts in high squeaky voices or in deep growls. They jig and dance, sing songs, peer close into a child's awe-struck face, and pat faded old cheeks mischeviously with snowy mittens. Juleboks are the only ones with the audacity to stomp across a clean kitchen floor with their overshoes on.

The family must identify each of the eight to ten people in the group before they will unmask, and the revelers roar with laughter at each mistaken guess. Sometimes they sing an off-key version of "Ja var sa glad" (a favorite: "I am so glad each Christmas Eve") and other Norwegian songs.

Since the Juleboks, or Christmas fools, come out between Christmas and New Years — during the traditional visiting period — they often invade fairly large social gatherings. This helps to make the evening more festive for all. Since Juleboks make an effort to stop at the homes of their various relatives and close neighbors, their identify is soon guessed.

On rare occasion they meet with resistance — as once when they invaded the home of a new bride. When her door burst violently open and the "monsters" crowded in, she grabbed the butcher knife to face them. Just in time her husband arrived, while the shaken Juleboks hastily unmasked.

When all are identified the hostess passes goodies, or perhaps if the group is older, small glasses of red wine. Brief jovial socializing follows, then the Juleboks shout farewells and are off to the next farm. *F.B.*

Her grandfather's memories turned always to the sea, says Walters, in such lyrics as these:

The skerry away in the fjord,
So deep in the sea's unrest.
In silence endures forever
The foam that beats on its
breast.

Other tales concerned the fog in which he was continually losing his flock of sheep. A folk belief held that the fog was a beautiful princess cast under a magic spell; her only hope of release was a young shepherd who for 17 years never complained about the fog.

Fierce sagas of war and conquest were passed on in North Dakota, as they had been in Iceland for centuries when in long winter evenings the warriors and skalds gathered around fires and fought again the old battles in song and story. It was Iceland which preserved and kept alive the ancient Scandinavian sagas until they could be recorded in the 12th century.

Iceland was colonized by Vikings from Sweden, Norway, Denmark and from earlier Viking settlements in Ireland and Scotland, in which was mixed the Celtic blood. A Swedish writer, Tre Tryckare, describes typical colonists leaving for Iceland in the 800s. "Rugged bearded men, young and old, girt with swords, carrying spears, axes and shields; women in full-length gowns of homespun, youngsters and babies. They are carrying all kinds of baggage and stores aboard. (Their ships are) shorter and wider, not so lithe and deadly-looking as the warships, but solid, sea-going vessels. Household articles of every sort (are loaded) and livestock: sheep, cattle, horses, pigs, even squawking chickens. They say goodbye to a group of friends; then the boat is pushed off and rowed out into the fjord."

Descendants of these early colonizers cast off from Iceland bound for America a thousand years later. For them, like Germans and Czechs from Russia, the move to North Dakota was but another historic move as land became scarce and cultivated lands overpopulated. But they kept faith with ancient tradition through stories and sagas still told in Icelandic communities. *F.B.*

Lute—a fiske troll—riles water

Lute prided himself as one of Norway's meanest trolls. Touchy, along with having the characteristics of carrying long grudges, made him a troll to be avoided.

Lute hated nicknames. To be referred to as "Shorty", "Stub" or "Beady Eyes" would send other trolls scurrying as he flew into a rage.

When aggravated, Lute would stuff both cheeks with a super-sized load of Copenhagen. (He would use both sides to make certain all Norskes would know he was on the level.) In the darkness of night he would climb the mountains surrounding the fjords and with the wind on his back would spit for hours into the icy waters with a primary goal of contaminating all the fish. He thought he was getting revenge by destroying the area's main food supply. The light of morning made him leap with joy as codfish floated belly up on beaches for miles around.

However, to his utter dismay, Norwegians from all the surrounding farms and villages soon crowded the beaches with pitchforks and loaded cart after cart with spoiled fish — They liked them!

In reaction, with his anger now increased fourfold, Lute decided to leave Norway. Hearing there was a group of Norwegians settled around Hettinger, ND, Lute crawled into a crate of pickled herring and immigrated.

Now in the Hettinger area, when he gets mad, Lute just spits into the water supply turning it brown and making it smell like rotten eggs. To his dismay they still drink it and use it to bathe. But he is satisfied in hearing them complain a lot about it.

Moral: All that smells rotten is not necessarily bad.

Robert Boxrud

The evil disposition of trolls who followed immigrants to North Dakota is revealed in story at left as well as in other modern tales collected by Valborg Fisher of Bismarck in "Trolls of District IV." The Sons of Norway book pictures this bewhiskered troll with bushy tail, by Magnhild Hegland, on the cover.

Belznickl, Kristkindl terrorize and fascinate children

As Christmas drew near the anxiety started building; our thoughts and talk turned to the "Belznickl" and "Kristkindl" who would soon be coming. As early as two weeks before Christmas the Belznickl would gather his chains, rattling and roaring at the window just to be sure we wouldn't forget he was coming. Now if anything can keep you from misbehaving, the Belznickl could. He was a threat not to be taken idly. After all, he could drag you away on Christmas eve. Usually the morning after the Belznickl rapped at the windows, we would check to see whether he left any footprints. But we never did find any.

Finally Christmas eve would arrive and our anticipation and apprehension was enough to drive everyone wild. The Belznickl would start early after the evening dinner. His rattling and growling would keep on for an hour or two. When he let up for a few minutes, we would worry that he had skipped our home and gone somewhere else. He and the Kristkindl did, after all, leave gifts and treats and we certainly didn't want to miss that. Usually preceding the actual entrance of the Kristkindl and Belznickl, we would furiously say prayer after prayer.

Finally the Belznickl came in with the Kristkindl behind. He was a furry thing that crawled on all fours, rattled his chain, and grabbed anyone or anything that got in his way. His objective was to get the bad kids and drag them away. Often he had to be held back by Mom or an older brother or sister. We'd pile on the bed, many times 10 or more of us kids, jump and wrap up in Mom's bedspread. He'd make a grab for us and we'd run.

The Belznickl was really our father but we didn't know that. We were so scared we didn't even recognize the big bear-like robe that we used on the bed for extra warmth at night. He'd tell us we'd better be good for the next year. Later Mother would remind us "the Belznickl will get you" if we weren't good.

Our first reaction to the Kristkindl was always what a beautiful angel she was. She was a neighbor woman dressed as an angel and would ask if we'd been good. If we didn't answer immediately that we had, she'd swat us with a little willow switch. She reminded us to say our prayers and this was usually followed by an Our Father and a Hail Mary. The Belznickl in this whole process would try to grab our legs in order to take us away. A great havoc was created with prayers being said amid screams of agony and peals of laughter. After the children received their gifts the awesome duo would leave and the evening settled down. Gifts were opened, songs were sung, and stomachs were filled with Christmas treats. It was always an evening filled with enough memories to last for a year.

Kas Greff
Ida Greff Heidt

Norwegians like Norski jokes

North Dakota Norwegians enjoy telling jokes on themselves. Favorites are the Ole and Lena stories. And although education has long been recognized as a strong goal among Norwegians, Ole and other Norskis are invariably portrayed as slow-witted and totally lacking in sophistication.

The thick Norwegian brogue with its quick accents is vital to telling these jokes well. No one can do it better than the second generation Norwegian drawing out the first and third syllables of "lutefisk," as in the following:

Ole was lying on his death bed. "Oh, Lena," he says. "Dat lutefisk you got cooking on the stove smells so good. Vould you get me a bowl of it?"

"No, Ole, I can't do that," says Lena. "I'm saving it for the people who come for the funeral." *F.B.*

Festivals celebrate ethnic themes across state

North Dakota's predominant ethnic groups, the Germans and Norwegians, have developed annual observances typifying their countries of origin.

An increasing number of communities heavily populated with Germans stage annual Oktoberfests, while the Sons of Norway lodges in Scandinavian areas faithfully celebrate May 17 as Syttende Mai, the Norwegian Independence Day.

Oktoberfest

The Oktoberfest celebration probably was first held in New Leipzig about a dozen years ago. Now it is observed in many cities, including Bismarck, whose second annual event was the biggest Oktoberfest in the state.

New Leipzig has preferred to keep its Oktoberfest a local affair, while Bismarck has tried to promote and expand its version.

Bismarck's celebration included a queen contest and pageant, dances and concerts by the Concord Singers of New Ulm, Minn., and the Little Dutch Band, a sellout German cuisine dinner, a farm equipment show, road races and a parade with 123 units.

Norwegian Independence Day is observed in at least the 30 North Dakota cities that have Sons of Norway lodges and probably informally in many more.

In most communities the observance includes a dinner of Norwegian foods, usually a dance and the wearing of Norwegian costumes, especially by the women.

Icelandic independence

North Dakota's oldest ethnic observance is held in one of the state's smallest communities. On Aug. 2 for the past 100 years or more the Icelandic people of Pembina County have gathered in the community of Mountain (population 146) to celebrate Icelandic home rule, granted by the Danish parliament a millenium ago.

The celebration features a parade, food, dancing and speeches. As Pembina County Auditor Bill Sturlaugson puts it, "Everybody is in a celebrating mood."

Showpiece of the parade the past 25 years has been a replica of a Viking ship. People dress in Icelandic costumes or old-fashioned clothes.

"There is a program at the public hall," Sturlaugson explains, "with speeches that would have been in Icelandic 25 years ago but are now in English."

There generally is a carnival and an old-time dance in the evening to the music of violin, accordion and piano.

An indispensable part of the celebration is the consumption of Icelandic food, including vinarterta (layered prune cake), pannukar (rolled-up pancakes), kleinur (deep-fried pastry), bread sausage and smoked mutton.

Sauerkraut Day

Businessmen in the German community of Wishek have expressed appreciation for their customers with a Sauerkraut Day on the second Wednesday of October for the past 56 years.

In 1981, some 2,200 people participated in the festival at which Wishek merchants dispensed 600 pounds of wieners, 100 gallons of coffee, 300 pounds of potatoes and 103 gallons of sauerkraut, to which was added 150 pounds of a bacon-based garnish called "speck."

Robert Zimmerman, editor of the Wishek Star, says details of the celebration's origin are hazy, but the format has been largely the same during its long history.

"It was too late in the fall for a parade but we have had talent shows and dances. This year the Plainsmen Shrine singers from Bismarck constituted the entertainment and in the past we have had dance bands like the Chmielewskis. This year there were door prizes for people who came the greatest distance, the oldest, youngest and longest married.

"It is primarily a Chamber of Commerce affair to thank our customers for their business."

Hostfest

Minot's Norwegians do their celebrating in the fall at a Hostfest, which Minot Mayor Chester Reiten claims is the biggest ethnic observance in North Dakota.

Meaning fall or autumn feast, the Hostfest is held on the last weekend in October and this year attracted 18,000 people to a 10-hour program in the All Seasons Arena at the state fairgrounds.

On the program were several Norwegian entertainers, including a cowboy singer, a dance band and two accordion bands.

Another popular feature is the parade of national costumes, with 50 women dressed in authentic Norwegian dress typifying the distinctive attire from different valleys of that country.

Reiten says the celebration started in response to interest indicated by third-generation Norwegian-Americans.

"The original Norwegians came here with a pride in Norway," he explains. "The second (generation) just wanted to forget it and become Americans, but the third generation realizes that we have roots in Norway.

"The program is not heavy and you have a chance to meet friends and eat Norwegian foods. In the back of the hall, church women sell typical Norwegian food like lefse and krumkake, which you can munch while visiting."

Norwegian crafts are an integral part of the activities. Spinning, weaving and rosemaling are demonstrated, and Norwegian art displayed.

Originally limited to Norwegians, the Hostfest has been expanded to include Swedes, Danes, Finns and Icelanders.

Reiten says the celebration has direct ties to Norway, especially with Minot's Norwegian sister city, Skein, whose mayor was the honored guest at the 1981 festivities.

Two years ago it centered on Sondre Nordheim, the "father of downhill skiing," who died virtually unknown on the North Dakota prairies and whose grave finally was located near Denby.

To reciprocate the Norwegian mayor's visit, the Minot State College Choir and some 150 other North Dakotans will tour Norway this year, concluding with a concert at Skein.

"The (Hostfest) celebration is very festive," Reiten asserts, "and people come from all over North Dakota, Minnesota and Montana."

As the Hostfest Asscociation's only president, Reiten has made three trips to Norway to promote closer ties. For his efforts, he was given the St. Olav Medal by Norway's King Olav for his work in cultivating cultural ties between the two nations. It is the highest honor Norway bestows upon a person living outside the country.

"Our ultimate goal is to establish a Norwegian heritage center at Minot in a building modeled after a Viking ship," Reiten declares, "but first of all to build pride in our Norwegian heritage."

Northwood has one of the largest percentages of Norwegians among the state's communities and three times in the past eight years has staged a Norwegian cultural day during October.

General chairman in 1981 was Mrs. Myrna Johnson, who reports the event was "a great big one," which attracted "thousands of people" from as far away as Arizona, Alaska and Florida.

"For the first time we brought in outside attractions," Johnson relates, "including an exhibit from the Vesterheim Norwegian-American museum at Decorah, Iowa, which came at no expense to us as an experiment in attracting more visitors to the museum. The director and curator came along and demonstrated weaving, textiles rosemaling and other crafts easy to transport. The community hall was filled and over 900 signed the guest books."

"There also was a group of 42 people from Norway who were touring the country with their 17-piece accordion band, and we had a ladies' chorus from the Sons of Norway lodge at Mayville, and a children's dance group from the Grand Forks lodge."

Campground is filled with tents and campers for United Tribes powwow, which brings together people of many tribes.

Other attractions included a woman telling troll stories and a bank-sponsored exhibit of 27 17-inch dolls from Norway wearing authentic district costumes.

Ethnic foods were available and the local church served a lutefisk, lefse and meatball supper to 900 diners.

Besides the faraway visitors, the affair attracted busloads of guests from nearby towns.

"Thanks to voluntееers and donations, the whole celebration cost about $200, which we raised selling buttons," she says.

"The object was to develop interest in the Norwegian culture, and I believe we increased it in some people and started it in some who didn't have any."

Robert Burns' birthday

The first settlers in the early days of North Dakota included a considerable number of Scotsmen. Each year on the anniversary of Robert Burns' birthday they would gather, listen to Scottish music and read the works of their nation's most famed poet.

That tradition continues, at least in Walsh County, where Scottish and non-Scottish members of the British Isles club gather on Jan. 25 to mark Burns' birthday. On March 17, they'll be together again to pay homage to Patrick, the patron saint of Ireland.

Jack E. Case

An immigrant drama, "Ach du Lieber," is staged in German for New Leipzig Oktoberfest; lower photo at left is from the marketplace. Below, audience fills the stands around arena at outdoor powwow.

In middle photo above, Donna Vander Vorst and Lorraine Wagner ladle borscht at Bismarck Oktoberfest. Eight thousand people fill All Seasons Arena in Minot, below, for Norsk Hostfest.

Interior of Klara Lutheran Church near Hamburg. Twenty of the 24 charter members of this church were born at Finnskoga in Varmland, Sweden, near the Klara River.

Church was social center

From territorial days, the church has been one of the most familiar landmarks in North Dakota.

And many a church stands alone upon the prairie, kept company only by a cemetery. The dates on the tombstones tell the wayfarer that people were here a long time ago. But the freshly mowed grass in the churchyard testifies that people still worship here. For in many places in North Dakota, the church was and is the community, and the community, the church.

The stranger to North Dakota might puzzle over those sights and the disproportionately large number of churches in cities and towns of small populations.

But to understand the endurance and the proliferation of the churches in North Dakota is also to understand its people.

The earliest settlers in what was to become North Dakota were Anglo-Saxon/Yankees, many of them descendants of people from the eastern seaboard who had over the years moved inland. The churches founded to serve them were mainly Presbyterian, Methodist, Episcopalian and Congregationalist.

Bewildered by this huge, treeless plain and a language they could not understand, the immigrants drew together in rural ghettos, finding comfort in the company of those who shared their nationality — its language, traditions and religious values.

But they still had to deal with the outside world, the government, the schools taught by English-speaking teachers, the banking system and the businesses in the infant towns where they traded.

Most of those institutions were controlled by Anglo-Saxon Americans. The one institution the immigrants could control was religion. And the church was one place where they could gather together to carry on traditions, speak their language, sing the familiar hymns and socialize, explains the Rev. William Sherman, a Catholic priest at Grand Forks who also is a sociologist and authority on North Dakota ethnic cultures.

A religious people

"They were strongly religious people. Their faith was a bulwark against the vicissitudes of the harsh life on the northern prairie, and the church was a little piece of the old country. So it was very important to them," he says.

Invariably, after the homes, the

Klara Church in 1957.

first building erected in those small ethnic communities was a church.

Catherine Omafray, born in a Ukrainian settlement north of Wilton in 1901, says the Ukrainians there were very poor and each family had to put a $50 mortgage against whatever property it had in order to buy lumber to build a church.

The little church, says Sherman, became the ethnic rallying point.

Young people usually found their marriage partners at church functions and, because mixed marriages were frowned upon by both families and the official church, especially among the Catholics and Lutherans, many of those ethnic communities retained a strong identity for many years.

The Protestant churches had their men's clubs, missionary and ladies aid societies, and the Catholics had their men's vereins and women's altar societies. Those and other church organizations supported the local church and also gave people the opportunity to come together socially.

One does not have to look far beyond the city limits of Bismarck and Mandan to find examples of North Dakota's church-centered, rural ethnic communities. And there are still first- and second-generation North Dakotans who remember the early days and what the church meant to them.

Rose Stein's family was among the many Germans from Russia who settled in western North Dakota. Now 80 and living in Bismarck, she recalls what life was like in the early days.

She grew up in the Judson area, some 15 miles west of Mandan, and before her marriage kept house for the priests of St. Vincent's of Crown Butte, a rural farming community a little farther to the north.

The St. Vincent community was so purely German-Russian Catholic that there was only one family of another nationality.

In those early years, says Stein, there were about 120 families in the community. But to this day it has consisted only of the church and the social hall erected by St. Vincent's Verein.

She remembers her mother-in-law, Anna Marie Stein, telling how after the people settled there, they built a small stone and sod church. A priest came to say Mass and hear confessions only once a month, but the people would come to the church on Sundays, by wagon in summer and sleigh in winter, and there they would say the Rosary and the traditional prayers and sing the familiar songs.

'Wonderful choir'

Of her own years there, Stein says proudly, "We had a wonderful choir, the best in the area. We used to practice once a week, sometimes for two hours. But it was a social time too. We would stop after about an hour and have coffee, and then sing some more. Music was a part of our lives."

St. Vincent's, like other churches, had its church fairs for which the women made fancywork to sell, sold raffle tickets for prizes donated by area businesses and served a meal that featured traditional foods.

"We had no running water so it had to be hauled in barrels and cream cans, and in those early days, the church had no kitchen so we brought in kerosene stoves to cook on. How they used to smoke and sputter," Stein recalls.

Her eyes light up as she remembers some of the church festivals that lent excitement and color to the lives of the people.

Corpus Christi parade

"In June we had the Corpus Christi parade on the Holy Day of Obligation. The little altar made by the men of the parish would be decorated with flowers and lace curtains and taken outside. Then the priest and the congregation would go in a procession to the altar with the priest carrying the sacraments and the little girls dressed in white carrying little baskets of flowers that they threw in path of the priest. And there was music — an accordion, clarinet and trumpets and bass. Oh, it was a happy time," she recalls.

She also remembers how in early spring, three days before Ascension Day, the people would attend church every morning and then go outside where the priest would bless the fields and pray for the spring rains, so vital to their existence.

Dominic Zander of Mandan, 75, who also grew up in the St. Vincent community, recalls the fun the young people had at the wedding dances.

"There was dancing to the piano and drum, and homemade beer, wine and whiskey. Like in the old country. You threw money in the bucket to dance with the bride. We still do that at wedding dances," he says.

Zander says the children of St. Vincent families were raised very strictly. "And we always went to church. A lot more than people do now," says Zander.

Neither he nor Stein could speak a word of English when they were youngsters. "Everything was German. The Mass, the catechism classes. They didn't start using English in the church until the early 1940s," Zander says.

Many people left the St. Vincent community during World War II to work in the aircraft factories on the West Coast and never returned, Stein says.

The small farming community of St. Anthony, 14 miles southwest of Mandan, was settled in the late 1880s by German-Russian and German-Hungarian immigrants.

For many years there was a parish boarding school founded in 1909 by the German-speaking Ursuline Sisters. Many farm families sent their children to the school to assure that they received a proper religious education, says the Rev. Florian Fairbanks, longtime parish priest. All classes were taught in the German language.

School in German

In 1942, the state Department of Public Instruction complained to the bishop of the Bismarck Catholic Diocese that the children were not learning English. The same complaint was registered about Saints Peter and Paul Catholic Church school at Strasburg. As a consequence, the Ursulines were replaced.

The Felician Sisters, who were Polish but spoke English, took over the school at St. Anthony and the Sisters of Notre Dame operated the school at Strasburg, explains Fairbanks.

The St. Anthony school was closed in 1968. The population of the village has dwindled to a mere 37 and only three businesses remain.

But the St. Anthony Church parish there still numbers 400 and its Verein, founded in 1911, is still very active with a membership of over 300.

The St. Anthony church fair is still held the last Sunday in September. Both dinner and supper are served and the women of the parish spend days in preparation. It is the biggest event of the year for the parish and attracts as many as 2,000 people.

Warsaw, in a Polish area in Walsh County, never was incorporated as a city, but the large and beautiful St. Stanislaus Catholic Church there is known far and wide as the Cathedral of the Prairie.

A fire gutted the Cathedral in 1978, but parish members, determined that they should not lose that vital piece of their heritage, rallied to rebuild it.

In the earlier years of their histories, many churches were destroyed by fire, usually caused by a faulty furnace or a lightning strike. To rebuild was a laborious task, both physically and financially. But the parishioners almost never questioned whether to do so.

St. Martin's Catholic Church of Huff is the focal point of that small community some 20 miles south of Mandan.

Rebuilt of stone

The church was struck by lightning and burned to the ground in 1940. The people of the parish, led by the Rev. Conrad Lotter, a great builder with rock, decided to put up a new church of native fieldstone.

Lotter donned overalls along with his parishioners and they laboriously hauled the rock from the nearby hills. The priest also built birdbaths and grottos, adding to the beauty of the site.

The Roman Catholics, mostly of German-Russian and German-Hungarian descent, are the second largest religious group in North Dakota, numbering some 175,000.

The largest, some 200,000, is composed of the diversity of Lutheran denominations — primarily descendants of immigrants from Norway, Sweden, Denmark, Germany and Finland.

Diversity from Europe

That diversity originated in Europe as a result of the Pietist movement of the 17th and 18th centuries, which people today would view as a deeply fundamentalist movement.

Its adherents sought a more personalized religious life and a church less creed-bound. They chafed at the state-controlled church, saying the laity should have more say about the spiritual life and government of the church.

As in any movement, people embraced the new philosophy in varying degrees and the new congregations that were formed in the wake of the movement followed the leaders that best represented their thinking.

As people from the Lutheran countries immigrated to America and settled in North Dakota, they also drew together in their own ethnic groups, often with people from their own region of the old country, and established churches of the particular Lutheran persuasion from which they had come.

The high church

From those congregations were developed the early Lutheran synods in the United States. The Norwegian Synod was referred to as the high church, more formalized in structure, more dogmatic theologically but with a more liberal view of people's lifestyle.

"It wasn't a sin to have a beer or dance," says Bishop Roy Gilbertson of Bismarck, who heads the Western North Dakota District of the American Lutheran Church.

The low church was known as the Hauge Synod, named for the great Norwegian lay leader, Hans Nielsen Hauge, who had been influenced by the Pietist movement.

It permitted more participation of the laity in the government and spiritual life of the church, and its adherents sought a more subjective, personalized religion based on the Scriptures. It was more puritan in its attitude toward people's behavior, shunning such worldly pleasures as dancing and card playing.

The United Lutheran Church, says Gilbertson, was somewhere in between. In 1917, the three synods were united into the Norwegian Lutheran Church.

A merger in the early 1960s joined that large synod with several smaller ones whose ethnic groups were mainly Danish, German and Norwegian. It became the American Lutheran Church, whose 165,000 North Dakota members constitute the largest Lutheran church group in the state.

The Lutheran Church in America is a union of Lutherans with mostly German, Swedish and Danish backgrounds, some of whom broke away from the old United Lutheran Church. It is more formal than the ALC but about equal in liberalism.

The Missouri Synod and Wisconsin Synod are basically composed of the descendants of people who came directly from Germany, and are low church, taking a fundamentalist view of biblical Scripture.

The German Lutheran immigrants from south Russia were descended from people who had migrated from a part of Germany where there was a freer low church emphasis than the Missouri and Wisconsin Synods, and they joined what was the old American Lutheran Church.

Norwegian still heard

The Scandinavians were not as protective of their ethnicity as the German-Russians and started holding church services in English much earlier, in the 1920s and 1930s.

But in some small communities, Norwegian still is heard on the streets and churches sometimes hold a service in the native tongue or include Norwegian songs in the services. Church suppers, featuring lutefesk and lefse, are popular and well-attended.

Although Morton County is heavily populated by people of German extraction, there are strong, small pockets of Norwegians west of Mandan. In fact, the first Lutheran church founded west of the Missouri River was the Evangelical Lutheran Church of Sims, once a bustling Morton County community along the Northern Pacific main line.

Now, nothing remains but the church, established in 1894. Both the Sims church and United Lutheran Church of Almont, a still active village only 3/ miles from Sims, are ALC churches. But the people of Sims take pride in their church heritage and there is yet no talk of merging with the Almont church. Indeed, the Sims congregation is looking forward to celebrating the church's 100th anniversary in 1984.

Some 10 miles southwest of Mandan, a group of Norwegian families, most of them related, settled in the early 1880s on land near the Heart River.

Services in the home

They were a religious people who met in the homes until they were able to build their small church on the banks of the river in 1910. They named it the Heart River Lutheran Church. It was served by the pastor of the First Lutheran Church in Mandan, who held services there on Sunday afternoons.

Clarence Hendrickson, a Mandan farmer whose father, Kornelius, was one of the church founders, says services were in Norwegian until the early 1920s. He remembers how everyone flocked to church on Sunday. It was a day of rest, worship, and of visiting with relatives and neighbors over coffee and lefse, he says.

The Ladies Aid society was a strong organization and, among its

Window in St. Benedict's, a French Catholic church at Wild Rice. Below, prayer book printed in 1866 was brought from Russia.

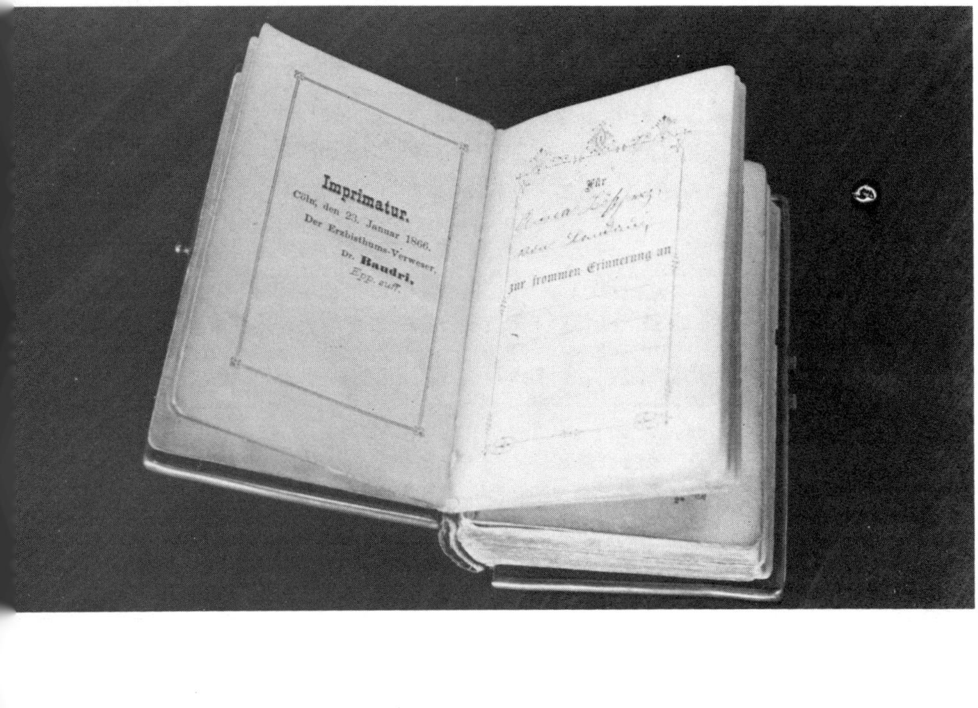

functions, raised money to help maintain the church.

Church attendance dwindled in later years as the younger people moved off the farms and other distractions pulled people away from a Sunday afternoon church service, says Hendrickson. The church was closed in 1950. However, the building is used occasionally for special events such as the funeral of an old-timer of the congregation.

Annual Picnic

And the grove of trees in which the church nestles is still the scene of the annual Heart River Lutheran Ladies Aid picnic, a tradition that has endured through four generations. In addition to being a picnic, it is a joyous reunion of the Norwegian clan.

Though one of the state's smallest ethnic groups, the Ukrainians still have a strong identity . They settled at Wilton and in the Belfield area west of Dickinson at the turn of the century, founding the communities of Gorham and Ukraina.

They brought with them their ancient faith and though priests of the Eastern or Greek Rites were few, mission priests traveled great distances to minister to the immigrants — baptizing babies, marrying young couples and reading prayers for the dead, often long after death had occurred, according to historical accounts by Frances Wold of Regan.

St. Demetrius Church at Ukraina and Saints Peter and Paul Church of Wilton were built in 1906 and St. Josephat Church at Gorham in 1912. A shared priest linked the communities and boys and girls often found their marriage partners through that link.

Wilton's Ukrainian Catholic Church originally was located 14 miles north of the community but in 1912, after many of the Ukrainians began working in the coal mine, it was moved to town.

Identity through church

The Rev. George Pruys, priest of Saints Peter and Paul at Wilton, says that because they are so small in number, the Ukrainians would have lost their ethnic identity long ago identity were it not for the church.

His congregation has books that give the service in both English and Church Slavonic, the traditional language of Ukrainian Rite churches. But most of the older members know the liturgy by heart and rarely refer to the printed word.

Emily Backman of Bismarck grew up in the Swedish community of Falkirk west of Wilton, served by the Birka Lutheran Church, now 75 years old.

In some years, as was true with many small North Dakota churches, Swedish Lutheran churches had no resident pastors, so religious instruction was conducted by the people of the parish.

The young girls, says Backman, looked forward to confirmation, knowing it meant getting a new white dress. Aware of the importance of that to young hearts, the Ladies Aid one year bought material and made a dress for a girl who otherwise would not have had one.

She remembers the church auction sales in the fall at which fancywork made by the Ladies Aid was sold to raise money for the church. People, she said, would come from miles around to attend.

Sunne Lutheran Church, five miles east of Wilton, was established in 1893 and is the oldest of three churches that served the Swedish-speaking people of the Wilton area.

Backman took on an important project for the Sunne church last year, translating from Swedish the early minutes of church meetings. Sunne discontinued services and meetings in the Swedish language in 1919.

Occasionally, a song in Swedish is sung at a funeral or golden wedding anniversary but only a handful of older people can still speak or read the language, according to Wold, a member of the church.

Lucille Hendrickson

Twin spires are western Dakota landmark

The twin spires of Assumption Abbey are a familiar landmark rising above the rolling prairie at Richardton. The story of this monastery begins with Father Vincent Wehrle, a Bendictine monk who came here from Switzerland. Wehrle first founded a community of monks at Devils Lake but moved to Richardton in 1899 because of the greater number of German-speaking settlers here.

Monks soon numbered 26. They opened a school for boys and settled homesteads to help finance their ambitious building plans. The twin-spired church was finished in 1910, with local brick fired at the abbey and faced with Hebron brick. Known as the "Gem of the Prairies," it was the largest church building in the state. Stained glass windows, wood carvings, oil paintings, stucco work, parquet floors and a superb organ are outstanding features.

At present about 65 members live in the monastic community, some serving as pastors and teachers outside the abbey. The once active high school, seminary and college are now closed. But monks still farm the land, raise beef cattle, till orchards and gardens. They operate a print shop and book bindery, and have an extensive research library.

Assumption Abbey now hosts many groups for meetings and retreats throughout the year. *F.B.*

Assumption Abbey and St. Mary's Church form a large quadrangle with inner courtyard. Farm and school buildings lie outside with grazing land beyond for 300-500 beef cattle. The church, of Bavarian Romanesque style with 120-foot spires, was completed in 1910.

‘Peace churches’ traditionally were rural

Brethren and Mennonites were among the homesteaders who came to North Dakota at the turn of the century, and their descendants still live in the state today.

Mennonites and Brethren share many characteristics, but developed in different places at different times. Both Mennonites, which includes Hutterites or communal Mennonites, and Brethren believe in adult baptism.

Brethren used to be called "Dunkers" because they baptised converts by dunking them three times, face forward. The religious rites in congregations include the washing of feet. The Brethren movement was later than that of the Mennonites, starting in Germany in the early 1700s.

According to J.B. Toews, Fresno, Calif., a Mennonite scholar, most of the Mennonites who came to North Dakota at the turn of this century were from Minnesota and South Dakota. These homesteaders — or their forebears — were mostly Germans or Dutch who came to America starting in the late 1700s.

According to scholars of the churches, the Mennonites in North Dakota are mostly of German-Dutch or German-Russian descent. The Hutterites are mostly German, with a little Swiss and Hungarian blood mixed in, and the Brethren are mostly German.

There aren't many members of these religious groups in North Dakota today.

According to statistics provided by several church archivists, North Dakota has at least 13 Mennonite churches, with between 1,200 and 1,500 members.

There are just three Church of the Brethren congregations, with 342 members.

The Mennonite membership figure includes five Hutterite colonies, all in southeastern North Dakota. Their membership is estimated at 400 to 500.

The more conservative of the Mennonite and Brethren homesteaders wore the traditional dress when they first came to the state. The Brethren who originally settled at Cando and founded the first church of their denomination, Cando Zion Church, in 1896, presented "sort of a spectacle" with broad-brimmed hats, beards and the prayer veils (little lace caps) worn by the women, according to the Rev. Glen Fruth, Abilene, Kan. who once served Brethren churches in North Dakota.

The Rev. William Sherman of St. Michael's Catholic Church, Grand Forks, who has mapped the ethnic distribution of North Dakotans, says the heaviest concentrations of Mennonites are in the northeastern part of the state in Ramsey, Cavalier and Pembina counties. They also are to be found in Walsh, Nelson, Grand Forks, Traill and Griggs counties.

In Pierce and Rolette counties of north central North Dakota, there are descendants of Mennonites who settled there starting in 1894.

Many of the Mennonites who settled North Dakota came from families that originally went straight from the Ukraine to Manitoba during the 1870s. Their industriousness as homesteaders was noted by historian Hazel J. Loynes.

The Mennonites became known for their long, low, sod dwellings, said Loynes. A typical Mennonite homestead had a house with attached barn, both covered by a thatched roof. Attached to the structure was a European brick oven fueled by a mixture of straw and manure. The Mennonites planted gardens and trees, built frame houses and cultivated yards as soon as they were able.

Their churches had two entrances and cloakrooms, one for the men and one for the women, and they sat segregated during services. By 1910, according to Loynes, many of the Mennonites were speaking English, although German remained the language of home and church for many more years.

Chiefly a rural folk, they homesteaded their way across the Midwest. According to Fruth, they spread out from their "mother" church at Cando. Many trainloads of Brethren came in boxcars, with teams of horses and equipment.

According to Beverly Lewallen, Cando, associate district executive with the church, at one time during the early 1900s there were 20 or more Brethren congregations, ranging from Williston to Devils Lake and as far south as Carrington. Now, the only remaining congregations are at Cando, Surrey and Knox.

The Brethren who came to North Dakota were moderates in their religion and many were more interested in farming than in retaining old customs, according to Fruth.

They live "most sensibly" and obtain "no superfluous or expensive luxuries, no fashionable clothing, or even costly — until they can afford them."

Church members did not hesitate to get involved in local public affairs, according to Fruth. He recalled that the Brethren in the Cando area had a temperance movement going in 1909 and a Child Rescue Work program in 1917.

According to several historians, a few old-fashioned Mennonites and members of the Brethren came to North Dakota expecting to continue the small-farm lifestyle that had been successful elsewhere.

But, as Bishop Eli J. Bontreger, who served several Amish (another denomination of the Mennonites) communities in Rolette and Pierce counties for many years wrote, "The novelty of farming those prairie lands, where four to six horse teams were needed, wore off after a number of years and a desire for farming on a smaller scale grew ... on some of us."

Many of the Old Order Amish in North Dakota dispersed after 1909. John A. Hostetler, a scholar on the Hutterites, concluded that "It was the cold, severe snowstorms and the low crop yields that loom large as the causes for the decline of the Amish community."

Only the Hutterites, the most conservative of the many Mennonite denominations, still live in colonies and wear the traditional plain dress. The men have full beards and wear black denim clothes. The women wear full skirts, long-sleeved blouses and scarves.

And while the strict Hutterite interpretation of Scripture requires nonconformity and rejection of most worldly pleasures, Hostetler notes that the proscription doesn't extend to the latest farming techniques and equipment — Scripture tells mankind to be efficient and industrious, say the Hutterites.

Pacifism is a matter of conscience for members of the "peace churches" — and , during wars, a number of members have refused military service.

John Pearson

Religion: traditional, Christian mix

Are the Sun Dance and Holy Communion compatible?

They are to some Indians, demonstrating that the religious beliefs and practices of contemporary Indians cover a broad spectrum.

On one end, one can find peyote users and Indian medicine men, and at the other end, Indians who are theologically trained pastors of Christian parishes.

Without getting into the intricacies of Christianity and Indian religion, there are some general observations to be said about Indians and religion.

• Like white people, most Indians are nominally Christian.

How many of them are actually active, church-going Indians deeply involved in their Christianity, and how many simply pay lip service to Christianity is as hard to answer as for the white population.

• There remains a strong undercurrent of traditional Indian spiritualness, including a respect for all that has been created and an emphasis on generosity.

In some Indian people, the traditional beliefs replace Christianity. In others, they supplement it.

Though it may seem strange to some white people, some Indians see no conflict between practicing such ceremonies as the Sun Dance and being active Christians.

In one area of the Standing Rock Reservation, many Indians practice Christianity, but others are bi-religious, notes Jim Walton, a white who has lived on the reservation for several years.

The bi-religious people "tend to be people who see the value of life, who see spiritual truths," says Walton. "They're not too concerned with the source or origin. If it's true, it's true."

Indeed, some Indians see a striking compatibility between their traditional beliefs and those written in the New Testament.

The similarity is one reason Indians took so quickly to Christianity, believes Donna Richardson of the Council of American Indian Ministry in Minneapolis, and a South Dakota Sioux.

"We could really empathize. We could see that there were so many similarities between our way of life and the Christian way of life," she says.

She points to the similarity between Christ dying on the cross and the Sun Dance, in which young Indians hang from a pole by leather thongs hooked into the flesh of their chest.

In the Sun Dance, participants are making a sacrifice, and in so doing they seek a blessing for the tribe and all living things.

Richardson also mentions Christ fasting in the desert and meditating as similar to the Indian custom of fasting and going out on vision quests.

There also are the similar concepts of afterlife. In both Christianity and traditional Indian belief, the soul or spirit lives on after the body has died.

Concepts of giving and selflessness are also common to both Christianity and Indian spiritual beliefs.

"There's no innate conflict between Christianity and Indian beliefs," says Richardson.

"Some of the (Indian) beliefs are more Christian than Christianity."

Sara Brown, a white and the minister of the Twin Buttes Congregational Church on the Fort Berthold Reservation, believes there is considerable difference between the average white Christian and the average Indian Christian.

She finds the average Indian Christian "a lot like the very first Christians."

She says this because she finds the Indians "not denominational the way we are," and because "their religion cannot be separated from their everyday living."

This second trait leads to the Indian Christian putting less importance on attending church on Sunday, she has observed.

Another pastor, the Rev. Innocent Goodhouse of St. Luke's Episcopal Church in Fort Yates, is one of the few theologically trained Indian ministers serving in Indian country.

Goodhouse believes it is mainly the younger Indian people who are resisting Christianity.

Some of them simply aren't religious, he says, but others have been drawn to traditional religious values as part of the Indian cultural resurgence of the 1970s.

"They feel that they are another religion or denomination, and they want to remain separate," he explains.

Goodhouse has nothing against traditional Indian religion. His mother practiced traditional religion, and, he says, in some of the churches he travels to, the old people like to incorporate old Indian songs into the liturgy.

It's not just the young people whose attendance has been poor, Goodhouse says. Like many congregations around the country, he sees his losing membership.

"I would like to see it change around," he says. "But as long as the adults aren't responding to the church, how can you expect the young people to?"

The main areas where Indians have conflicts with Christianity appear to be over what some of the missionaries did, especially in their suppression of Indian culture, and the difference between what the New Testament says and the way many white Christians live.

One mild criticism of Christianity came from an old Christian Arikara woman on the Fort Berthold Reservation, who preferred not to be identified.

"The white man thought he taught us about God, but we already knew about him," she says, referring to assumptions made by missionaries.

One Indian who has turned from Christianity is a Bismarck woman in her 40s. She has lived in an urban setting for a long time. She also did not want to be identified.

She says many Indians she knows practice Christianity "and there's nothing wrong with that."

But, she adds, "I would say most people I associate with are in a period of spiritual growth and are to some degree dissatisfied with Christianity."

Part of the dissatisfaction, which she sees in her age group on down, relates to the resurgence of Indian culture and pride during the past decade.

"For the first time in our lives, we realize we do have some control over our destinies, and this is one way of taking control."

"I started feeling a close relationship to everything, the earth, the animals. I have somewhat of an understanding of my relationship to the earth. I know that everything is alive, and the earth takes care of us; it provides everything we need."

Other urban Indians aren't church-going Christians, but not for the reasons the above woman gave.

According to CAIM's Richardson, many Indians who have gone to church on the reservation simply stop going once they move to a city like Bismarck.

The reason? As Indians, they just don't feel comfortable or welcome in an all-white parish.

Greg Turosak

Jewish population too small for rabbi

When the Temple B'nai Ephraim, Bismarck's synagogue, was built in 1930, there was concern about its size.

"When it was built, they didn't think it was big enough because over 200 would come for the holidays. It was built when there was a larger Jewish community," says Sol Wezelman, an insurance executive who has conducted many of the services at the synagogue since arriving in Bismarck 25 years ago.

But now that the number of Jewish families in Bismarck has dwindled to about 20, the size of the temple no longer is a problem.

The small size of the Bismarck Jewish community makes it difficult to justify having a permanent, full-time rabbi, and there hasn't been one since Rabbi Marshall Berg departed in the early 1950s. He now lives in Des Moines, Iowa.

None of the five North Dakota synagogues has a full-time rabbi any more. The last to leave the state was Rabbi Jerald Brown of Fargo.

"He had established the reputation as the rabbi of North Dakota," says Wezelman, noting that Brown was based at the Temple Beth El in Fargo but traveled to Bismarck, Grand Forks and Minot several times a year.

But the lack of a rabbi hasn't stopped services at the synagogues in North Dakota. Lay persons such as Wezelman are able to perform ceremonies during the major holidays or at special events such as bar mitzvahs and funerals.

Wezelman recalls that during his early days in Bismarck there were 30 or 35 Jewish families, and others attended the synagogue's services from such cities as Dickinson, Wing, Solen, Mott, Tuttle and Robinson.

These days, the biggest activity is the Sunday school, which each week attracts about 15 children. The teaching is done on a voluntary basis by people such as Kathy Kamins, Sherry and Joe Kashinejad, Brenda Shark, Shelly Bank and Sybil Wezelman.

Temple Beth El in Fargo is the largest and most active Jewish congregation in an area that includes North Dakota and western Minnesota. The membership is around 120 families. Fargo has a second group, the Fargo Hebrew Congregation.

"Judaism does not have a priestly system," notes Fargo's Ruth Landfield. "No one stands between a Jew and his or her God, whatever one's concept of God happens to be.

"Any lay person can rightfully perform all religious services in Judaism — organized religious Sabbath and holy day observances, marriage, burial, brit, Bar or Bat Mitzvah, confirmation, etc."

It is traditional that Jews be buried at Jewish cemeteries, and there are several in North Dakota.

Fargo, for instance has three, and the other major cities in the state have at least one each. Others are located near the sites of Jewish colonies that were established a century ago.

One is located in Burleigh County in Canfield Township, three miles northeast of Regan. Abe Kamins, father of Bismarck's Norm Kamins, donated land for the cemetery.

Although the cemetery didn't incorporate until 1909, the earliest birthdate on a marker is 1903. Because a rabbi wasn't often in the area, funeral services were conducted by laymen.

Abe Winter

Czech headstone in New Hradec cemetery.

Church history marked by conflicts

"Isn't it nice that we can sit together and all speak the same language," said Oscar Hegstrom to Catherine Omafray.

This conversation took place at the senior center in Wilton. a small town 25 miles north of Bismarck.

Hegstrom, as his name suggests, is Swedish, and Omafray is Ukrainian. Both have lived in Wilton since its early days.

There is a significance in Hegstrom's remark that goes even deeper than language. It speaks to the many differences that once isolated North Dakota's ethnic groups from each other.

A major influence

The church has always been a major institution among the people of North Dakota, sustaining them spiritually against the harsh environment in which they live and preserving their ethnic cultures.

But by their very strength in people's lives, religious beliefs and the official church helped to cast a shadow across the relationships of North Dakota people for many years. Church-centered ethnicity caused polarization of community groups and fostered enmity between families and neighbors and personal heartbreak for young people who dared to climb the walls of religious and ethnic prejudice.

The children of immigrants who defied the church and family to marry someone from a different ethnic-religious group often became outcasts. Only in recent years have the problems created by mixed marriages eased.

Church and governmental records and historical publications only occasionally allude to the impact that dissension between and within churches had on the social, political and even economic life of North Dakota people.

Wounds went deep

It is only in talking with older generations or drawing on one's own memories that much can be learned. Laymen and clergy are willing to speak of those things now. But the past is still so recent and where wounds were deep, few of them are

St. Demetrius north of Belfield has distinctive onion-shaped dome, is extensively landscaped.

An altar screen across front of eastern-rite Ukrainian church has doors through which priest passes during ritual.

willing to let their identities be known.

In many North Dakota communities there was for many years a line of demarcation between Catholics and Protestants, even when the ethnic background was the same — German Lutheran vs. German Catholic. And religious differences set apart even people of the same broad religious background — for example, high church Lutheran vs. the more fundamentalist low church Lutheran.

Wilton is a microcosm of the ethnic-religious separation that existed in so many North Dakota communities and still lingers in some towns.

Wilton was settled at the turn of the century by three major ethnic groups — the Ukrainians who took up homesteads north of town, the Swedish farming community to the south of town, and the Anglo-Saxons who came first and established businesses.

Opening of the Washburn Lignite Coal Co. mine at Wilton drew other immigrants in smaller numbers — Norwegians, Bulgarians, Germans and Romanians.

Most of the town's "elite," were Anglo-Saxon and members of the Presbyterian Church, established in 1900, one year after the town was incorporated.

People of immigrant backgrounds say they were looked down upon by the town establishment.

Gottlieb Hochhalter, retired Wilton banker, has long been active in the church. He himself was raised in a German Baptist home but after moving to Wilton joined the Presbyterian Church of which his wife was a member.

Some of the early Presbyterians, he says, were very temperance-minded and didn't believe in dancing, drinking, smoking or playing cards.

That helped create a division between them and the Ukrainians.

The Ukrainians began moving to town as the men took jobs in the mine, and they made their homes on the north side. They had built their church 14 miles north of town in 1906 and in 1912 moved it to its northwest Wilton location where its onion-dome steeple has been a landmark.

The work in the mines was hard and dirty and most of the eastern European immigrants liked a beer at the end of the long workday. The three-day wedding with dancing and liquor flowing freely also was a part of their tradition.

Scathing editorials

The other townspeople looked askance and labeled the Ukrainian neighborhood "snake town" and the train that transported the miners to work as the "garlic special," Hochhalter relates.

The editor of the local newspaper was a Presbyterian and married to the mine manager's daughter. He wrote scathing editorials about the "Russian weddings" and scolded "our young men" for attending and imbibing.

He concluded one of those editorials by saying, "If our citizens would let these people of foreign customs alone, they would carry on their celebrations more peaceably and the inhabitants of Wilton could enjoy their slumbers without being frequently disturbed by those who do not seem to have any respect for themselves or for the town in which they live."

On May 23, 1919, a notice signed by the mayor of the town appeared in the local newspaper: "All celebrations in connection with so-called 'Russian weddings' will not be permitted to continue after midnight Saturday, and any disturbances or jollification on Sunday will not be tolerated hereafter."

Omafray, now 80, remembers the strained relationships that resulted.

"They (the Anglo-Saxon townspeople) never socialized with us. A lot of people who came couldn't talk the language. And if they didn't pay for their land they lost it," she says, referring to hard times. "Some of the business people were bad, and some were good and tried to help us."

The Ukrainians, she says, got on well with the Swedes and with the people of Sacred Heart, the town's Roman Catholic Church.

The Sacred Heart people shared the Ukrainians' Catholism, and the Swedes, who also couldn't speak English, shared their immigrant status.

Although church beliefs called for a far more conservative lifestyle among the Swedes, they lived mostly in the country, away from Wilton's Ukrainian north side, says historian Frances Wold.

However, the people there got up in arms if a Swedish girl married a German or Ukrainian.

Despite their robust pleasures, the Ukrainians were a deeply religious people who attached great importance to their church traditions. One priest served the Ukrainian Catholic church at Wilton and the ones at Ukraina and Gorham in the Belfield area west of Dickinson.

On the Saturday before Easter in 1916, he traveled the 200 miles to Saints Peter and Paul Church at Wilton and, because of poor travel connections, did not make it back to the two other churches for Easter.

A rift begins

That was the beginning of a rift between the people of the Ukrainian churches in both communities, which eventually led to a split. Those who had come from families of the Orthodox church, which does not recognize papal authority, formed their own churches in both Wilton and Ukraina.

Rev. Carlot Wisness dons stiff pleated frill collar to preach in Norwegian in one of many Lutheran churches he served in state. Typical of these churches is semicircular altar rail. At right, Ukrainian Greek Orthodox Church at Wilton retained eastern-rite rituals and domed spire, but the tilt of lower crossbar shows it is no longer under authority of the pope.

One longtime member of the Wilton community said the rift there stemmed partly from family jealousies about who should be cantor, the highest position in the church next to the priest.

The Orthodox churches are closed, though the buildings still are maintained. Prejudices of the two groups were passed on to the young, and even to this day there are some dormant feelings.

The Swedish Lutherans had their differences, although not so traumatic.

The immigrants came from diverse parts of Sweden and their religious beliefs differed. Some belonged to conservative, low churches in the old country and disapproved of "worldly pleasures." Others belonged to the more formal but liberal high church, and that created disagreements that led to splits in the church, explained Frances Wold, a member of Sunne Church.

Sunne Lutheran Church, now of the Lutheran Church of America, was founded in 1893. Two years later, a group broke away and with other unaffiliated Swedes built the Swedish Mission Church, regarded as more fundamentalist than Sunne.

Among other things, the Lutherans argued about changing the language of church services from Swedish to English, and sometimes left a church over that issue.

The Wilton Ukrainians were not the only immigrants made to feel inferior by other ethnic groups.

In many communities, the German-Russian Catholics were called "Roosians," a label that had derogatory implications.

A Mandan woman who lived at Dickinson as a small child recalls Protestant children standing across the street from a group of German-Russian children and yelling, "Cathliker, Cathliker."

Bishop Roy Gilbertson, who heads the North Dakota District of the American Lutheran Church, grew up at Binford, a community of 400 people in Griggs County.

"There were three Lutheran churches and each was suspicious of the other. The Catholic families in town — and there were only two — knew what it meant to be an oppressed minority," he says.

Parental prejudice

Gilbertson remembers how parental prejudices were instilled in children. "To hear my parents talk, the Catholics were trying to take over the country.

A Bismarck resident recalls that when he was a boy growing up in the Wells County village of Skyeston, the Catholics lived on one side of town and the Protestants on the other.

"And when the kids went to the movies, the Catholics sat on one side of the theater and the Protestants on the other," he says, adding that people voted in town and school board elections not on the basis of candidate qualifications but along religious lines.

Mandan, with three Catholic churches now, has always had one of the largest German-Russian Catholic populations of the major cities of the state. For many years the Protestant vs. Catholic issue had a considerable impact on the lives of people there.

Collins Avenue, running through the center of town, separated the German-Russians on the east side from the blend of Anglo-Saxons, Scandinavians and Irish Catholics.

People kept to their part of town socially, and in the very early days the German-Russian people did not enter into the political life. A majority of the businesses were owned by Protestants and Irish Catholics.

The first priests of St. Joseph's Catholic Church were Irish. That did not sit well with the German-Russians, who pressed for and eventually got German-speaking priests.

Like the fathers in German-Russian families, the priests were very authoritarian. German-Russians expected them to act that way and looked up to the priests as their leaders in all matters for they were not only the father figures but usually the best-educated people in the ethnic communities, explains the Rev. William Sherman, Grand Forks sociologist and authority on North Dakota's ethnic culture.

A political priest

German-Russian immigrants had a dim view of politics, remembering the corruption of the government under which they had lived in south Russia. They rarely voted and had no say in the community affairs that affected their lives.

> *"Kids from the other side of town knew more, had nicer clothes."*

The Rev. Hildebrand Eichkoff, Catholic priest at Mandan for many years, was determined to do something about that.

"It was in Mandan that I first met a political priest," Abigail Quigley McCarthy says of Eichkoff in her autobiography "Private Faces Public Places."

She had come to Mandan from Minnesota in the late 1930s as a teacher and got to know Eichkoff well. She writes that the round, balding German Benedictine had a passion for improving the lot of his people and a great contempt for the "cheeseknifers," as he called the Protestants of the town establishment.

Mandan had no Catholic high school and Eichkoff, concerned about the effect on young minds of the Protestant-controlled public high school, urged some of his parishioners to run for the school board. He then encouraged his parishioners to vote, McCarthy says.

Protestants in town were upset when they learned that the priest was not only urging his parishioners to vote, but telling them who to vote for in both school and city elections, recalls a Mandan Presbyterian.

Protestants were about equal in voting numbers to the Catholics. But although they griped about the Catholic clergy's influence in elections, the Presbyterian says, they sometimes were lax about going to the polls. As a consequence, the Catholics soon were the power group controlling the city commission and the school board.

As the German-Russian people became better educated and more politically sophisticated, the clergy no longer dictated their voting choices. But even in more recent years, elections have hinged on the Catholic vote.

A Mandan Protestant recalls the time in the 1950s when he served in a local public office and at the end of his term decided not to seek re-election. Catholic-Protestant tensions had begun to ease, and he had the admiration of a German-Russian member of the board who urged him to run again, offering as an inducement to "get you the whole East End."

Religious conflict also affected other facets of community life. Mandan had a rumpus back in 1945, well-remembered by those who were leaders of its first Community Chest drive.

Four organizations, including the Salvation Army, were to be the beneficiaries.

The Sunday before the drive was to begin, the Catholic priest told his parishioners that, because the Salvation Army was a beneficiary, they should not contribute.

Nearly half of the Catholics who had volunteered to help with the drive withdrew and some of the Catholic businessmen who had made advance pledges informed the campaign committee they would hold up their donations until the matter was clarified.

Two campaign leaders paid a visit to the priest and asked him if he thought his feeling against the Salvation Army was typical among the Catholic clergy. They pointed out that various Catholic prelates in this country and in Europe had often allied themselves with Salvation Army efforts and that the bishop of South Dakota only recently had given the speech at the dedication of the Salvation Army temple in Watertown, S.D.

The priest replied that he didn't care if even the pope supported the Salvation Army, it was *his* parish. He finally compromised with the committee, agreeing to tell his people they could contribute to the drive, except for the Salvation Army.

That meant new cards had to be prepared to permit designation of donations, and many people of the parish ignored the priest's second round of instructions.

The Chamber of Commerce had several Catholic members and, says the Mandanite, "the whole affair caused such a rumpus that a number of Protestant businessmen resigned from the chamber."

Because the German-Russian young people had lived within their sheltered ethnic environment, the impact of suddenly being thrust into a high school with diverse ethnic groups often was difficult for them.

A Mandan woman who grew up on the east side of town recalls the feelings of those students.

"The girls and boys from the other side of town had nicer clothes, and because many of their parents had had more education, they were often better students. They knew more about a lot of things, were more cultured. It made the kids from the east end feel inferior," she says.

Mixed marriages painful

As Catholic and Protestant boys and girls made friends outside their ethnic groups, it inevitably led to mixed marriages, which were upsetting to the families, particularly among the German-Russians and Lutheran.

When the babies came, the real problems began, especially over the issue of baptism. Many a Lutheran mother, urged on by grandmother, rushed her child to the Lutheran minister for baptism while the Catholic father was out of town — and vice versa — creating an enmity between families. That kind of incident was repeated across North Dakota, involving various ethnic groups.

One of the few written records of the religious conflicts in North Dakota is Berneice Lunday's book, "Unblessed," which offers a look at the extreme in strife created by mixed marriage.

The Bismarck author tells of the experiences and emotional confusion that her mother, Margaret Elderman, suffered for years after she married outside her ethnic-religious group.

Born into a German-Russian family in the Dickinson area, Margaret fell in love with a young German Lutheran farmer, Jacob Schoen. When her father threatened to shoot her suitor if he ever showed up on the place again, the couple eloped.

They made their home on her husband's small homestead in the same farming area, living in a two-room shanty. One day her younger sister raced over by horseback to warn her that the family planned to set the place afire.

The couple was uneasy, the author wrote, but did not think it would come to that. In the middle of the night they awoke to find their home burning.

The author relates other incidents, including the deliberate poisoning of the young couple's cow. Defeated by the violent hatred, they went to his father's place near Dodge and he took them in while they searched for a new farm.

Her husband's Lutheran relatives were kind but tried to convert Margaret to their faith and told her that if the children were not baptized they would be damned.

On their new place, Margaret became acquainted with a Seventh-day Adventist neighbor who argued that one gains salvation through conversion and adult baptism. As they discussed religion, the neigbor quoted Scripture and advised Margaret to read the Bible, saying it held the answers to her questions.

Margaret told her neighbor she had never read the Bible because the priest at home had said they shouldn't: they wouldn't understand it.

She spent hours poring over the Bible seeking the answers that had so long eluded her as she searched for a religion she could believe in. She eventually joined the Adventist Church.

Lodge secrecy condemned

The negative stance of Lutheran and Catholic churches toward some organizations, particularly the Masonic Lodge, was often a divisive factor in a community's social relationships. The Masons were frowned upon for their secrecy, and viewed as anti-church.

In Mandan, the Catholic priests would forbid teen-agers to attend the dancing parties regularly held by the Rainbow Girls and Order of DeMolay, both youth Masonic organizations.

Like the Lutherans, the Catholics had internal strife but of a different nature.

In many places the German-Russian immigrants resented the Irish priests.

There was an old saying, said the Rev. E.J. Becwar of Bismarck, that "The Irish love their priests but not necessarily the church, and the German Russians love the church but not necessarily the priests."

The late Rev. Robert Feehan of Bismarck was the priest of St. Mary's Catholic Church for nearly half a century — well-liked by the people of his parish and a favorite cleric among the Protestants.

But when Feehan came to Bismarck as a young priest, said the Rev. E.J. Becwar, he had a very difficult time. He was not cast in the authoritarian mold to which the people of his parish were accustomed and, because he was Irish, didn't speak their language.

"Father Feehan tried very hard, hearing their confessions in German even though the language was a struggle for him. But some people left the church," Becwar recalls.

Money was often a matter of internal strife in the Catholic churches in the early days, as attested to by several longtime Catholic clergymen of the state.

The parish trustee boards were composed of the local priest, the bishop, the bishop's vicar general, and two lay people, usually leaders in the community. But the real power was in the hands of the two lay trustees because priests came and went, and the lay trustees kept the local accounts. They had continuity so they could control the finances of the parish, said Becwar, a Catholic priest at Bismarck.

If the congregation didn't like a priest, they could withhold funds for maintainance of the rectory and keeping food in its kitchen. They could and did sometimes force a priest out of the parish, said the Rev. William Sherman.

Lucille Hendrickson

Moslem services were held at Ross in this building which may have been the first mosque in the United States.

Arab mosque built here in 1929

Moslem services were held each Friday at the basement mosque in Ross, said a WPA interviewer during the 1930s, with a member of the congregation officiating and using the Koran printed in Arabic.

Before coming to worship it was the custom for everyone to wash hands and feet, then clothe themselves in their cleanest clothing, he said. Worshipers brought small rugs on which they knelt, facing east, to offer their prayers. Men and women were separated during these prayers.

For Ramadan — the ninth lunar month of about 30 days, according to the Moslem calendar — members of the Ross congregation would fast, eating only after dark. At the end of the month they celebrated with a feast.

The mosque was built in 1929. It was never domed or completed and has now disappeared. But though another mosque, built in Cedar Rapids, Iowa, in 1934, is called the first building designated as a mosque in the United States, many Arab Americans recognize instead this place in North Dakota as the site of the first Moslem mosque in the nation.

Gates of the Moslem cemetery nearby were spanned by a wrought iron arch set with the symbols of Islam — the star and crescent moon.

Moslems believed they should not take interest for money borrowed, the interviewer noted, nor should they eat pork or drink liquor. "They feel a duty to contribute one-tenth of their income to the salvation of the poor, to help each other and also their neighbors and friends," he said, noting that often they do give aid "either to their own nationality or other nationalities by money or work donations in time of distress."

F.B.

Care of dead reflects view of life

"Cemeteries say a lot about how a people look at life as well as death. You can walk through them and trace the changes by the changes in the markers," says Tim Kloberdanz.

Kloberdanz, assistant professor of sociology at North Dakota State University, adds that, "Regardless of customs, funerals and weddings represent security for the individuals and strengthen their ethnic bonds."

Kloberdanz says the German-Russians accepted death realistically without excessive emotion and had a saying that "Death is free of charge but costs you your life."

"When a person was dying," he relates, "the whole family would gather at the house of the dying, but it was not considered good to cry a lot because that would hold back the death of someone who was suffering. Their culture is against display of emotion."

He says the German-Russians felt there were omens of death, including three mysterious knocking noises in the house, a bird flying toward the window, the hooting of an owl or the howling of a dog late at night and the sole of a boot coming off while walking.

In the early years, coffins were custom-made by local craftsmen to fit the dead person. If a small child died, the godparent of the same sex would carry the coffin on his or her head to the cemetery.

At the cemetery, there were prayers and songs as the coffin was lowered into the grave. Many people found it so moving they would have to leave the ceremonies. During the ceremonies, the singers would "take the voice of the deceased" and tell the others that fate would spare nobody,and that they, too, someday would join the dead.

German Catholics particularly sought to discourage suicide and would bury people who committed suicide in the far corner of a cemetery or outside it.

Children were baptized as soon as possible, because unbaptized children would be buried in unmarked graves.

In the early years, graves were marked with crosses of wood because it was the most readily available material. Later, wrought iron crosses made by the local blacksmith were used. Up until the 1920s, the crosses often were filled with old symbols.

Those crosses were succeeded by iron crosses cast in a foundry and finally by the concrete and stone markers used today.

P.V. Thorson, associate professor of history at the University of North Dakota, says that many of the Norwegian congregations shared the German Catholic distaste for suicide.

He says he has heard of instances where the bodies of suicides were denied admission to the cemetery by the front gate and their coffins had to be lifted over a back fence for interment in holy ground.

"Scandinavian funeral services continued to use the language and liturgy of the native church until after World War II," says the Rev. Duane Lindbergh of Waterloo, Iowa.

Lindbergh served several churches in North Dakota and has written a book on the Norwegian clergy.

"It is important to the Norwegians that funeral services be conducted in the church building, and many of

Early day funeral scene at Fort Yates Catholic cemetery as filmed by Frank Fiske, post photographer.

them still use something in the mother language like a solo, the Lord's Prayer or a Norwegian hymn like 'Behold the Host.'

"The funeral itself always involved a sermon, and it was not generally considered in good taste to overeulogize the deceased. The services always involved some congregational singing and solos.

"The body originally would be at the home, and friends would call at the home and bring gifts of food. The coffin would be open at the church but closed when the services ended.

"After the committal services, the congregation would return to the church to eat. It was important that the people gather together as a vehicle for a community symbol of the end of the world. It was the 'banquet of the lamb of God,' the fulfillment of heaven."

An account of the first Norwegian settlement in the Cooperstown area recalls that one Norwegian custom that has died out was the issuing of special invitations to funerals.

The invited friends assembled in the forenoon, bringing with them cakes, sandwiches and other food with which a sumptuous dinner was prepared.

"Scandinavians are by and large stoic, and you could not measure the degree of love by outward evidence of tears. They have a controlled response to death ultimately rooted in the faith that (death) is the road to heaven," says Lindbergh.

He says the original Norwegian immigrants were rural people whose basic goal was "160 acres or more of good land," and their churches were rural.

Tombstones were sometimes hand crafted of petrified wood or stones. Note candle design on either side of cross. Broken glass probably held inscription, possibly a photo.

"The cemeteries often surround the church," Lindbergh explains, "but this concept wasn't practical when the churches moved into the towns, because there wasn't sufficient land. Ground used for cemeteries is considered hallowed and holy."

He notes that the Norwegians put great emphasis on the care of graves. "Living members of the families continue to maintain the graves and keep them up," he says.

Lindbergh says that, through the years, efforts were made to mark all of the graves, orginally with wood markers and later with stone, which was used in native Norway.

"Gravestones often have Scriptures or some other message in Norwegian," he says.

Funeral customs and philosophy of North Dakota's Hutterites are described by author John Hostetler, who writes: "Death to the Hutterites means termination of earthly struggles and a beginning of paradise. They prefer a slow death with time to consider eternity and make everything right. The Hutterites bury their dead men in a white shirt and black trousers and their women in a black dress. Wakes would be held for two nights before the funeral, with alternate hymns and Scripture reading. The Hutterites have an emotional acceptance of death."

Nicholas Vrooman of the North Dakota Arts Council is studying ethnic cemeteries and notes that the Metis people of the Turtle Mountain area, who have French and Chippewa ancestors, are noted for distinctive tombstones.

"They made a lot of tombstones cast from a slab of concrete with colored glass bottles imbedded in them and often inlaid with colored pebbles," says Vrooman.

Prior to the coming of the white man, both village and nomadic Indians of North Dakota practiced scaffold burials, relates Mary Jane Schneider, chairman of Indian studies at the University of North Dakota.

"The Arikara, Mandan and Hidatsa village Indians practiced scaffold burials as late as 1900, and often had 'cemeteries' of scaffolds," Schneider says. "The scaffolds had religious significance but they were also practical because for much of the year the ground is frozen in North Dakota and it was very difficult to dig graves with bones or sticks as tools.

"Lewis and Clark noted the scaffold practice in their journals. The Indians believed that persons who died with a leg or arm missing would go to a different place in the hereafter than the others, and thus the scaffold protected the bodies from dogs and wolves.

"The Sioux also buried their dead on scaffolds, though they had no cemeteries, but in the eastern part of the state as late as 1850 the Chippewa placed their dead in 'grave houses.' They would build a little peaked house over the grave in the ground, and then place in front of it a stick with the tribal totem on it."

Schneider says that both the nomadic Sioux and the village Indians practiced "ghost keeping" in which a bit of hair and other articles of the dead person were made into a bundle. The bundle was kept for a year or more, given food and talked to until the tribe deemed that the time had come to end the mourning, release the ghost and relieve the family. At that time the family would give away things that belonged to the dead person and new things would be given the family.

"Modern Indian burial customs are quite similar to the white people's and depend upon whether the Indians are Protestant or Catholic," Schneider says, "but the gift giving is still done today."

The Mandan and Hidatsa give items away right after the funeral, but the Sioux usually wait a year or more. A feast always accompanies the gift-giving, which includes shawls, star quilts and war bonnets. At the time of a death, friends and relatives rally around the family and bring food.

Schneider notes that earlier among the Sioux, a person who died suddenly would simply be left undisturbed in his tepee. The body was left behind when the tribe moved.

She says many modern Indians are outraged that whites have excavated Indian grave sites, and are reluctant to discuss burial customs or locations that remain undisturbed.

The Ukrainians who came to southwestern North Dakota around the turn of the century brought their Byzantine Rite religion with them and conducted services in "church Slavonic," which is to Ukrainian what Latin is to Italian, says Agnes Palanuk of the Ukrainian Cultural Institute in Dickinson.

Palanuk says Ukrainian cemeteries are distinctive for their wrought iron crosses, which are taller than those found in German-Russian cemeteries. Those from the early times are elaborate with filigree. The inscriptions are in Ukrainian and the crosses often contain a photograph of the deceased, taken before death and preserved against the weather.

Jack E. Case

Nationalities

People from many nations and continents came to settle here.

Those with a common language and heritage often settled together, forming ethnic communities which are still recognizable today. They built a church — or perhaps a synagogue, a mosque, a sun dance arena. And they continued traditional ways of celebrating their holidays and rites of passage. They adapted to new lands and changing times, yet they have kept the clear character of the state's ethnic mosaic.

Other nationalities were also here from earliest settlement times and, though not portrayed here because their numbers were few, also contributed much to the development and character of this state.

Joe Albert, a Syrian bear wrestler from Dunseith, gave "strong man" shows during 1930s around the state.

JR.

Earthlodges at Slant Indian Village near Mandan appear to be simple dirt mounds, but interior view reveals massive structure held up by four huge cottonwood posts. At left, Delberta Larrabee reigns as Junior Miss United Tribes.

Just what is an Indian anymore?

"Being an Indian is a state of mind."

Perhaps that reaction from a Bismarck Indian best summarizes just what it means to be an Indian.

What's left to being an Indian when you look at a way of existence completely changed — a mixed-blood line, a new everyday language, the trappings of a white technological society and tattered cultural remnants?

What continues to make Indians different from white people?

Legally, a person has to have at least one-fourth Indian blood to be enrolled in a tribe.

But it is the philosophical rather than the legal boundaries that really are more valuable in defining the line between white and Indian.

The most common difference one hears from Indians is that they are less materialistic.

This value difference is closely related to others — more respect for the land, greater emphasis on the family, less concern for personal aggrandizement.

One also hears that Indians are more concerned with short-term goals, while whites place more emphasis on long-term gains.

It's hard, though, to generalize. Indian values differ from tribe to tribe and among individuals.

Values differ among Indians just as they differ among whites.

But there are common threads, and one hears remarks about materialism over and over.

"If you put the white man's values down, you have the almighty dollar for the god, while the Indian people care more about sharing and helping each other," says Oliver Eastman, a 77-year-old Sioux.

Whereas some white people view the grand giveaways some Indians indulge in as backward, Carl Whitman, an older Indian on the Fort Berthold Reservation, sees them as a sign of cultural advancement.

"It's better to give than to receive," he says. "To me, that's a graduation from animalism."

Vance Gillette, a young Indian attorney raised at Fort Berthold Reservation and now living in Bismarck, says Indian values have changed a lot since his grandfather's days.

But some of Gillette's values echo Eastman's, who is old enough to be his grandfather.

"When you're growing up, you're instilled with certain personality traits," says Gillette. "With Indians, it's more of a communal base. They like sharing and generosity.

"Whites are more into materialism. With white people, it's 'me.'

Greg Turosak

Differing lifestyles on the reservation

Because reservation Indians tend to live a segregated life, it does not necessarily follow that they all have the same lifestyle.

Today's Indian people share a basic culture, but from that point on their lifestyles differ, in some cases by choice and in other cases by circumstances.

There are the traditionalists, mostly older people, who embrace the Indian religion and, as much as possible in this day and age, live according to the old ways.

There is a growing segment of young people, often well-educated, who have made a conscious effort to learn more about their roots and are trying to blend old ways and values into a modern lifestyle.

There are people, but they are few in number, whom Indians themselves call "apple" Indians. It's a derogatory word to describe fellow Indians who give lip service to Indian values but who in reality put self-interest first.

And "commercial" Indians. Those who delight in wearing the trappings — braids, beadwork — but whose dedication to Indian values also is suspect by fellow Indians.

And, finally, there are some non-traditional people of Indian blood who have become so integrated into the white culture that they have retained little of what can be called Indian.

There are few if any rich people on North Dakota's Indian reservations.

Those who live the most comfortably are usually successful ranchers or people with good government positions, usually with the Bureau of Indian Affairs.

The majority live in modest economic circumstances or in poverty.

George and Elizabeth Azure live modestly in a home at Sioux Village, a housing development at the turn of the road going into Fort Yates on Standing Rock Reservation.

They regard themselves as fortunate because George, who was in road work for many years for the Bureau of Indian Affairs, has a BIA pension and draws a modest Social Security paycheck every month.

They value old traditions but have succeeded in melding those with a lifestyle similar to that of any small-town North Dakota family.

As she kneaded dough in her neat kitchen, Elizabeth talked about the changes she has seen on the reservation since her childhood on a farm near Fort Yates.

She and her husband both grew up on farms and were educated in boarding schools. Life was simple and they worked hard for a living.

"Life nowadays isn't as good as it used to be," said Elizabeth. "There was a time when people lived near the river. They planted their gardens and stored vegetables in the root cellars for the winter. Most people had a team, some chickens, a milk cow, maybe a pig or two. They didn't depend on the government."

The drought and the depression of the 1930s wiped people out, and then came Oahe Dam, she said.

"Now there are food stamps and surplus commodities, and the root cellars are used for storm shelters," she said.

Those earlier days were better, agreed her husband. He grew up on his family's cattle ranch outside Fort Yates. But with the continued drought, there was no feed, the cattle were starving, and they had to sell most of their land just to survive.

They moved to town and he got his job with the BIA .

The Azures view with dismay the dependency of so many of the reservation people on government assistance for the basic things of life. They are disturbed by what they see alcohol doing to family life.

Their neighbor, Shirley King, who had dropped by for coffee, nodded her head in agreement, saying family life has been weakened by alcohol.

"The grandmothers and grandfathers, they used to be the teachers, and they taught the children to have great respect for their elders. Although you could say children were raised permissively by their parents, the respect they were taught served as a restraint on bad behavior. I remember my grandmother teaching me.

"Now the older people are dying off, and with the alcohol problem in some families, what you have now in too many families is the permissiveness, but without the respect. So some young peple are out of control," she said.

The problem is alleviated somewhat by the Indian tradition of the extended family. When parents, for whatever reason, are incapable of raising their children, a grandmother or other relative takes over, it was explained.

Looking at reservation life today, the Azures said the automobile and televison have brought the world closer, and while some students still go to boarding school, there are buses nowadays that transport children to day schools.

Most families have some kind of transportation so they can get off the reservation to shop, go to a movie, visit friends and relatives.

Indian foods, like wojapi, a kind of chokecherry pudding, and wild turnips and dried meat are served in many homes.

But like other Americans, Indian people like pizza, hamburgers and tacos, especially "Indian" tacos made with frybread.

Lucille Hendrickson

Making the urban transition

When Connie Fox's mother comes to visit her, she stops at the outskirts of Mandan to telephone a family member for an escort.

Just the volume of traffic in the Bismarck-Mandan area can' be intimidating to an Indian who has grown up on a reservation, Fox said.

As director of the Peace Pipe Indian Center in Bismarck, Fox is well-acquainted with the problems some Indians have in making the transition from reservation to urban living.

According to the Peace Pipe staff, about 1,500 Indians are living in the Bismarck-Mandan area.

The 1980 census — which Indian officials say did not give an accurate enumeration of residents of some of reservations — counted 20,119 Native Americans living in North Dakota.

Close to 8,900 of those are living off reservations.

And many more could be considered transients, people who move to a city for a few months and end up returning to the reservation for a variety of reasons, Fox said.

The North Dakota Indian Affairs Commission and Dakota Association of Native Americans (DANA) sponsored a conference in June to examine the problems Indians encounter off the reservation.

Lack of job opportunities and housing were listed as some of the

Connie Fox and Alvina Patneaud of Peace Pipe Indian Center, Bismarck, help others adjust to urban living.

primary concerns. Discrimination was cited as a factor in many situations.

The conference also noted that the tribes should provide career counseling and job and living skills information to their people in preparation for off-reservation living.

"I think one of the biggest problems people have is they are unaware" of what is involved in living in a city, Fox said.

Alvina Patneaud, the Peace Pipe outreach worker, added, "A lot of Indian people say, 'We just can't make it here. It's too expensive to live.' Some come and get an apartment for one month, find they can't pay next month's rent and go back."

The center tries to "ease the transition for them" by referring them to employment agencies, helping them find housing, outlining what types of benefits they may qualify for or what type of educational programs are available, Patneaud said.

But, many of the Indians the center deals with "really haven't decided" to live in a city environment and may make several moves between the city and reservation before settling, she said.

Harriet Skye, DANA's director since 1979, said she made four moves between her home at Fort Yates and several cities, before settling in the Bismarck area.

Her first time off the reservation came during the 1950s as part of the government's relocation program. At the time, Skye said she was unprepared to deal with urban living — particularly in a city the size of Los Angeles.

"It gets a little tough, so you go back home" and acquire more education, or more confidence, before trying again, she said.

Two other "urban" Indians also said attitudes have much to do with how well an individual adjusts.

Adrian Crowfeather, civil rights officer with Job Service, said his adjustment to non-reservation life — living as an Indian in a non-Indian environment — came when he was attending college in South Dakota during the 1960s.

In his 15-year tenure with Job Service, Crowfeather has lived and worked in Fort Yates, Minot, Washington and for 10 years in Bismarck. The only difficulty he has had was adjusting to the "crowdedness" of Washington, he said.

But, making the switch requires a "lot of perseverance. (You've) got to keep hoping; if it's a bad situation, it will get better," he said.

Leroy Gray moved to Bismarck from a Montana reservation last January to take a course in power plant technology at Bismarck Junior College.

Financially, it has been a lean year for his family, Gray said, though both he and his wife work part time. But, Gray said, he has found people in Bismarck to be "pretty friendly."

With a positive attitude, "most people, if you meet them halfway, are not going to turn away," Gray said.

He will be returning to Montana after he finishes the course because the tuition was paid by a power plant's scholarship program under the condition he work for the plant for two years.

His family, particularly his three daughters ages 2 to 8, will miss the city, Gray said. They've become used to the attractions a city has to offer, such as the zoo and the variety of movies and shows that come into town, Gray said.

While Crowfeather said he didn't have difficulty adjusting, he pointed out that many Indians may have difficulty because of what he called a "spillover of this dependency type of thing on the reservations." What motivated him was the encouragement of people, he said.

To ease the transition, Crowfeather said, it helps to have "somebody there who says you can do it."

Juanita Helphrey, director of the state Indian Affairs Commission, pointed out that many come to the city "out of pure frustration" with the limited opportunities on their reservations.

Because many are unprepared for city life, they face problems obtaining jobs, finding housing and dealing with prejudices, members of the center and Helphry noted.

Rosemary Lynch

Turtle Mountain reservation: cultural melting pot

The reservation is small and, for North Dakota, densely populated. It covers just 72 square miles and is home for about 8,300 Indians who live on or near it.

Most of them are a mixture of Chippewa and French blood. The reservation is, in effect, a "mini melting pot" of Indian and European cultures.

"That's how we got such a large population," says tribal Chairman Jim Henry, his tongue firmly in cheek. "That French blood comes out; we're lovers, not fighters."

Outwardly, the Belcourt community, population 1,900, seems reasonably prosperous and similar to most North Dakota towns of its size.

Although some of the people on the reservation live in poor quality housing, about 800 new homes have been built on small individual land parcels, in rural housing clusters and in Belcourt during the last 15 years.

Several businesses and industries provide jobs close to home, but unemployment remains a serious problem. Unemployment, about 40 percent, has risen with a decline in seasonal farm work brought on by the continued mechanization of agriculture, according to the North Dakota Indian Affairs Commission.

Turtle Mountain tribal leaders are trying to find out what oil and other resources might be hidden under the scenic landscape, resources that could help support the reservation's large population.

Tourism — the reservation is eight miles from the International Peace Garden — is seen as a potential source of jobs that hasn't been developed.

Says Henry, "We don't have the (large) land here. We have the people, so we have to develop industry."

To that end, Henry led an effort that resulted in building an industrial park that currently houses the Turtle Mountain Manufacturing Co. The company employs Indians to make trailers for the military and some private business.

A shopping center, completely operated by Indian businessmen, was established in Belcourt.

The business community, hospital, housing, radio station, rural water system and other facilities combine to set Turtle Mountain apart from other reservations in North Dakota, where business and services are less developed, not always accessible and generally operated by non-Indians.

Turtle Mountain reservation with its many lakes and wooded hills is part of a scenic area that includes the International Peace Gardens.

Only one business in Belcourt is owned by a non-Indian, while several businesses in neighboring off-reservation communities are owned by tribal members.

"I think we're head and shoulders above any other reservation in a five-state area," says Henry. He also says he believes the state of North Dakota is "probably 10 or 20 years ahead" of Montana and South Dakota in working with Indian people.

Farrell Gourneau, vice-chairman of the tribal government, says the reservation community has a number of Indian contractors in construction, trucking and other basic industries. The reservation also has skilled seasonal workers who travel to energy development towns in other areas of North Dakota during the summer, he adds.

Some members of the Turtle Mountain Chippewa Band live on or own land allotments in the Buford-Trenton area on the border of North Dakota and Montana.

Those allotments came about because Congress failed to set aside enough land on the Turtle Mountain Reservation to provide the 160 acres each Indian was to receive under federal law.

Many Indians, like the parents of tribal council member Ray Parisien, sold their allotments in Montana sight unseen, rather than leave their traditional homes in the Turtle Mountains.

Parisien notes that oil wells are now pumping on the land his parents sold.

Despite Turtle Mountain's accomplishments, it still has social problems, such as those involving alcohol and drugs.

But Henry says there is less tension between Indians and non-Indians in the Turtle Mountain area than elsewhere in North Dakota.

Perhaps part of the reason for the Turtle Mountain Indians' adaptability to white society is cultural.

The people tend to be more outspoken and aggressive than other North Dakota Indians, and outwardly they seem quite similar in attitude to non-Indians.

Most of the people are a mixture of Chippewa and French, with some Norwegian, Spanish and other ethnic origins thrown in.

Many families formerly spoke French, but the language has largely died out over the years since the fur-trading days. French names are commonplace, however.

Almost lost in the French-Chippewa culture are people like Leo Wilkie, who consider themselves of a different racial and cultural background from the reservation majority.

Wilkie, a sculptor of Ojibwa descent, says there is a struggle by Ojibwa, Cree and other segments of the reservation population to achieve racial identity.

Larry Johnson

Above, New Town high school in break between classes; the school is about half Indian and half white.

A ranch in the rugged country of Fort Berthold Indian reservation near Mandaree.

Potential's the word at Berthold

One word that comes to mind as one travels through this rugged, sprawling reservation is "potential."

That's not to say things are hunky-dory on this reservation — home to 3,500 of the remaining, mostly mixed-blood population of the Mandan, Hidatsa and Arikara Indians.

Another 3,000 or so enrolled tribal members live off the reservation.

This reservation shares problems common to all reservations in North Dakota.

There isn't enough housing, and much of the existing housing is poorly maintained.

There are far too few jobs.

Unemployment was up to 63 percent in 1981.

Some 15 percent of those employed are involved in agriculture, about 12 percent in retail and about 10 percent in construction and industry.

Most of the rest are involved in government jobs — tribal, federal, state or city — or in services such as school employment.

There are health problems, including alcoholism, and the reservation has no hospital.

Those problems exist in the face of a rapidly growing Indian population — from 2,713 in 1970 to a current tribal estimate of 3,500.

Almost half the Indian population is under age 15.

Despite the problems, one gets the feeling that given time and effort, the potential of this beautiful area and its basically friendly people may yet be realized.

One sees the potential in the quality grazing land of the Missouri and Little Missouri River breaks. One sees it in the hint of oil development that is starting to creep onto the reservation, providing jobs. One sees it in the broad expanse of Lake Sakakawea, with its potential for recreation and irrigation. One detects it in the Indian high school students, whose education is a road from the past to an undefined future. One sees it in the tribal government, its ranks swelled with young, educated Indians who have ideas and hopes for implementing them.

True, the reservation is stagnant in many ways. But there are signs all around that point to a potentially better future for the Fort Berthold Indians.

It's important to keep in mind that Fort Berthold is a reservation still seeking to hit its stride in the wake of the greatest social and population displacement in the state's history.

Prior to the closure of Garrison Dam in the 1950s, the Three Affiliated Tribes — who, unlike the Sioux, were never at war with the white man — led a peaceful existence along the bottomlands of the Missouri River, in pleasant communities like Elbowwoods, Independence and Nishu, all long since inundated.

Though they had moved onto the reservation from other areas along the Missouri, the Mandans, Arikaras and Hidatsas were pretty much able to continue the sedentary farming lives they practiced prior to the white man's arrival.

Everything the tribes needed was along the river — lignite and wood for fuel, bottomlands for crops, shelter for their livestock. Extended families could stay close. There was little need for money.

Then came the dam.

A full 90 percent of the population had to move to higher elevations to escape the flood.

Instead of a rural country existence, close to extended family members, many Indians found themselves in unfamiliar, detached locations.

A lifestyle reinforced through centuries was drastically uprooted.

Indians and whites were thrown together in a new town called, imaginatively, "New Town."

There was little for many of the Indians to do.

The problems became ones not only of economics, but of mental attitudes.

To hear many people describe it, the loss of the bottomlands created a feeling of aimlessness, bitterness and apathy — all helping to weaken the social fiber and add to such problems as alcoholism.

The flood, plus the Indian relocation program of the 1950s, caused many to leave the reservation.

It is only now, still in the first generation since the Great Disruption, that the reservation is beginning to find something new.

And only now that some of the young people who went off to school are back and holding positions of responsibility and authority within the tribe.

This young, activist tribal administration is interested in creating jobs, improving living conditions, fostering Indian self-pride through role models, promoting education and having Indians take control over their lives on the reservation.

Greg Turosak

The upper midwest's best preserved military post is at Fort Totten. Below, a scene in the town of Fort Totten.

Fort Totten aims for self-reliance

Driving through the small towns on the Fort Totten Reservation, you are sure to notice the children.

Small groups of youths, fishing along the shores of Devils Lake, playing ball on the scruffy patches of grass surrounding the housing complexes, tinkering with a bicycle on a street corner.

Members of the Devils Lake Sioux Tribe are quick to point out the youthful composition of their reservation. Of the approximately 3,000 enrolled members of the tribe, about 1,250 are between infancy and high school.

The increase in the birth rate was a major factor in deciding to build a $14 million community school, now under construction.

Tribal Chairman Carl McKay believes a community school will help foster a community, tribal spirit — a spirit that government policy has worked against in the past.

But, the major focus of the tribal leadership is economic growth on the reservation.

"It is so darn important for a tribe to become independent economically of the federal grant," McKay said. "Individual tribes have to develop their own financial base, provide for themselves."

In the past decade, the tribe has undertaken several ventures designed to improve the economics of the Devils Lake Sioux people.

The Devils Lake Sioux Manufacturing Corp. is the major change.

But, the tribe also has branched out into farming and is constructing a $900,000 shopping mall, financed by federal loan programs.

Warren Sogard, a Fargo attorney who serves as counsel to the tribe, said, "This tribe has quietly been going about its business for 10 years and getting its act together."

Seven years ago the tribe's income was about $50,000 a year, McKay said. This year, he expects it to hit about $1 million.

McKay has great hopes for farming on the reservation. Since 1976, the tribe has been repurchasing some of the 130,000 acres of land originally assigned to the Devils Lake Sioux Tribe under an 1867 treaty. Much of the land was redistributed as a result of various government policies designed to spur assimilation of Indians, and some was homesteaded to white farmers and ranchers.

The tribe has been buying and putting into tribal ownership individual Indian land that had been fragmented through inheritance.

The tribal farm, which employs nine persons, has about 7,000 acres of cropland under cultivation. This past summer the operation branched out into ranching.

Since most of North Dakota is keyed toward agriculture, McKay believes "we (the tribe) need to be getting into that business."

The farm has proved to be a financial success, officials say. And McKay hopes the tribal farm will encourage more individual farming by promoting a cooperative-type management system for use of equipment.

The major economic impact, though, has come from the eight-year-old Devils Lake Sioux Manufacturing Corp. Its major contract is with the Defense Department for production of camouflage material. The tribe owns 51 percent of the company; the Brunswick Corp. is the other shareholder.

The company employs about 330 persons, about 60 percent of them Indians, according to Rex Moore, manager of corporate responsibilities.

The annual turnover rate is about 52 percent, and absenteeism averages about 6 percent. Those figures, according to Moore, compare with 200 percent and 20 percent, respectively, in the corporation's first years of operation.

Company officials tried a variety of methods to reduce the absenteeism and turnover rates, including work-incentive programs, counseling, workshops and liberal rehiring policies, Moore said.

"The sudden change is really unexplainable. No one applied method can take credit," Moore said. Part of the change may be attributed to the workers adjusting to the nine-to-five schedule, he said.

The early high rates are "just a general condition of a society not acquainted with the industrial environment," Moore said.

The plant also has brought tribal members back to the reservation. Moore himself is a member of the Devils Lake Sioux Tribe who left as a teen-ager because there were no opportunities.

Mary Swigart, who works in the engineering department, returned to the reservation along with several members of her family during the 1970s. Many are working at the plant, and Swigart sees the plant as one of the factors keeping her extended family on the reservation.

"So many of us in the family depend upon the plant," she said.

Rosemary Lynch

Small girls are elegantly dressed for powwow. Below is a view of Fort Yates, on Standing Rock reservation, with Oahe reservoir in the background.

Standing Rock Sioux: trying to build a new way of life on the reservation

When the waters of Lake Oahe are high, Fort Yates, headquarters of Standing Rock Indian Reservation, is a veritable island, connected to the mainland only by a causeway.

In some respects, the reservation itself is an island where Indian people strive to maintain their identity while coping with the problems of living in a space-age world dominated by the white man's culture.

In 1890, the Hunkpapa, Blackfeet and Upper and Lower Yanktonnai Bands of the Teton Sioux were moved onto Standing Rock Reservation straddling the North Dakota-South Dakota border. The government said they were to leave the old ways behind and become small farmers.

There have been many hard times since a new way of life was forced upon the Indian people. Most devastating for the Standing Rock Sioux were the Three Ds — drought, depression and the dam.

During the Dirty Thirties, many who had become farmers and ranchers had to sell their land and livestock to keep from starving.

In the 1960s, 56,000 acres of the reservation's Missouri River bottomlands were inundated by Lake Oahe, created by the closure of Oahe Dam near Pierre, S.D. The flood forced the relocation of 21 percent of the people.

Despite the reverses it has suffered, the tribe has persevered. The people now have considerable control over their own affairs. Their leaders are steadily gaining management expertise and have expressed a determination to build a better life for future generations.

Two counties, Sioux in North Dakota and Corson in South Dakota, lie within the boundaries of the reservation. U.S. Census Bureau figures put the total population in 1980 at 8,816, of whom 4,800 are Indian. But the tribe says the Indian population is more like 6,000, according to its census.

Money received as compensation for the Oahe flood and federal anti-poverty programs begun in the 1960s have helped to improve living conditions.

Hundreds of new homes have been constructed in the past 15 years, and sewer and water systems have been installed in the small outlying communities. But plumbing currently is a big issue. The systems often break down, and both the tribe and the Indian Health Service, which installed it, claim the other is responsible for major maintenance.

There is a beautiful new multi-million dollar high school at Fort Yates, and the community college offers academic and vocational education opportunities for reservation people of all ages.

Business and industry ventures have had less success.

Unemployment is high. Normally around 60 percent, the unemployment rate is now more like 80 percent, mainly because of recent federal cutbacks in programs, tribal officials say.

The frustrations of unemployment and poverty have contributed to alcoholism and its related social ills.

Most of the Standing Rock people who do have work are employed in government jobs or are engaged in agriculture, usually cattle raising.

The tribe is focusing its economic development on the reservation's major natural resources — land and water.

The rolling grasslands and readily available water from the Missouri River create a potential for livestock ventures. Proposed are production of feed crops through irrigation, a cattle herd, improved range management and a feedlot operation. From that is envisioned a potential spinoff into a meatpacking operation.

A start was made a few years ago with the cooperative tribal-community college cow-calf operation, now self-sustaining.

Land consolidation is viewed as essential to agricultural development, and a program to buy back Indian trust lands has been under way for some years.

When its boundaries were set, the Standing Rock Reservation encompassed 2.3 million acres.

Over the years, trust lands were reduced by nearly two-thirds through white settlement and the sale of individual Indian allotments. Much of the Indian-owned land is leased to non-Indians.

As a result of reacquisition, trust lands now total some 850,000 acres, about 350,000 owned by the tribe and the rest by individuals.

Everett Iron Eyes, natural resources director for the tribe, said that because irrigation is essential to agricultural development plans, and the tribe's claim to Missouri River waters bordering the reservation is being challenged, it is vital that studies of the reservation irrigation potential be completed.

Preliminary studies show there could be as much as 100,000 acres of irrigable land, he said.

Glancing at the photo of his five children on the wall beside his desk, Iron Eyes said, "We must have something to assure the future of our children. All we have is the land and the water."

Lucille Hendrickson

At right, clockwise, Justin Gray Hawk, 21 months, holds grandmother Agatha Chapman's hand at Bismarck powwow. Housing development at West Twin Buttes on Fort Berthold. A young contestant with beaded finery at United Tribes' powwow. Craft sale attracts many prospective buyers. Women's traditional costume winners, Debbie Hall, Linda Gorneau and Brenda Hall.

"It still hasn't worked its way through ourselves that it's OK to be Indian, because just a few years ago, it wasn't OK. For me, the biggest thing is realizing that Indian people weren't wrong when they were fighting for the land and the things they love."

—Harriet Skye

Harriet Skye of Bismarck, director of Dakota Association of Native Americans (DANA).

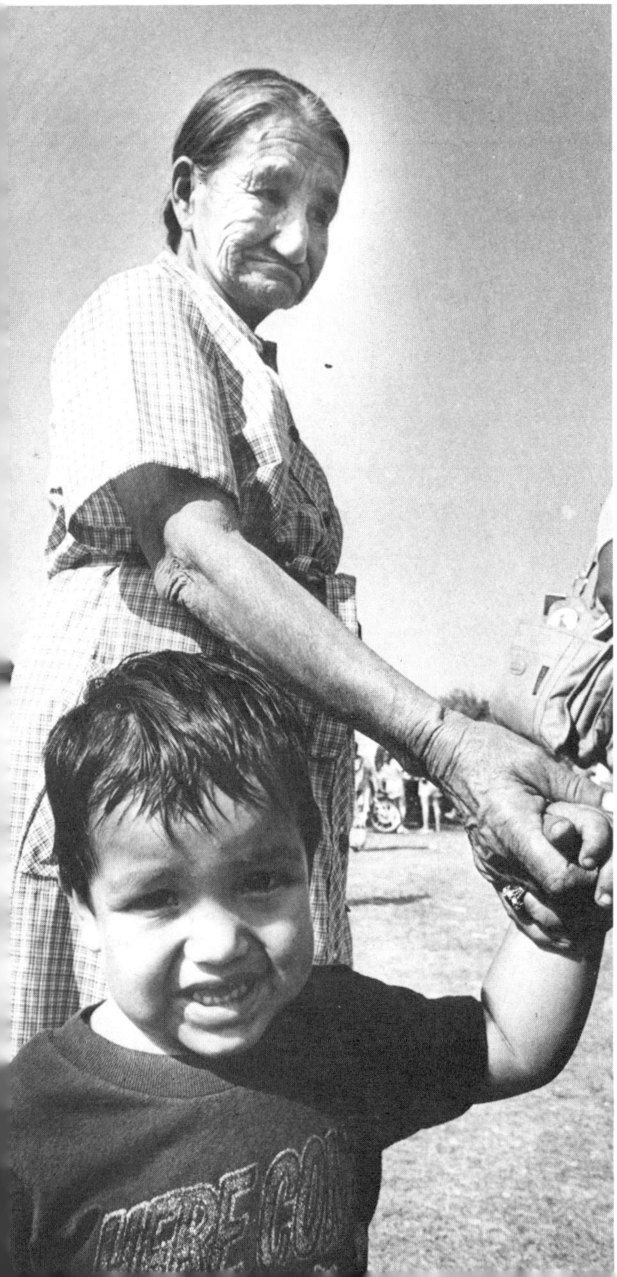

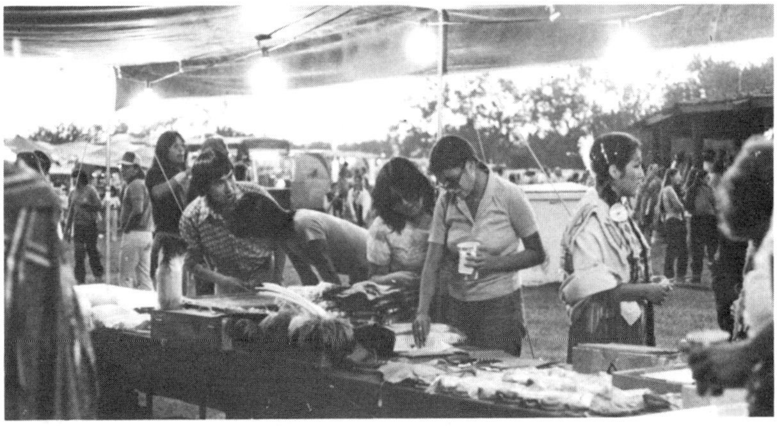

Metis say Indian side of culture resurging

Tom Davis can trace his "roots" back to the late 1600s, when they start branching out to opposite sides of the Atlantic Ocean.

It was about three centuries ago that an English fur trader named David Davis took an Indian wife, whom he renamed Josset.

"We've come as a Davis clan, all the way to right now," says Tom Davis. "There is a great number of Davis people on this reservation."

Davis, tribal planner for the Turtle Mountain Band of Chippewa in Belcourt, says the Indian half of the mixed-blood, or Metis, culture at the reservation is regaining strength, after paternalistic policies by the federal government destroyed much of it during the first half of this century.

"Within the last five or six years, a great portion of this reservation has turned back to their Indian, Ojibwa, ways," says Davis. "I would say there is a split in the population here, in identifying themselves" as Indian or of the mixed-blood culture.

Even those who identify with the French side of their heritage remember their Indian blood and take pride in it, he continues.

"Seven or eight years ago, the realization finally hit these people of what they are," he says. "You start seeing bumper stickers, 'I'm Chippewa Indian and I'm proud.'"

The approximately 8,300 tribal members who live on or near the reservation are known as Metis, a mixture of French, British and Indian — mostly Chippewa, Ojibwa and Cree.

Metis also live around Walhalla, in the Buford-Trenton area near Williston, in the state's major cities, on other Indian reservations and in Canada.

Descended from marriages between early fur traders and native Americans, the Metis developed a hybrid culture and their own identity and language.

In North Dakota, they worked as buffalo hunters, made pemmican for trade and were the "truckers" of the prairie, operating caravans of Red River ox carts until the coming of the railroad in the late 1800s.

Most Metis went to the Canadian side of the boundary in 1824 to retain trading ties with the Hudson's Bay Co.

But as the end of the fur trade approached, the Metis began to fall on hard times. Many tried turning to agriculture, with some success. But their riverfront farming operations were disrupted in 1869 when the Canadian government purchased Metis land from the Hudson's Bay Co. and European settlers began moving in.

Twice, in 1870 and 1885, Metis in Canada rebelled under the leadership of Louis Riel, who sought to establish a "New Nation."

In 1885 the Metis, who were mostly Catholics, also announced the fall of Rome and the establishment of the "Living Catholic Apostolic and Vital Church of the New World," apparently because the Church opposed their rebellion.

The "New Nation" was quickly defeated in both instances, the first in Manitoba and the second in Saskatchewan. Riel was convicted of treason in Canada and was hung on Nov. 16, 1885.

The Metis and Indians lost their land base in northern North Dakota in the 1880s. They once held claim to 10 million acres of reservation land in the North Dakota region. But executive orders in 1882 and 1884 reduced their base to the present 6-by-12-mile reservation in the Turtle Mountains.

The United States and the Turtle Mountain Band of Chippewa currently are working out the final stages of a $52 million settlement for the land that was taken.

Davis says nearly total dependence on the federal government since about 1915 and more recent boarding school and relocation programs destroyed much of the Indian heritage of the Metis.

But, he says, the treaty settlement is one of the factors helping to restore Metis pride.

Perhaps the biggest factor, he says, has been a program of cultural studies from kindergarten through college on the reservation. The tribal government also tries to hold seminars to foster cultural awareness, he adds.

Davis considers language the key to cultural identity. "Once you lose your language, you lose the basis of

Metis families with their Red River carts. Their colorful dress might include "six or seven gaily colored petticoats," observed a WPA interviewer during the 30s, noting a love for singing and dancing. "They are a happy and fun-loving people. It is not uncommon to see them decorated with flowers. All use a dash of red on their clothing." In the old days the carts were taken on big twice-yearly buffalo hunts and used to haul pemmican and buffalo hides as far as St. Paul.

your culture," he says, such as prayers and songs.

Most Metis have lost their Indian languages, he says, but many are still able to speak a mixture of French and Indian called "michif." Davis says michif was the only language used in his home until he was about 7 years old, and some of his older relatives still use it almost exclusively.

Family names, food and attitudes are other distinguishing characteristics of Metis culture.

Names such as Bercier, Gorneau, Belgarde and Decoteau are obvious signs of French influence.

Davis lists traditional Metis foods such as "boullettes" (meatballs), "bangs" (a type of frybread), blood sausage, head cheese and a mixture of fat and berries that resembles pemmican.

Physically, the Metis vary from blonde and blue-eyed to very dark complected.

In attitude, they differ from traditional Indian culture by being more aggressive and competitive in business, and more at ease with white culture.

Davis isn't sure what the future holds for Metis culture.

"The culture is rich," he says.

"They're going to have the freedom of choice of what they want to be."

Larry Johnson

The last of a past generation

Sitting with Harry and Lillian Swift Horse in front of their log house above the Missouri River bluffs outside Cannon Ball and talking about the old days was like turning back the clock.

Lillian sat with her beadwork loom upon her lap; and now and then, when they came too close, Harry yelled at his cows browsing on the hill behind the house.

The sun was low in the sky and the mosquitoes had begun their nightly forays. Harry, who has a salty sense of humor, said with a mischievous glint in his eye that in the old days Indians went barechested because they believed that if they were bitten by mosquitoes they wouldn't get hypertension.

Harry and Lillian were born on Standing Rock Reservation more than 80 years ago. They have been married for 57 years.

They belong to that rapidly diminishing generation of Indian people whose parents were the last to have known the freedom of the plains and the first to reside on the reservation.

They are among the few left to pass on to younger generations their knowledge of the old Indian culture.

There is dignity and pride in their bearing.

They long ago made an accommodation with life, clinging to much of Indian values and lifestyle and accepting what they felt was worthy from the white world.

Harry doesn't see much that is worthy. A Yanktonnai Sioux who has the deep reverence for nature of the traditional Indian, he has considerable scorn for the white race.

"This is God's country, Yanktonnai country. The white man has ruined the land," he said.

The dead trees standing in the Oahe Dam backup waters, which cover what had been a fertile river valley below his home, are to him a daily reminder of the white man's folly.

Lillian was born at Wakpala, S.D. in 1900. Her mother, Mary One Bull, was a niece of Sitting Bull. She's proud of that lineage. Her father, Herbert Welsh, attended school at Hampton, Va., and became an Episcopal minister.

"She was going to be the first Episcopal woman priest until I got in the way," cracked Harry.

Both Lillian and Harry were educated in Indian boarding schools.

Lillian said she couldn't speak a word of English when she started school at St. Elizabeth's Mission at Wakpala. So learning was slow, she said, especially since the students had classes only half the day and spent the rest of the day on work detail.

The Catholic sisters who ran the school, she said, were strict. The children were punished if they spoke their own language. "We had our mouths washed out with soap if they caught us at it," Lillian recalled.

But she appreciates the education she received. "I liked that learning. It helped me a lot. When I was 18, I could talk to white people."

Harry, who started school at Fort Yates and later attended the Indian school at Bismarck, remembers all too well the hard discipline and the work details.

He said he was so young and small when he helped with the breadbaking that he could scarcely lift the dough in the big tubs.

"We milked cows, hoed and cultivated, shingled the roof, made storm windows, worked in the laundry, shoveled coal."

The worst, he said, was cleaning the water tank. It was dangerous and hard work. It meant climbing the wooden ladder to the top of the tank and balancing oneself precariously while trying to use the broom and shovel to clean it out.

As a young man, he spent a lot of time on the rodeo circuit. At one time, he was part of a Wild West show that performed during the summer at county fairs. In one of the acts, he said, he was one of five cowboys who rode in a pyramid on three horses while galloping around the ring.

"I did everything — bareback and wild horse racing, rope spinning. But one thing I didn't do. I stayed away from women."

That is, until he met Lillian. They were married March 3, 1924.

They settled down to farm and ranch, and in winter, Harry earned a little money hauling coal from the railway station at Cannon Ball to Fort Yates.

He gained a reputation for his skill in breaking horses, and to this day, he says, people bring him horses to gentle. He says he can tell by the shape of the head what kind of disposition a horse has.

Harry and Lillian Swift Horse, above and right, cherish their Indian values and life near Cannon Ball and Missouri rivers.

Harry is a colorful personality with his leathered face and tall, proud carriage; his braided hair and well-worn cowboy hat.

Lillian's mother taught her the Indian homemaking arts. How to dry meat and the wild fruits, how to make "wojapi," a kind of chokecherry pudding still liked by Indian people.

Wild meat was plentiful then. "We had venison, prairie chicken and pheasant. People ate healthier in those days," she said.

It was from her mother, too that she learned how to tan hides and do beadwork, arts she has passed on to younger women.

And she learned how to prepare Indian medicine from roots and herbs.

Of her long years with Harry, she said with a grin, "He was smart to marry me. I have always taken good care of him."

She said she still uses some Indian medicines to treat their illnesses.

But Indian medicine could not make her babies well. Only one of their five children survived infancy.

"In those days, when children got sick there was no car to take them to the doctor and the roads were bad," she recalled.

Sorrow they have known.

And hardship.

But Harry and Lillian Swift Horse have lived their lives of frugal independence close to nature, and with the pride that has been a part of their inheritance.

Lucille Hendrickson

Earthlodges along the Missouri were home of farming Indians, the Mandan, Hidatsa and Arikara. Variation in teepee designs of nomadic plains Indians is seen near Williston at Fort Union, an important fur trading post from 1829 to 1865.

Recalling yesterday's Berthold

Paige Baker Sr. has reached that relaxed stage of his life.

The 68-year-old Indian rancher lives comfortably with his wife Cora on their land near Mandaree on the western part of the Fort Berthold Indian Reservation.

Maybe Paige's life isn't the kind that makes the history books, but he seems at ease with himself and his life.

To understand what has happened to the Fort Berthold Reservation and its Indian people in one short lifetime, it helps to talk to people like Paige.

Another good person is Matilda White, one of the last of the full-blooded Arikaras, who lives in White Shield.

Paige is more than willing to enjoy a conversation about his life and reservation on the back flap of his pickup.

The setting is pleasant, in front of Paige's and Cora's modest home.

The land is hilly. There's a nice breeze blowing through the spruce, cottonwoods, lilac, Chinese elm and caragana, most of which Paige planted himself.

Cora is busy inside when the visitor first arrives, so Paige and the visitor chat outside for awhile.

Paige has been ranching all his life.

"I was born and raised as a ranch kid," Paige says. "That's all I could do — pitch hay. It takes an education to get off the reservation. Ranching is about the only thing I do."

Paige and Cora used to have more than 100 head of cattle, but because Paige is getting older, that's down to 14 head.

Though Paige likes some of the changes that have come to the reservation, he looks back fondly on his childhood in the bottomlands — before the Garrison Dam flooded out Independence, his birthplace, and Elbowwoods, where he and Cora first lived.

"As a kid, I enjoyed my life," says Paige. "We had a lot to do to keep out of mischief," playing and exploring in the bottomlands.

"We didn't have too much trouble with alcohol or drugs."

Like almost anyone on the reservation who is over 30 years old, Paige has a clear vision of the flood and what it meant to people's lives.

"When the Indians moved from the bottomlands to the top, they had no land and just money in their hands, without having any knowledge of any business of any kind.

"Money wasn't the problem for Indians many years ago. They didn't need money. Their wealth was counted in blankets and horses."

Adds Cora, later in the visit, "We were happy down there. People didn't have a town to hang around and get drunk in. We used to have more neighbors and we'd get together."

"You would have seen some happy people," says Paige of the old existence in the bottomlands.

Cora says Indians were at a loss to explain why white people would flood out their reservation.

"When people like George Catlin and the steamboaters came by, we always treated them with open arms," says Cora.

"We never expected they would do this to us."

Matilda, the older woman from White Shield (named after her great-grandfather, White Shield), lives a little differently than the Bakers.

She and her family too used to live in the bottomlands, in an area known as Timber Coulee. Now she lives in an old house in White Shield with her son, daughter-in-law, two grandsons, a cat and a dog.

Matilda remembers the days when she was a young girl and lived in the bottomlands, and how her father, Lee By Waters, had 1,400 head of sheep, as well as cows and chickens.

They lived in log houses, heated by coal. Water was clean and plentiful.

Observing the lives of her grandchildren and other young people in White Shield, she says:

"Children seem to be disturbed; they don't know what to do with themselves. There isn't a thing to do.

"And this housing. It's too close together. They get into trouble with nothing to occupy their time.

Aside from the change in physical surroundings, Paige, Cora and Matilda all have seen cultural changes too.

"We try to respect our old ways," says Matilda. "We try to tell our children who you are, what you are, where you come from."

But things are changing.

"It's going to be hard to keep our culture," says Paige.

"A lot of these college kids are trying to go back (to the old cultural ways), but I don't think they can do it. They just don't get the swing of it. I think we're losing our grip on it."

Greg Turosak

Judge Louis Gipp, son of two cultures

People still call Louis Gipp of Fort Yates "Judge" Gipp.

Well-known on and off Standing Rock Reservation, Gipp served as tribal judge for 15 years.

He was the first mayor of Fort Yates when the village was incorporated as a city. After his years on the bench, he was the first Indian named to the North Dakota Parole Board, serving part of his five-year tenure as chairman.

He also was a member of the tribal delegation involved in Oahe Dam settlement discussions with federal officials in Washington.

Gipp, now 70, is a product of both the Indian and white cultures and views himself as lucky to have lived in both.

His grandmother, Mary Fighting Woman, was a 14-year-old girl in the huge Indian encampment at the Little Bighorn during the battle against Custer. She later married William P. Zahn, a soldier with Reno's forces in that campaign.

His mother, Josephine Zahn, and Frank Zahn, celebrated Indian historian-interpreter-artist-musician, were brother and sister.

His father, Albert Gipp, was the son of a German homesteader near Fort Rice.

From his mother, Gipp gained his knowledge and appreciation of Indian culture. His home is filled with prized Indian artifacts.

He recalled how his mother made a conscious effort to please her husband, fixing white man's meals for him and the ranch hands — roast beef and mashed potatoes.

"But when my grandmother came to visit, she'd take us children and go down to her teepee so she could eat Indian food," he said with a grin.

After his father died, when he was only 15, his mother reverted more to Indian ways.

"I still like Indian food," he said, adding that he especially likes to dry round steak and fix it with wild turnips.

Asked about fry bread, Gipp said it did not become the staple of the Indian diet until after the people were placed on reservations.

"The Sioux were nomadic, depending upon nature for their food. When rations were distributed to the reservation Indians, they didn't know how to use the flour, so the government sent out women to show them how to bake bread.

"When the women got there, they found the Indian woman had no ovens, no bread pans. All they had were kettles over open fires. So the government women melted lard in the kettles and fried the bread. That's how we got fry bread," Gipp said a chuckle.

Gipp got part of his education from the Roman Catholic sisters at boarding school.

"They could be hard disciplinarians," he said, recalling the time one of them ripped his earlobe she tugged on it so hard in punishment.

"But they taught us responsibility, and how to work," he said.

His many associations with non-Indians over the years helped him gain an understanding of the white culture and respect for its work ethic.

"We can blend our way of life if each is willing to sacrifice a little," he said.

He thinks it's fine if Indian people go off for the weekend to powwow, and he's proud that his two sons and their families have taken an interest in their Indian heritage and participate in the dancing contests.

"But you should show up for work on Monday morning," he said.

There is much that is admirable in the Indian tradition of sharing, said Gipp. But he pointed out that the communal way of life can cause problems in this day and age.

"I used to have young wives come to me in tears, telling me that so-and-so (relatives) wouldn't leave, and there wasn't enough food in the house to feed everyone.

"I'd tell them that system worked when the buffalo was here," he said, "but that now it's dollars and cents, and their first obligation is to the family," he said.

He said he thinks the people are gaining on that problem.

Indian people know a lot more about money management these days, too, he said.

In past years, he said, people who suddenly received compensation money from the government for land or water settlements often squandered it.

"They weren't used to having money and didn't know how to handle it," he said. "Many became victims of unscrupulous salesmen who sold them things they couldn't use — like refrigerators to Indians without any electrical hookups, or a car, knowing full well they could later take repossession of it.

"Indian people fell for those things because they represented wealth in the white man's culture."

Gipp thinks it is unfortunate reservation people are so isolated.

"We have not yet mastered living off the reservation," he said, pointing out that when Indian people do that, there are many things they must learn about — paying taxes, for instance.

But with the lack of employment opportunities on the reservations, he thinks young people should learn to live off the reservation.

"But they should live close enough so they can come home periodically to be with their people. We have certain traditions that we can find nowhere else, and if they move too far away, they're apt to get homesick and move back.

"I lived in Chicago for a year and nearly died," he recalled.

Gipp says it is vital that Indian young people get an education.

He quit school to help support the family after his father died. But he got through the eighth grade, and through avid reading, he became a self-educated man.

"An education is something no one can take away from you," he said, "and it is the one thing that can help young people succeed in the white culture."

Lucille Hendrickson

Louis Gipp, retired Sioux tribal judge, at home in Fort Yates.

For the young, a look to the future

At 20, Emerald Spotted Horse has a pretty good idea where she would like to be in a few years.

Except for brief periods living in California, Chicago and Minneapolis, she has spent most of her youth on the Fort Totten Reservation.

And she plans on returning to the reservation after she completes her training for a nursing degree at Haskell Indian Junior College, Lawrence, Kan.

"I'd like to be a nurse ... get married ... have kids ... live a normal life."

She spent this past summer working in the Bureau of Indian Affairs office in Fort Totten. She has worked in the tribe's halfway house for alcoholics and as a nurse's aide at the tribe's nursing home since she was 16.

Emerald recognizes the problems of the reservation — unemployment, boredom, alcoholism, drug abuse — and some of the prejudices Indians encounter outside the reservation.

She said she chose Haskell's program in licensed practical nursing "because it's all Indian."

As an Indian, Emerald said she has encountered prejudice, an instance in a restaurant when a white woman refused to be seated near her table, for example. But, she belives, the prejudice is not among "the young kids. It's the older people. Like if you're sitting in a restaurant, they stare at you."

Emerald likes life on the reservation.

"It's more reassuring. You feel a lot better being around people you know."

However, she would like to spend some time in a city, just for a different experience. Many of her friends have left the reservation "for a while; they always come back."

Her father, Emerald said, has told her life in the cities can be "very hard. He's had it hard all the time." Her parents, "they're always worried about bills," she said.

If she did spend some time working in a city, Emerald predicts she would return to the reservation. "My main concern is the people," she explained. She wants to return to the nursing home and work with the elderly people there since they often seem "lonely."

The reservation has problems, some of which she thinks may stem from the traditional Indian culture.

"I know a lot of Indians who don't like to work. ... don't work ... or work enough to get the first paycheck," Emerald said. "Maybe it's the way the Indians used to live a long time ago ... get enough to live for today."

She also thinks the alcohol and drug problem is increasing, since younger children seem to be getting involved. But, such problems, she pointed out, are hardly confined to Indians. Whites and other nonwhites in similar circumstances experience such problems, too, she said.

Emerald believes she had some advantages that not all the other youths on the reservations have had, such as having two parents who were rather strict. And her parents instilled in her an importance of religion, she said.

Many of the people her age, married and unmarried, are now parents themselves. If parents "talk to their kids a little more ... love or something," maybe the children would not turn to alcohol or drugs, Emerald said.

But, "a lot of these kids try ... and a lot make it too," Emerald said.

Rosemary Lynch

Kindergarten youngsters at United Tribes Educational Technical Center, Bismarck, show delight at the quilt they designed. Each child completed one square; their teacher sewed blocks together and finished the quilt.

Norwegian immigrants wanted their own land

The earliest Norwegian immigrants reached North Dakota and Cass County in 1869. The first areas they settled were along the Red, Goose, Sheyenne and other rivers.

Good farming land with availability of wood and water were primary factors in choosing the site for a new home. Thus, the Norwegian immigrants looked first at areas along rivers and streams, with a secondary influence being the railroads.

About 10 years later the best land in the east was taken, and Norwegians immigrants began to settle farther west. By 1900, they were well-established across the northern tier of the state, including Divide County.

They soon had also become widely dispersed throughout the southwestern area of the state. Large concentrations of Norwegians, beginning in about 1883, settled near Stanton, Taylor, Dunn Center, Bucyrus, Reeder, Almont and Sims.

The Rev. William Sherman, a Grand Forks sociologist, notes that Norwegians also were the first immigrants to join the Anglo-Saxon "rough country" ranching enterprises of the southwest in any great numbers.

The greatest numbers of Norwegians came to North Dakota after 1880 and through the turn of the century. In the period from 1892 to 1905, Scandinavian immigration equaled 47 percent of the total immigration to the state. Norwegians formed 42 percent of that Scandinavian immigration.

Since 1891, Section 15-11-06 of North Dakota law has decreed that: "The state board of higher education shall cause the Scandinavian language to be taught at the university, and for that purpose, a professor learned in that language shall be employed as one of the teachers of the institution."

There is no "Scandinavian" language, and they certainly weren't talking about Danish. What those pioneer lawmakers meant was Norwegian.

University of Minnesota historian Carlton Qualey, in a 1930 piece written for the North Dakota History magazine, estimated that if

Norwegian immigrant family of nine. The girls and their mother wore dress caps with scarf tie at crown.

American-born sons and daughters were counted, 30 percent of North Dakota's population then was of Norwegian stock.

A 1965 survey coordinated by Sherman concluded that 30 percent of North Dakota's rural households were still of Norwegian ancestry.

"The Red River Valley is one of the largest concentrations of rural Norwegians anywhere," says P.V. Thorson, associate professor of history at the University of North Dakota.

And, in pioneer times, the Sheyenne River Valley also was considered solidly Norwegian.

But today Divide County, in the northwestern corner of the state and as far away as one can get from the Red in North Dakota, is the most Norwegian area of the state.

It is a proud heritage. "They (in Divide County) wear it on their sleeves," says Sherman.

Sherman's 1965 survey showed that of 46,486 rural North Dakota households, 13,879 were of Norwegian ancestry.

That study counted more than 72 percent of the 619 rural households in Divide County as being Norwegian.

For Norwegian immigrants, North Dakota was a place to farm. So, like other settlers, they were attracted by the availability of free or cheap land.

"One thing that was uppermost in the minds of all Norwegian immigrants that came to the farming country in America was to go out west and get a homestead, to get his own farm," wrote Edward Lian, in an unpublished autobiography of his life at Fairdale.

Oman B. Herigstad, who wrote a history of the first Noregian settlement in Griggs County, said it wasn't political or religious conditions that prompted Norwegians to emigrate, but rather what they saw as more promise in America.

Norway was crowded, there were requirements for military service and, in general, it was difficult to make a living there, he said.

During the period 1869 to 1883, when large numbers of Norwegians began coming to America, Norway was experiencing a period of depression. Forests had previously been seen as an important source of national wealth, railroads were built and people speculated wildly in land, borrowing money to meet expenses.

But, said Herigstad, the forests soon were exhausted and the average farmer had overestimated his resources and was unable to pay off his loans.

Few of those first immigrants came directly to North Dakota from Norway. They first lived for a time in states like Minnesota, Iowa or Wisconsin. To their advantage, many of them thus knew a little more about America than did members of some other ethnic groups.

Qualey suggests that before 1869, Norwegian immigrants preferred more wooded areas of America and many considered North Dakota a vast prairie roamed by Indians and unfit for cultivation. The move to North Dakota, he says, was actually the third and fourth stages of immigration by Norwegians westward across America.

Norwegian journalist Paul Hjelm-Hansen visited the Red River Valley in 1869 and his writings thereafter attracted many of his countrymen to the region.

He noted in Norwegian-language newspapers that "The whole prairie, which does not have the slightest bulge or rise, is the most fertile land one could wish. ... The soil is fertile to the highest degree and is exceptionally easy to cultivate, for there is not as much as a stone or stump in the way of the plow."

He also advised his countrymen that "A man can take 160 acres of homestead land and, if he has the opportunity to do so, he can in addition buy 160 acres for $200. With an area of 320 acres of this land, every family that does not care to live too pretentiously can make a confortable livelihood."

Letters and articles written by Hansen were read by thousands of Norwegians in both America and Norway.

At the same time, other Norwegians were learning of the opportunities in America through letters from relatives and friends and information disseminated by railroad companies and immigration bureaus.

The Northern Pacific, according to Qualey, maintained agents in several European countries and in 1884 was advertising in 32 Scandinavian-American newspapers.

Newspapers themselves — both those in English and those in the Norwegian language — were active propagandists for the region.

Norwegian-language newspapers continued to flourish during the pioneer years and Thorson estimates there at one time may have been as many as 55 in the state. One of the largest and most popular was the Normanden, published at Grand Forks.

Norwegian immigrants had come from a rural and crowded country that was slow to industrialize. Even though only about 3 percent of Norway is arable, most of its sons who came to North Dakota had a farm backround, perhaps as laborers or renters of land.

Historians have concluded that 78 percent of the Norwegian immigrants in America were from rural areas of Norway. It is likely that the percentage was even higher among those who came to North Dakota, because rural land was what the state had to offer.

Norway lost more than 900,000 people in the 19th century through emigration, more than any other country except Ireland.

For the immigrants, owning land in America was "instant status, besides being able to feed your family," says Thorson.

Despite the immigrants' depressed economic stature, illiteracy was virtually unknown among these Nordic settlers. Norway had in 1836 enacted a law requiring all people to be confirmed in the state Lutheran church and had established public schools three years later. The church, in turn, required confirmants to be familiar with the teachings of Luther, the hymnbook and Bible.

The North Dakota Norwegians were instrumental in organizing local schools and stressed education for their children at the high school and college levels. Thorson says the Norwegian-Americans didn't really feel at home in North Dakota because they couldn't speak the language, and thus they "wanted their children to be accepted."

Ole Lima, who came from Norway to the Cooperstown area in 1886, wrote in a letter to his Norwegian father that education was perhaps more important in America than in the old country. "Many a penniless young boy here in America has by working in summer and going to school in winter for several years, procured for himself education and training sufficient to hold high and remunerative positions in society."

Despite striving for an education in English, the Norwegian immigrants at the same time held on to their native language. It was preserved in part because the Norwegian settlers tended to live in rural areas, near other immigrants from Norway.

Many also recorded their experiences and impressions of pioneer life. Thorson notes that "50 to 75 years ago people were writing novels and poetry here, in Norwegian, and getting them published."

Sherman's studies have concluded that most of the land settled by Norwegian immigrants is still owned by people of Norwegian ancestry. Norwegian-Americans tended to stay on their farms, while greater percentages of their kinfolk from countries like Denmark or Sweden moved into more urban areas, where their ethnic identify was more easily lost.

Illiteracy was virtually unknown among Nordic settlers.

In those early farm communities, summer parochial schools were taught in Norwegian and Lutheran church services were in Norwegian. In some areas, libraries carried large numbers of volumes written in Norwegian, and later-arriving immigrants from Norway also helped perpetuate the language.

Joanna Johnsrud, Grand Forks, who grew up in Fairdale, says her parents spoke and read Norwegian at home. "My dad read a lot and we kept an old Norwegian newspaper, the Decorah (Iowa) Posten — that was a paper that was common all over the Midwest among Norwegians," she recalls. "In those days there was a little novel in each edition and some of the stories were interesting to me so Dad and I read them together, and that's one way I learned the language so well."

"Norwegians saw to it that the state was dry. They were the backbone of the temperance movement."

Despite their farm backrounds, for immigrants from a country of high mountains and deep fjords the flat and treeless prairies of North Dakota were something new.

Lian said he never had seen wheat before coming from Norway to the Fairdale area in 1906. Where he grew up, barley, oats and rye were raised.

He and a brother walked 18 miles to Fairdale after getting off a train at Edmore. Along the way, Ed Lian observed "a lot of little animals about the size of a rat were running all over the prairie and sometimes they would look at us, curious and pretty."

Historians say Norwegian immigrants were more nationalistic in the last half of the 19th century than were the Swedes or Danes.

Norway was a part of Denmark for 400 years until 1814 and then, despite having a constitution, remained under the rule of a Swedish king until 1905.

The later-arriving Norwegians had a greater desire to preserve that spirit of independence achieved in the 1905 emancipation of their homeland.

They had "an aggressive national spirit — part and parcel of that was to get an education," says Thorson. It also inspired them toward political and moral activism.

"Scandinavians in general, and Norwegians in particular, saw to it that the state was 'dry' until the 1930s. They were the backbone of the temperance movement," Thorson says.

The women and their pastors had prohibition societies in Norway, it was "something they brought with them and carried on," Thorson says.

Norwegians rapidly became interested in politics and social reform.

A predominant characteristic of the Norwegian immigrant was his deep religious conviction.

Some Norwegians felt that during the last century of union with Denmark, the state Norwegian Lutheran church had lost its spiritual appeal and was concerned mainly with everyday matters and material problems.

Hans Nielsen Hauge, a farm boy, traveled all over Norway preaching the gospel and exhorting Norwegians to cease their sinful drinking, fighting and immorality.

Clergy and Danish bureaucrats feared this would jeopardize their influence and had Hauge imprisoned.

Norwegian immigrants of the Haugian, or "low church," persuasion thought activities like drinking and dancing were sinful.

Followers of the Norwegian state church enjoyed playing their fiddles or other instruments and attending a Saturday night dance that might last until sunrise.

Bertha Ravnaas of Turtle Lake wears embroidered wool dress from her native Norway with delicate silver bangle jewelry for special occasions.

They feared losing their Norwegian culture and were instrumental in organizing and patronizing private colleges like Luther College, in Iowa.

Despite being broken into a number of differing synods, the Lutheran church is credited with being the foremost ethnic organization for Norwegians and it played a large role in preserving their heritage.

Bob Jansen

Wide open spaces amazed immigrants from mountain lands

Sig Peterson, a second-generation Norwegian-American, says than his generation may be "better Norwegians now" than the original immigrants, who were striving to be "100 percent American."

But Sig is first of all a North Dakota rancher-farmer, semiretired, and is not given to pretentiousness.

He knows that changing times and good fortune have given him opportunities not available to either his parents or his Norwegian kinsmen.

Indeed, the attention that Sig and Marge have devoted to their heritage is a luxury made possible not just by their own years of hard work, but by the efforts of their parents and other immigrants, Norwegian and otherwise.

Sig was born at Sims, though he moved at an early age to a farm near Almont, where Marge was born and raised. Both of those Morton County towns had predominantly Norwegian-American populations.

Sig's grandfather, a sailor, first came to America in 1882. He temporarily left his wife and family in Norway, although as an ex-sailor he had free passage on trans-Atlantic crossings and shipped back to Norway several times.

Then, in 1888, finally ready to settle down, the sailor sent for the family to join him in North Dakota.

"It must have been a shock to see these wide open spaces," Sig says of the immigrants, who had come to the Great Plains from a land of rugged hills and ragged coastlines.

To illustrate the point, he tells of a Norwegian woman coming west by rail. Apparently, the train reached the end of its line in North Dakota at about the time that the woman was arriving at her wits' end. She reportedly stepped off the train exclaiming, "Oh, not a tree to be seen, I want to go home."

Sig's family did not go home, but neither did members break their ties with Norway.

His father, who was 16 years old

Arland Paulson, Maddock, sports a Viking costume and thick red beard for local celebration and parade.

when the family emigrated, had an especially good reason for maintaining ties with the homeland.

According to family legend, he had left behind the Norwegian girl that he had chosen for his bride.

She must have been a lovely and faithful lass too, because when Sig's father finally was able to return to Norway 10 years later, he married that girl.

At least, so says the legend.

He definitely married someone, but Sig and Marge disagree on whether it was the same girl. Sig favors the legend; Marge just asks, "Well, who knows?"

She laments that so much family history is lost with the passing years, sometimes never to be regained.

Marge's family also was immigrating to America near the end of the last century, and her ethnic heritage is somewhat more varied than Sig's.

Her maternal grandmother was a Swede "who thought of herself as a Norwegian," Marge says.

This cultural crossover came about because after the woman's Swedish father died, she was brought up by an uncle in Oslo. "She herself said she was Norwegian," Marge explains.

The grandmother immigrated to St. Paul, Minn., in the 1880s and married a Norwegian seaman she met in St. Paul.

But Minnesota did not prepare Marge's grandmother for North Dakota, the family's next stop.

"My grandmother was an art teacher in Oslo, moved to St. Paul, a city, and then came to these plains, where she just about went crazy," says Marge.

Sig suggests that very few Norwegians may have owned a farm before arriving in the United States because "only 3 percent of Norway is tillable land." In any case, he says, the steep hillsides make farming in Norway very different from farming on the prairie.

In the United States, there was not only the promise of a good wage but of 160 acres of free land to those who would work for it. Congress had passed the Homestead Act in 1862 and this legislation more than anything had spurred the first wave of Norwegian immigration.

"Back in Norway, a five-acre farm was pretty big," says Sig.

The enthusiasm with which Norwegians entered into farming in North Dakota is symptomatic of the strength and determination of the people.

Sig's and Marge's families came to farming relatively late.

His father worked for the railroad for many years and also owned a small coal mine. It was not until becoming ill around 1916 that Sig's father turned to farming.

Marge's Swedish grandmother and Norwegian grandfather moved from St. Paul to Sims in 1905.

The next year, her Danish grandfather and grandmother, who had already lived in Chicago and Iowa, also decided to settle in the new town of Almont, starting a hardware and farm-implement business there.

Marge's mother was one of the last area recipients of land via the Homestead Act, having filed for the tract in 1912.

Marge's father served in the Navy for four years during World War I, then coming back in 1918, he went into business with his father and did some farming on the side. He turned to full-time farming when the family got its homestead.

In 1968, the original 12-foot-square shack that stood on Marge's mother's homestead came back into the family, and later it was moved to the Peterson ranch.

Sig and Marge have restored it, rebuilding the chimney, replacing the floor, papering the walls, and furnishing it with precious antiques and a wood-burning stove. On one wall hangs the land grant signed by President Woodrow Wilson.

Surrounded by manifestations of the Norwegian culture, as he was in Sims and then in Almont, Sig long took that culture for granted.

Marge says, for instance, that one well-known characteristic of Norwegian-Americans is hospitality.

Another trait that Marge notices in Norwegians is that they are "always busy with their hands, doing things, beautiful things — knitting, crocheting."

Sig agrees. "My mother's mother had nine girls and she told them 'Your hands must never be idle,'" he says.

Nor do the men seem to be exempted from this business of busy hands: Sig like so many other Norwegian men has taken up woodcarving and has fashioned a number of troll figurines out of basswood as well as a startlingly realistic pair of cowboy boots from cottonwood.

The Petersons note that another perceived trait of the Norwegian people is common to all Scandinavians — a love of music.

He and Marge are the living proof. Together, they perform an act composed of Norwegian songs, yodeling and humor. Sig plays a rare Hardanger fiddle, inlaid with mother of pearl, that was bought in Norway. The act gives them an opportunity to share their love of Norway with others, in addition to being fun.

Their fame as entertainers has spread. Gov. Allen I. Olson invited them to perform at an April 1981 reception honoring Rolv E. Ryssdal, chief justice of the Supreme Court of Norway.

Sig and Marge both came from musical families; Sig says he could read music before he learned to read English.

Sig was taught English in school but he also spoke some Norwegian — at least, the dialect of Norwegian that his family had carried with them from Southern Norway. The dialect shows a Danish influence, and Sig says it differs from standard Norwegian so much that he would go to church at Sims, "not understanding nearly a word" because the Lutheran sermons were delivered in the formal Norse tongue.

However, speaking Norwegian had not meant much to him as a young man.

He remembers an incident that occurred some years ago in the eastern part of the state, where Norwegians settled in greater density that did in the Almont area.

"We wintered cattle in 1937 south of Devils Lake and the young men were all talking Norwegian, and we thought 'this is strange!'"

The Petersons also were among many in Almont last November to help put on the lefse and lutefisk supper, an annual tradition of more than 20 years' standing.

If the coming generation shares the community spirit and vitality of Marge and Sig Peterson, then that tradition can be expected to continue for years to come.

Frank Miele

Life in North Dakota Norwegian community gives sense of belonging

Norwegian community life centers easily around the church. Typical of many rural Norwegian communities across the state is Viking, a prosperous and close-knit farming community south of Maddock. It focuses on the Viking Lutheran Church, to which literally everyone in South Viking township and the surrounding area belongs.

Norwegian phrases are commonly heard in the homes. Children understand these as well as jokes told in Norwegian. Almost every home has Norwegian articles in daily use or display: inscribed silver serving spoons, bread trays with Norwegian phrases, cheese cutters, heavy hand-knit sweaters, home-loomed wool blankets shrunken through the years and used as padding in cushions or quilts, hand carved nutcrackers and trolls, photos of the old home in Norway on the wall.

Friends still greet each other with "Tak for sidst," meaning "Thanks for the last time I saw you." As in the past, the coffee pot is always on.

Viking settlement began in 1886 when six Norwegian men came west after a stop over in the Norwegian community of Spring Grove, Minnesota. They drove covered wagons and claimed homesteads according to a criteria explained in the 1936 book "Viking: Early Settlement Days":

"All six men were practical farmers wanting good farm land without too many rocks to dig out, some meadow or land bordering a big slough and assuring them a supply of hay for their stock. They also wanted to settle close together so as to be near neighbors."

They built six sod houses, averaging one each day. For these they plowed strips 16 inches apart, cutting blocks two to three feet long. According to the record they paid $6.25 per shack for the lumber used for doors, windows, rafters and roof. Then they returned to Spring Grove for the winter and came back in spring with families and household goods.

Relatives and friends from Spring Grove soon followed; many were newly arrived from Norway and eager for land. In many cases these people knew each other in Norway so they brought not only a single culture but, in a sense, a settled community. Social patterns changed little except that these young families started new life on equal footing.

Sunday evenings and long winter days were often spent visiting and planning for community needs. One pioneer, Timan Quarve, wrote in the Viking book, "Many a winter evening saw a large group of man gathered at our homes, holding debates. The subjects were usually of a political nature, such as dividing the territory into states, or later, the question of writing prohibition into the state constitution."

Early community projects included plowing and leveling a road to make the trip to Maddock with oxen easier, plowing a fire break around the entire community, establishing school and church services. A post office, general store, meat market and blacksmith shop were soon in operation.

Land for a school was donated by one of the original six settlers. Children studied by day and at night adults came to learn English, American History and government; church services were held in the school on Sundays.

The Viking church was built in 1903. In 1909 it was the site for the first meeting of the Norwegian Evangelical Lutheran Church in America for all the states west of Wisconsin and including western Canadian provinces. The building is now listed in the National Registry of Historical sites. In church men sat on the right, with women and children on the left. Until 1962 only men were allowed to vote in church affairs.

Land stays in the family and is rarely sold, even to neighbors.

In Viking, as in other Norwegian communities across the state, young people grow up with a strong feeling of belonging. Relatives and extended family ties are close, but it is the community and church, not family, which mark the milestones in each person's life with appropriate ritual.

News of a birth sweeps quickly, bringing expressions of pleasure and a host of gifts as neighbors stop to greet the new arrival. Baptism makes everyone feel more comfortable and brings the baby into full membership.

Baptism day can be strenuous for the new mother as she tries to keep the baby sleepy, full and clean (in the heirloom baptism gown) while preparing dinner for the dozen or more guests who will accompany the family home from church. Baptism itself is short and formal. In recent past the baby was not taken by parents to the baptismal font, but rather by one of numerous godparents. Sometimes parents did not go forward at all.

The baby is the center of attention, after services, as the congregation clusters around for a closer look amid speculation on which Viking relative it most closely resembles. If the baby cried, someone always remembers the father cried in just the same way at his baptism.

Confirmation is the next milestone in a young person's life. Traditionally the two-year preparation was called "reading for the minister," and the final ceremony at about age 15 marked a kind of growing up or graduation. Again relatives, close friends, godparents and pastor gather at the home for dinner and an afternoon of socializing and gift giving. Other neighbors come during the afternoon, staying for a meal of meats, salads, open faced sandwiches, cake and an assortment of Norwegian delicacies.

Marriage marks the third milestone which the entire community celebrates. The pastor issues a general invitation to the wedding from the pulpit and everyone expects — and is expected — to attend.

"Having a shower on" the couple is a vital feature of each wedding, whether it is a son or a daughter of the community who marries. In Viking these are no small intimate groups of female friends of the bride, but rather are big affairs in the church basement honoring the entire family. Showers begin with a program of entertainment to include musical selections and usually a skit depicting significant or embarrassing experiences from the young couple's past, portrayed in a familiar and affectionate spirit.

To open gifts, both bride and groom sit with their mothers at a table. Small nieces or nephews scurry back and forth bearing gifts and passing them up and down the audience rows. This may take a very

Viking Lutheran Church in 1962 celebrating its 75th anniversary. Three-day program included tours of newly built sod house and museum, a parade, stagecoach rides, musical entertainment, religious services and picnics. Church was newly remodeled and painted and a local family with two small children spent seven days retracing, via the covered wagon seen at far right in this picture, a pioneer grandfather's 200-mile trek from Hickson.

In Norwegian communities every home has items like these in use or on display. From left, 1873 round wooden box, handcarved nutcracker from Norway, covered wood cake box with rosemaling decor.

long time, as there are many. Though a groom might be uncomfortable, spotlighted in this somewhat unmanly role of fussing over presents, sons of Viking obviously enjoy the event. Again comes the inevitable food line, with a generous array of foods including the Norwegian fattigmand, sand bakkelse and rosettes.

Most couples are also honored with a surprise chivaree, although this is being replaced by the wedding dance. The chivaree begins with noise-making and pan-banging and includes good natured harassing of the young couple, such as a ride in the manure spreader or a farmhand lift onto an outbuilding, a session of beer for the men outside, socializing inside for women, and finally food and coffee for everyone.

Silver and golden wedding anniversaries are duly celebrated for all couples. These are similar to showers with an affectionate program. Many couples thus feted were married in the Viking church.

When a person dies in Viking, the funeral marks his or her last rite of passage. In the days of party lines, an impending death meant neighbors left phones off the hook to monitor emergency calls and inform the community, which then converged on the bereaved family offering sympathy, help and food.

For close neighbors a funeral responsibility is gathering at the church for grave digging. The gravesite is likely an old family plot or another nearby selected by the one who is to occupy it. The grave diggers must cope with familiar problems such as hard frozen earth in winter, solid rock, or cornering on another coffin inexplicably in the way.

The funeral is attended by the entire Viking community as well as others from afar. Afterward the ladies' aid serves a big meal of hot dishes, salads, sandwiches (open faced) and desserts. The expressed purpose is to feed those who have long distances to travel, but it also serves to lighten the somber mood and ease the family back to normal living. Left-over foods are taken to the family home where large numbers of relatives and neighbors gather in the evening.

In this way a life passes in Viking. A man or woman is born, confirmed and, usually, married. From the first this person belongs to the community in the fullest sense of the word, and the ties are repeatedly reinforced in both formal and informal ways. At last comes death and a final resting in the graveyard at the community's pulse center — the Viking Luthern Church. *F.B.*

All-girl group performs Swedish folk dance in native dress.

Swedes brought smorgasbord of aspirations

Swedish newspapers in about 1840 began carrying accounts of America's resources and opportunity. The first permanent Swedish immigrants came in about 1851 to Illinois, and soon the newspaper stories were supplemented by letters from friends and relatives who had emigrated.

More than 1 million Swedes came to America between the Civil War and World War I. The peak year was 1882, when 64,607 people left for the United States.

Swedes were drawn to the Midwest because of a climate comparable to their homeland and, more importantly, cheap and fertile land.

Chicago was an early center for Swedish immigrants. Later, St. Paul, Minn., became a focal point.

When the railroad began operations in the Red River Valley, it actively recruited settlers. The Northern Pacific's agent for Swedes in St. Paul was a Mr. Blomquist, who told the immigrants that there was land available in North Dakota and that others from Sweden were there already.

The earliest Swedish settlers in North Dakota were the sons of Hakon Hicks, who, with Bernt Bernhardson, left Goodhue County, Minn., in 1869 and claimed land on the Minnesota side of the Red River. Land was taken by sons of Hicks on the Dakota side of the river and later a Cass County community was named Hickson.

At about that same time, August P. Laudblom and Hans Hoglund left Iowa and filed claims in the Harwood area, which, like Hickson, is near Fargo.

The early communities settled by Swedes were along the tracks of the Northern Pacific, primarily in Cass County. After 1900, Swedish immigrants moved beyond the Red River Valley, into western and southwestern areas of the state, Bemis noted.

Blomquist advised some Swedes to take land near Bismarck. In the 1965 survey, Burleigh topped all counties with 102 rural Swedish households. The bulk of them, according to an ethnic distribution map drawn by Sherman, were in the northwestern area of the county.

Sherman notes that in 1882 a group of Swedish settlers, eventually perhaps as many as 40 families, began moving into the Fort Clark area west of Washburn. A handful still live on land along the Missouri River northwest of Fort Clark.

The settlement, Sherman suggests, probably had close ties with a much larger group of Swedes that lived across the river between Wilton and Coleharbor.

John and Peter Ostlund, railroad

construction workers, were the earliest Swedish settlers in Bismarck. Ostlund became one of the city's first draymen.

Bemis recounts the story of A.F. Djuberg, a cabinetmaker and businessman in Gothenborg, Sweden. In 1881, he decided to emigrate and upon his arrival in St. Paul was persuaded by Blomquist that there was land and other Swedes in the North Dakota community of Sanborn.

Upon arriving in that small Barnes County village he learned that claims already had been filed there and the nearest suitable land was 10 miles away. Constituting that "large Swedish community" promised by Blomquist were but two bachelors, Gust Anderson and Peter Shoberg.

Djuberg did stake his claim, but grasshoppers that first summer nearly devastated his 15 acres of oats. However, he was able to sell $60 worth of potatoes and other vegetables in Sanborn.

Swedish immigrants to North Dakota tended to get lost in a "sea of Norwegians."

So observes P.V. Thorson, who teaches Scandinavian history at the University of North Dakota.

Thorson suggests that in addition to being much fewer in number than their Norse neighbors, Swedes were quick to integrate with other groups and did not preserve their ethnic identity.

Norwegians, coming from a very rural country, tended to settle on farms. Although also heavily agricultural, Sweden was more urbanized than Norway, so it wasn't unusual for more Swedes to become city dwellers and businessmen, says Thorson.

Other historians point to the large number of active Norwegian heritage groups, compared with fewer for the Swedes. That, they say, is in part because more of the Swedish immigrants ended up in cities, where they integrated and lost their ethnic identity.

A 1965 survey by the Rev. William Sherman, a North Dakota State University sociologist, counted 1,598 "rural" North Dakota households of primarily Swedish descent. That amounted to 3.4 percent of all rural households.

In contrast, there were 13,879 rural Norwegian households, or almost 30 percent of the total. In proportion to its total population, North Dakota is the most Norwegian state in the nation.

Myrtle Bemis in 1910 wrote for the North Dakota State Historical Society a comprehensive history of Swedish settlement in North Dakota.

She attributed emigration of the Swedish people to limited opportunities at home, an inability or unwillingness by those in power at the time to give the poor man a chance to get a home and the inherent characteristics of the Scandinavians to "roam about on this earth."

Contributing heavily to those Swedish economic woes was a shortage of arable land. Other factors inspiring emigration were religous unrest, temperance agitation and low wages.

A further cause of discontent in Sweden was compulsory military service, which did not exist in America. Adolph Benson and Naboth Hedin, in the book "Americans from Sweden," note that it was not so much the military duty that drove young men from the country, but rather the excessively harsh discipline imposed by the upper-class officers.

The Rev. Alf Bergin, who served various eastern North Dakota parishes between 1893 and 1896, recalled that Swedish settlements then were very small. "Only a few families lived at each place and nobody could be induced to come out and increase the settlement. Land agents and money lenders had been unreasonably severe to the poor pioneers and interest was exorbitant and sheriff sales plentiful," he said.

An extreme example was a settlement named Sweden, just west of Grafton. John Almen, who established a post office there in 1879, named it for his native land.

Shortly there were — in addition to the post office — two stores, a blacksmith shop and a couple of saloons. But the post office was moved to Grafton when the railroad came through in 1882, and North Dakota's Sweden soon disappeared.

One year after statehood, the 1890 census counted 8,419 foreign-born Swedes in North Dakota, equaling 2.6 percent of the state's population. Cass County had the most Swedes, but Burleigh County recorded a greater proportion of Swedish, 25.5 percent, among its foreign-born population.

That same census listed 44,698 Norwegians in the state.

In his "History of North Dakota," Elwin B. Robinson lumps immigrants and their American-born children together, thus computing that in 1910, the ethnic groups together constituted 71 percent of North Dakota's population.

Using that measurement, the 29,000 Swedes here in 1910 were 5 percent of all North Dakotans. The 125,000 Norwegians constituted 21 percent.

Benson and Hedin suggest that Swedes, like most immigrants, came from the so-called lower classes and initially appeared to others to be naive or simple-minded, but they also were shrewd.

Records of children with Swedish ancestry in schools, colleges and universities show their grades usually among the highest, Benson and Hedin say.

They suggest that Swedes, like Germans and Scandinavians in general, were usually free from illiteracy and practically all could read the Bible and other religious works.

The physical sturdiness of the Swedes, like other Scandinavians, is almost proverbial.

Although they see him as having an innate shyness, Benson and Hedin conclude that it goes against a Swede's instincts to welcome a visitor to his home without offering something to smoke, eat or drink. The "smorgasbord," they suggest, "is an expression of this desire for display."

There have been Swedish pioneers in all of the state's counties. That 1965 survey showed concentrations of North Dakotans with Swedish ancestry still exist in northwestern Burleigh County, the Kintyre area of Emmons County, Kulm area of LaMoure County, near Oakes, several areas of Cass County and various scattered pockets throughout the northern portion of the state.

Bob Jansen

Midsummer Dagen Fest colorful with maypole

Midsummer Dagen Fest was a favorite Swedish holiday, held June 24 to celebrate the longest day of the year — a time of almost no darkness toward the northern part of the Scandinavian countries. It was celebrated in Swedish communities throughout North Dakota with all night dancing beneath a maypole decorated with green leafy garlands and wild flowers. People dressed in their holiday attire played games, picnicked and sang Swedish folk songs. The Vasa Swedish Lutheran church near Esmond kept this midsummer festival as an annual celebration, holding it in a shady grove nearby and featuring every year a "fancy work" auction. *F.B.*

This Danish mill, once used for grinding flour, stands in center of town square at Kenmare.

Easy-going Danes shed identity

Heard any good Danish jokes lately?

Probably not.

North Dakota pioneers from Denmark were much fewer in number than those from, say, Norway.

In addition, Danes tended to quickly become "Americans" and shed their ethnic identity. So, humorists aren't likely to single out this nearly invisible nationality.

"The Danes have assimilated better than almost any (other) ethnic group in the country bar none," says P.V. Thorson, an associate professor of history at the University of North Dakota.

Danes, like Swedes, came from a more urbanized and industrially developed country than did Norwegians, who tended to settle on North Dakota farms.

Thus, in proportion to their numbers, more Danes became businessmen and city dwellers than did the Norwegians.

Thorson says that of the five Scandinavian countries, immigrants from Denmark were the most "easy-going."

Among immigrant groups, Danes generally were quick to learn English and drop old-country customs.

That conclusion is supported in comments from Christus Jacobson, who was interviewed by a field worker with the Works Progress Administration program that operated from 1935 into the 1940s.

Jacobson came to North America with his family as a young boy in 1889. After living for a time in Iowa, they moved to a farm in the Bluegrass area north of New Salem.

"So far as I know, there are no Danish customs practiced by former Danish residents in this region," he told the government writer. "After we got settled, my father decided that all his ideas of government and former methods of life were to be changed and the old life forgotten as far as possible."

Nels P. Jensen, then of Hazen, told the WPA interviewer of coming in 1901 to Albert Lea, Minn., where a brother and several other Danes lived. Jensen, who homesteaded in Oliver County, said he left Denmark because he didn't want to spend three years in the Danish military.

For him, too, the transition was easier than that experienced by some immigrants of other nationalities. "American customs are rather free and easy and not too hard to take up," he said.

"And the language never seemed to be so hard to learn, at least I never had a great deal of trouble."

Denmark was the oldest kingdom in Europe, unlike Norway, which had been under the rule of Danish and later Swedish monarchs. Thus, said Thorson, the Danes who emigrated didn't consider themselves oppressed and didn't bring with them a strong spirit of nationalism.

Jacobson noted that in Denmark it was a custom to keep photos of Danish monarchs. "But after we came to America, the pictures of the royal family were given to the children to play with ... and it was not long before they were destroyed by the children."

Waldemar C. Westergaard, writing in the North Dakota Historical Quarterly about Danish settlers in Cass County, suggests that most people in the old country were either artisans, petty tradesmen or householders with a few acres of land.

The earliest Danish immigrants, who came to North Dakota in the late 1870s, left their homeland for two reasons, Westergaard says.

Those from Schleswig, a Danish province that had been acquired by Germany, came primarily to avoid German military service.

The other reason was that in both Schleswig and Jutland (Denmark), wages for common laborers were very poor.

The census of 1890 counted 3,915 foreign-born Danes in North Dakota, out of a total white population of 182,719. But many of the immigrants called Danish actually were Icelanders living in Pembina and Cavalier counties. They were listed as Danes by the census because Iceland was under the control of Denmark.

One of Cass County's earliest Danish settlers, Chester Westergaard, is said to have lived first in Chicago, where he became acquainted with Marcus Thrane, a Norwegian revolutionist who began publishing a radical newspaper in 1869.

Westergaard in 1873 began working as a typesetter and printer and eventually became editor. He moved in late 1876 to Sherbourne County, Minn., where he continued the paper.

A subscriber in the Red River Valley offered Westergaard financial assistance to settle in the Valley after he had discontinued the paper in February 1878. He homesteaded along the Maple River in Cass County and later was joined by relatives from Minnesota.

Danes from Schleswig began arriving in the county in 1879.

Waldemar Westergaard notes that "people of the settlement took up the English language easily."

Although Danish and Norwegian newspapers were kept in nearly every home, "children rarely spoke to each other other than in English."

There were more English than Danish books read by the early settlers. Westergaard says the library in the local school district had only three or four Scandinavian books out of more than 400 volumes.

A few years later, Danes came to the Kenmare area and nearby Bowbells. According to Ward County's 75th anniversary book, a committee of three elders from the Danish Lutheran Church visited the vicinity in 1896 looking for a place to establish a colony.

Robert Cory, who compiled the book, said the churchmen surveyed Oklahoma, Michigan and other states before deciding to locate immigrants at Kenmare.

In the spring of 1897, a large group of Danes arrived and settled in what is now Denmark Township, Ward County.

In 1910, Danish immigrants constituted 19.8 percent of the foreign-born population in Ward County. A census 10 years earlier counted just six Danes in all of Ward.

A survey completed in 1965 by the Rev. William Sherman, a North Dakota State University sociologist, counted 588 North Dakota "rural" households of primarily Danish descent. That was equal to 1.3 percent of all rural households.

Largest numbers of rural Danes were north and northwest of Minot, in Ward, Burke and Renville counties, and in Cass County.

Sherman's 1965 survey showed that only one of the state's 588 rural Danish households was in Pembina County, where the 1890 census had identified greater numbers of Danish immigrants, many of whom really were Icelanders.

A Danish mill has been restored and is maintained in Kenmare as a tourist attraction and monument.

Bob Jansen

DANISH MILL

Finns steamed up on saunas, politics

Wouldn't a nice hot steam bath feel good on a subzero winter night in North Dakota or after a sweaty summer's day behind the plow?

North Dakota's immigrants from Finland thought so.

The sauna, it seems, is the most remembered aspect of Finnish culture.

To a lesser extent, some of the North Dakota Finns also were known for getting steamed up in another way. During the early years of this century, a few of them had a reputation for radicalism and heated political activism.

In 1903, members of the William Harju family were among the first Finnish immigrants to homestead in northeast Burleigh County. Otto Harju was born two years later in the family's sod house in Trygg Township, about midway between McKenzie and Wing.

"When they landed up there, they also built the sauna ... my folks always had a sauna," Otto Harju says.

However, it was not a family to get involved in politics, he recalls. Apparently, it was some Finnish immigrants and other farmers from the Belden area of Mountrail County who, in an effort at bring about social reform, delved into socialism and even communism during the years of the Depression and Dust Bowl. Economic conditions during those years produced particularly severe hardship for that northwestern sector of the state.

Harju thinks most Finns were, like his parents, not particularly interested in politics.

The earliest significant Finnish settlement in the state was in Dickey County. It was an extension of an immigrant community across the border in South Dakota.

The cooperative movement flourished there, but apparently stopped short of embracing communism.

In 1902 the area also saw the establishment of a Savo Finnish Creamery Co. Finnish cooperative telephone companies on both sides of the border, a cooperative elevator, mercantile company, oil company and livestock association followed.

Likewise, in Mountrail County the Belden Shipping Association was organized in 1921. Members bought cream and poultry from farmers and purchased binder twine and other materials by the carload.

Oscar Niemi, who homesteaded at Belden in 1905, was making weekly use of his sauna in 1968 when this picture was taken.

A similar organization near Belden was the Fairview Farmers Club, a social organization for making cooperative purchases through carlot buying.

But, back to the steam bath.

For the Harjus, that first sauna — like their first home on the prairie — was made of sod. It was later replaced by a wood-frame structure that, although no longer used, still stands.

The primary fuel for the firebox to heat the sauna's rocks was "prairie coal," also known as cow chips.

Harju recalls the Saturday night visits of neighbors who came "to sauna." It was a ritual, usually by lantern light, after the day's chores were done.

Afterward, there would be coffee and a snack.

Harju left the homestead at 17 and has lived in Bismarck since then. "The wife and I frequently went to the farm on Saturday nights for a sauna," he says.

The former Minnie Wick, now deceased, grew up in the Scandinavian-American community of Adams and met Otto, who became her husband, in the Capital City where she was a nurse. "When we were going together, I took her to the farm and she got introduced to the sauna," Harju recalls.

Steam baths also were popular with Finns elsewhere.

Oscar Niemi, who homesteaded at Belden in 1905, was making weekly use of his sauna in 1968 and shared it with other Finnish-Americans, according to an interview then with the Minot Daily News.

Niemi, who immigrated to America in 1899, lived for a time in Minnesota and South Dakota before settling at Belden.

A few Finnish immigrants also settled in the New Leipzig area of Grant County, but most had left by the end of the 1930s.

According to the Rev. William Sherman, a Grand Forks sociologist, most of those New Leipzig Finns came from Finnish communities in northern Minnesota. But they, too, are remembered for their saunas.

Interviewers for the Works Progress Administration compiled information about the New Leipzig Finns and noted that there had been four or five saunas in the settlement.

"Should other nationalities be taking a bath, the strongest Finn holds the door, because a person who is not used to the baths gasps and howls for breath, and tries to get out as the heat increases," said New Leipzig resident Aarne Frobom.

In another WPA interview, Finnish-American Oscar Billey of rural Ellendale noted in 1939 that his family's sauna was "a public area as a number of others come for baths."

Generally, Finns were latecomers among the European groups immigrating to America. Before arriving in North Dakota, most lived for a time in other states like Minnesota, Wisconsin and Michigan, where many worked in mines or the lumber industry.

The Finns were relatively few in number when compared with Norwegians and most of their descendants have scattered. "I would say there's not any Finns around here anymore," says Harju. "What's left here is a Duke's mixture."

The family sauna was a public place.

Athough a farmer in Finland, when William Harju arrived in America he worked in copper mines near Calumet, Mich. But it wasn't a steady job, and Otto says his father probably felt that Calumet was a tough saloon town and "the environment there was not good for the family."

On the train west, William Harju and Jacob Erkilla from Calumet met two other Finns, Jacob Neimi and Henry Inget, who had been working in mines near Ely, Minn. The four families homesteaded, and soon were joined in the area by relatives and other Finnish immigrants.

Harju, while living in Michigan, had come a couple times to the Savo community in South Dakota to work at harvest.

Some of the Finns who later came to the settlements in Burleigh and Mountrail counties settlemnts had first stopped for a time near Brocket, in the eastern part of the state.

Edward Banttari, writing for a history book of the area, estimates that more than 115 Finns settled in eight townships between Wing and McKenzie from 1903 to 1915.

William and Marja Harju wanted their children to learn English, and Otto thinks most other Finnish immigrants had the same attitude. "All their interests and all their hopes were in this country. They didn't continue to live in the old country; their heart wasn't there."

The Finnish that was spoken within the family wasn't understood by the Irish, German and Norwegian settlers in the area. "When you're brought up in a community like that, there was only one language we could converse with, and that was English," Harju says.

Yet, at the same time, several of the Finn farmers cooperatively stocked a library with about 300 books written in the Finnish language about Finland's history, folklore, poetry and fiction.

An exodus of Finns from North Dakota farms that began in about 1918 continued through the drought years of the 1930s.

Banttari notes that by the 1930s, there were fewer Finnish-Americans living in the area, and those who remained were less able to read the language. The library was eventually moved to a retirement home in New York Mills, Minn., where several pioneer Finns lived.

Finnish immigrants were Lutheran, but there were differing beliefs within that religion.

William Harju was the first lay preacher for the Apostolic Lutheran Church south of Wing and Otto is called upon periodically to officiate at funerals there.

Harju and members of the apostolic church practice a fundamentalist type of religion that frowns upon certain types of entertainment like dancing, drinking and music.

Other Finnish immigrants belonged to a more moderate Suomi (Finnish) Lutheran congregation, which eventually merged with an Evangelical Lutheran church in the community of Wing.

The Belden Apostolic Lutheran congregation, which also embraces a fundamentalist doctrine, was founded in 1906. Services were held in private homes or the Finnish Hall until a church was built in 1949.

In addition to being a religious meeting place, the Finnish Hall was, for some free-thinkers in the Belden community, a place for advocating social reform. The hall was built in 1913 by a group calling itself the Finnish Farmers Association.

A special observance for the Finnish immigrants was Midsummer Day, celebrated on June 24. It was a time for social activities like picnics, church services and meetings or merely calling on neighbors.

A survey coordinated by Sherman shows that descendants of Finnish immigrants still live in several rural areas of the state. They include the Burleigh County settlement south of Wing, the Belden group, remainders of the Savo community south of Ellendale and Ludden, and smaller pockets east of Rolla, south of Kintyre and south of Gackle.

A monument to North Dakota's Finnish immigrants was dedicated near Rolla in 1956.

Bob Jansen

On a hot day in mid-summer a cool, smooth bowl of Icelandic skyr (a yogurt-like dish), topped with rich cream, sugar and freshly picked juneberries, and slices of brown bread with smoked meat makes a fine lunch. Icelanders, like Finns and other Scandinavians, enjoyed loaf sugar dipped in coffee and held in the mouth to slowly dissolve as coffee was sipped from the saucer.

Finns like their coffee with sugar cubes

"Whenever a Finn visits a Finn he would be very disappointed if coffee were not served," said a WPA writer investigating the Finnish community near New Leipzig during the 1930s. "It is always served regardless of when the visitor comes. Everyone drinks his coffee out of a saucer with a lump of sugar in his cheek."

The Finnish families were noted for the rag rugs on their floors, made at three carpet looms in the community. Common foods were buttermilk, fish, coarse bread and potatoes; Sunday dessert was a raisin and prune dish stewed on Saturday afternoon. Finns also prepared and ate a thick clabber dish, considered a healthful food.

Finns were great believers in dreams, noted the interviewer. "When two Finnish women talk about dreams it is well for bystanders not to listen. They believe in signs of the stars, moon and northern lights. Some of the older people still believe in witchcraft," he wrote.

Each North Dakota Finnish community had several saunas, usually located by a creek, to which neighbors came on Saturday nights to sauna and socialize. A sauna in Mountrail County is described by another WPA writer as being a dugout built into a sidehill. In the center was a trench, with shelves or reclining seats around the walls. Large hot rocks were placed in the trench. In other cases, a center pit was filled with rocks, heated for hours by a wood fire built among the rocks. When hot enough, the ashes were raked out and the rocks doused with dippers of water to make a dense hot steam.

The bathers reclined on the shelves, without clothes, for a half hour or so, beating themselves about the shoulders with leafy branches. When finished they took a cold bath or plunged into the creek. F.B.

Icelandic immigrant women wore these black caps with tassels and short tight wool jackets with white blouses and aprons. Silver clasps on the tassels and gold and silver embroidery on vests and hems sparkled in the morning sun. The patriotic eagle on the chair in lower photo suggests the eagerness of Icelandic settlers to become American.

Icelandic immigrants included poetic souls

In the ethnic mixture of North Dakota's pioneers was a group of people from a mountainous, volcanic country known for adventure sagas and lyrical poetry.

Immigrants from Iceland began coming to the northeastern counties of Pembina and Cavalier in 1878; about 10 years later that area had become the largest and most significant Icelandic settlement in the United States.

Early federal censuses categorized Icelandic immigrants as Danish because their homeland was under control of Denmark. Thus, it has been difficult for historians to get an accurate count of immigrants from Iceland.

Estimates are that between 25,000 and 30,000 Icelanders came to the North American continent between 1870 and 1900, the majority of them ending up in Canada.

The few rural Icelandic settlements in the United States, in addition to the North Dakota group, were primarily in Minnesota, Utah and on the Pacific Coast.

The first North Dakota Icelanders initially had settled in Manitoba, along the western shore of Lake Winnipeg, at a place they called Gimli, a name for paradise in Icelandic mythology.

However, the Gimli colony was far from a paradise. The poverty-stricken immigrants suffered from extreme winter and summer temperatures and smallpox contracted from Indians claimed more than 100 lives.

By early 1878, some of the Manitoba Icelanders decided to move to the United States and were advised that land was available near Pembina, in the northeastern corner of Dakota Territory.

Later that year, the first Icelandic home was built at Hallson, five miles west of Cavalier. A large number of settlers from Gimli came to the area between 1878 and 1881.

The Rev. Pall Thorlaksson, one of the founders of the Dakota settlement, encouraged other Icelanders in 1879 to abandon their colony in Wisconsin and move west. They did, and were joined in Pembina and Cavalier counties by Icelandic immigrants who had been living in Minnesota.

Already in the area were Norwegians, Irish and French-Canadians, but by the end of 1879 the communities of Hallson, Mountain, Akra and Gardar were well-established as predominantly Icelandic.

Eventually, there were significant numbers of Icelanders in Svold, Hensel and the larger communities of Cavalier, Pembina and Grafton.

Later, a concentration of Icelandic immigrants sprang up in McHenry County, north of Upham. Most of those Icelanders had lived earlier in the northeastern part of the state.

P.V. Thorson, associate professor of history at the University of North Dakota, notes that the Icelanders had a remarkable tradition of in-home education.

Also, Thorson says, since the Middle Ages there had been an Icelandic literary tradition. Reading and writing poetry and prose, he says, was "something an Icelander is supposed to do."

Thostina Walters, an Icelander who grew up on her family's homestead along the Tongue River near Akra, agrees.

In her book, "Modern Sagas," she notes that the living room was where young Icelanders received their groundwork in learning. The system served well in preserving and continuing the centuries-old literary tradition.

Walters says children were expected to read Icelandic by age 8 and were accustomed to being questioned by their elders about books they read.

After learning to read, they were encouraged to familiarize themselves with all the books in the family library, including the Bible.

Sara Ferber, writing for North Dakota History magazine, says the homes of Icelandic pioneers "were veritable social, educational, religious and industrial centers."

She notes that "the good mother was usually the tutor but if her time did not permit, a substitute was engaged, often an elderly person who was glad to thus earn board and room."

The Mountain school district was organized in 1881 and others soon followed. Walters says it was the efforts of the Icelandic settlers that were responsible for the number and variety of library books in schools of the area.

The elders, even after their youngsters began attending classes, in essence continued the tradition of in-home education by discussing the daily lessons with their children and questioning them on subject matter.

In 1886 a debating society was organized at Mountain.

That same year a log structure built there became the first Icelandic church in America. Church services had been held in homes since 1879.

Group singing and playing of musical instruments were popular and a number of plays from Iceland were rehearsed and staged in the North Dakota communities.

Walters writes that poetry was prominent, much of it dealing with the daily life of the settlers. "It was not uncommon for the pioneer to discover a poem about himself pinned to a tree when he emerged from his cabin at daybreak," she says.

Icelandic families are described as close-knit, with a strong emphasis on religion.

The first Independence Day celebration in the Icelandic community was held at a homestead near Gardar in 1880, just two years after the pioneers arrived. Settlers came from all of the newly organized communities and a distance of up to 30 miles to hear Thorlaksson trace the events that led to the establishment of the Fourth of July as Independence Day for the United States.

In the early years, adults participated in school programs by delivering speeches in Icelandic on American heroes, often comparing them with characters in their own sagas.

Walters recalled hours of listening to her father recite sagas of old Iceland and tales of men of American history, like Washington and Lincoln.

"He connected Iceland skillfully with America through his narration of Leif Ericsson and other Vinland heroes of the saga period. He drew inspiring pictures of the American shores with their verdant beauty smiling upon those who looked toward America as a land of new endeavor."

The Grafton Icelandic Lutheran Church listed 80 members in 1895. That number may have reached about 125 before the congregation disbanded after slowly losing membership, financial support and its ethnic identity.

A heritage of Viking adventure, along with the literary tradition and emphasis on education may have helped inspire the accomplishments of well-known North Dakota Icelanders like Vilhjalmur Stefansson, the Arctic explorer; Sveinborn Johnson, former justice on the North Dakota Supreme Court; poet Stefan G. Stefansson; and several other prominent members of the academic, legal and medical professions.

Vilhjalmur Stefansson, noted Arctic explorer. At right, an Icelandic immigrant girl chops wood with double-edged ax.

A continuing monument to the Icelandic pioneers is Icelandic State Park, west of Cavalier, and the Gunlogson homestead and arboretum within the park.

Bob Jansen

Icelandic women added 'dottir,' kept maiden name

Icelanders came to northeastern North Dakota from a cold wet climate where sheep and dairy cattle were raised, where the main crop was hay and where barley was the only grain grown. Garden vegetables consisted mostly of potatoes and turnips. Thorstina Walters recalls in her book "Modern Sagas" her mother's pleasure at the gardens of her German neighbors in North Dakota and how she quickly acquired a taste for the strange beets, carrots and cabbages. But Walters' uncle, newly arrived from Iceland, turned up his nose at saurkraut and declared "I did not come to America to eat grass."

Icelanders had traditions of learning and independent spirit. The desire for individualism, says Walters, was retained in their preference for country life. Urban life was seen as stifling to the initiative, casting everyone in the same mold; Icelanders, she said, wanted to be masters of their own destiny.

In school, Icelandic children had difficulty understanding English. Their teachers, in turn, had trouble with Icelandic traditions, especially the seemingly-independent way the women had of retaining their family names by adding "dottir" rather than "son" to the father's name. Walter explains:

"A case in point is that of little Sigurdur Jonsson who protectively led his small sister, Thora, to school. The bewildered teacher learned that the boy's name was indeed Sigurdur Jonsson, but his sister, on the other hand, was Thora Jonsdottir (Thora daughter of Jon). Presently, the teacher met the parents of his pupils, only to become further confused for the father went by the name of Jon Sigudsson while his wife was Gudrun Helgadottir. The pedagogue had just become reconciled to these strange 'folkways' when Sigurdur's older brother, Arni, began atending school. Arni had become sufficiently Americanized to wish to have the same surname as his father, accordingly he was registered as 'Sigurdsson,' while his younger brother continued to sign himself as 'Jonsson,' faithfully following the patronymic system. The two boys were, however, very much annoyed if some one suggested that they were not full brothers."

F.B.

Germans built Missouri Synod Lutheran churches

A German is a German is a German.

Well, not really.

In North Dakota, there are Germans in the generic sense, but they actually are a collection of German-Germans, German-Russians, German-Hungarians and a few small groups of other people who lay claim to Germany as their old country.

German-Germans, who are referred to simply as Germans in the rest of this story, settled mostly in inconspicuous pockets within larger ethnic communities. Although the Germans are not highly visible, Rev. William Sherman, who has studied and mapped North Dakota's ethnic distribution, says all the small pockets add up to at least 10 percent of the state's population.

Sherman says it is difficult to accurately count the numbers of Germans and Germans who came from Russia because the German-Russians often identify themselves simply as being German.

The German-Russian immigrants differed from the Germans in many ways, however. To Germans, they represented a cultural anachronism because of their conservative background and their lengthy isolation from mainstream German society. They left Germany in the last half of the 18th century and lived in Russia for 100 years, strongly resisting assimilation and preserving their lifestyle.

"To them, to be German meant to do what their forefathers had done," says Tim Kloberdanz, assistant professor of sociology at North Dakota State University.

When the Germans and German-Russians came into contact again in North Dakota, they tended to stay aloof from each other.

Germans tended to view German-Russians as being backward because of their old style of language, dress and food. "The fact that they could retain those customs might be a mark of achievement, but other Germans looked on them as backward," says Kloberdanz.

He says the distinction between the two groups no longer is as sharp as it once was, but it does exist.

Like other immigrants, Germans came to North Dakota basically for free land.

Most of the better U.S. farmland similar to that back in Germany already had been taken, but North Dakota farmland was being highly acclaimed and promoted by the railroads, which advertised heavily in the German language.

So Germans came to North Dakota from Germany and from previous settlements in the eastern United States to homestead and make their living.

Many of them did quite well for themselves, says Sherman.

Starting in the 1870s, they settled in small pockets throughout North Dakota.

"They didn't seem to feel the need for the ... large-sized compact settlements" that Norwegians and German-Russians did, says Sherman.

The three largest pockets of German settlements in North Dakota are in southern Richland County, the region from around Langdon to Dresden and a spot in central North Dakota that includes New Salem and a swath north through Hannover and Hazen in Oliver County.

Sherman says that Germans usually are found wherever the Lutheran Missouri Synod church is found, that the two are almost synonymous in North Dakota.

Many Germans were able to prosper in the immigrant society of early North Dakota, says Sherman. He says German-Americans from crowded settlements in the eastern United States had advantages over the North Dakota immigrants because they spoke English and were familiar with the American system.

An added benefit was the strongly ingrained German work ethic, according to Sherman.

Even Germans who came "right off the boat" sometimes did well, he continues. A few of them were successful enough to stand right in there and compete with the American-born Anglo-Saxons, Sherman says.

Anton Klaus, called the Father of Jamestown, was an example. "This guy was a whirlwind," says Sherman. "He was in hotels, mills, stores."

Another highly successful German was John Wishek, called the Father of McIntosh County because of his efforts to establish settlements and help the mostly German-Russian settlers.

By and large, the Germans did not came to North Dakota to escape deprivation and persecution as many immigrants did.

"It was probably just the ballyhoo of the railroads, and, like all of Europe, where does the second and third son go when the (home) farm goes to the first son?" says Sherman.

Many immigrated to the large cities of the United States, but others were farmers who wound up in North Dakota because other states were settled up.

Larry Johnson

Kids' parade at Oktoberfest in New Leipzig features German costumes and signs.

Immigrant's son learned politics at home

America is a land where a poor immigrant's son can grow up to be ... governor of North Dakota.

John Link probably wasn't thinking about that when he left Germany in 1900.

Also, he probably didn't expect to end up a farmer, on the prairie of northwestern North Dakota.

Johann and Anna Link, John's parents and the grandparents of former Gov. Arthur A. Link, were cotton weavers in a German area of what is now Czechoslovakia, where John was born. With hopes of bettering their life, they migrated to the Bavarian city of Augsburg, but found living there wasn't much better.

Arthur Link, a man of rugged physical features, has throughout his long political career been portrayed as a common, down-to-earth figure, known for speaking with an uncommon degree of sincerity. It is with some visible emotion that he tells of the economic conditions that made his parents forgo schooling to work in the European mills at the age of 9.

The former governor grew up on John Link's homestead in Randolph Township south of Alexander. The land now is farmed by two of his sons, Walter and Donald.

Recalling pioneer life, he suggests that "one of the most lasting customs, if you call it a custom, was that of being quite thorough, particular and exacting in whatever they did."

He explains that trait was a carry-over from hard times in the old country. It meant being "conservative, in terms of saving what you could, being careful with what you had."

John Link's family, like other European factory workers, lived in small villages. "When the farmers finished harvesting, they (peasant villagers) would get permission to glean the fields," says his son.

"They would walk with a sack and pick up any stray heads, take the wheat home and thresh it by hand." It then would be ground into flour.

"They knew that a few heads of wheat gathered up meant food."

The same tradition continued after the Links homesteaded on a North Dakota quarter-section in 1907.

The former governor notes that some heads of grain always fell out of the bundles during threshing. "After the grain was hauled in ... we would take a team of horses and rake the shock rows." The process was called "threshing the rakings."

Another example of conservation by the poorest immigrants was the care taken in butchering a cow or hog. Rather than throw the head of the animal away or toss it to the dogs, the Links would put every usable morsel of meat into sausage or head cheese.

"They were generous in terms of what needed to be done. They just didn't waste anything."

John Link met Anna Mencl in Augsburg. They came to America in 1900, were married in New York City and worked in textile mills at New Bedford, Mass., before moving to North Dakota.

They had heard that land was available in North Dakota's McKenzie County, and spent their first winter with friends at Cartwright. They couldn't find water on the land they were hoping to homestead there, so they settled 15 miles to the east, near Alexander.

Until their one-room, roofing-paper claim shack could be built, they lived in a semi-dugout made of sod and wood by John Jiricka, a bachelor neighbor they had known in the old country.

By the time their only son was born, in 1914, a lean-to had been added to that shack, which became a part of the farmhome that still stands today.

Link feels his parents "wanted their children to acquire the English language and American ways so they would not be handicapped, as they probably felt they were."

The old country wasn't entirely forgotten. The family subscribed to three German-language newspapers, and John would read aloud from them and letters from German relatives.

John Link, at least indirectly, influenced his son along a path that led to political and public service.

The elder Link was Randolph Township treasurer and clerk of the local school board for more than 30 years.

"As long as I can remember it, I was aware of township government and the school board — we kind of lived it," says the former governor.

"Because of his involvement in local government affairs, I don't remember my folks ever missing an election.

"When the Nonpartisan League organized, he joined that and went to meetings. At a rather early age I would go along with him."

After being a leader in his township and local Farmer's Union organizations, Arthur Link in 1946 was elected to the Legislature; through 1980 his career had included eight years as governor and one term in the U.S. House.

He was first identified as a Republican, when the NPL was allied with the GOP, but moved along with the League to the Democratic column.

The Links were patrons of the "consumer store" at Alexander, where farmers could exchange produce for groceries.

They also were members of local grain and live shipping cooperatives and the Farmers Union.

Link says the background of poverty probably was what encouraged his family and others to embrace those progressive, self-help organizations.

Despite those humble economic roots, a family violin was passed on to young Arthur by his maternal grandmother.

Beginning at age 8, he would weekly, usually on Saturday, travel by team and buggy the six miles into Alexander to take lessons from a Norwegian-American, the Rev. Ofaf R. Svore.

As the story goes, it was later, while playing violin with a local orchestra at a Farmers Union social and dance that Link met his future bride, Grace Johnson of Cartwright.

Grace's ancestors, Link points out, were in the area even before the immigrant "squatters and sodbusters."

Her maternal grandfather, an Englishman, had come from Saskatchewan to North Dakota as part of the Hyde, Wood and Slater Cattle Co.

Like many of us, the former governor now realizes he should have been more conscious of his ethnic heritage as a youngster.

But he doesn't forget about those few heads of wheat that weren't wasted.

"We have moved a long ways away from the very conservative, saving nature of the immigrants who came to this country," Link says.

"Too many times it's quantity and volume that counts. We haven't time to be conservative with the little things."

Bob Jansen

German-Hungarians settled southwest corner

You probably have German-Hungarian blood in your veins if your name is one of these:

Balog, Burger, Buschbacher, Drachil, Duppong, Fetter, Filibeck, Kaip, Kaufmann, Martin, Meissner, Muller, Navratil, Prunkl, Seeberger, Schirado, Schneider, Sibla, Streitmatter, Thiel, Tschida, Walery, Weizman, Yambra or Youngheim.

Or: Bayer, Gion, Goetz, Grundhauser, Haas, Harle, Herold, Hess, Jesch, Kelsch, Kilzer, Koenig, Krier, Kronberger, Krumenacher, Lampl, Lindemann, Link, Mayer, Pechtl, Reiner, Schinal, Schmitt, Schroeder, Wehner or Wotreng.

These German-Hungarian surnames are commonly found in southwestern North Dakota, principally in Morton, Stark, Dunn and Hettinger counties. Most of the German-Hungarians settled in a belt southeast of Dickinson and many of them later moved into that city. They founded the German-Hungarian Club at Dickinson.

There also is a small group of German-Hungarians in Barnes County in eastern North Dakota.

The German-Hungarians should not be confused with Germans from Russia. Because both ethnic groups had a similar history, they were known as "pioneers on two continents." Their forebears developed settlements in wildernesses of eastern Europe a century or so before they came to the American West.

But they are distinctly different groups of Germans. The Germans from Russia began to arrive in North Dakota at about the same time as the German-Hungarians and many of them also settled in southwestern North Dakota. But they came from German settlements in Russia.

The German-Hungarians, mostly Catholic, spoke a dialect distinctly different from other Germanic people. They emigrated from the Banat, a river basin in the Austro-Hungarian Empire near the Turkish border. Many of them came to North Dakota during the late 19th and early 20th centuries.

They were descendants of southern Germans, many from Alsace-Lorraine, who had settled the Banat during the late 1700s. The uninhabited land had been ceded to Austria by the Turks and Germans were among several ethnic groups invited by Hapsburg Empress Maria Theresa to develop farms and communities on idle lands there.

Primarily farmers and tradesmen, the German-Hungarians adapted well to the swampy but rich river tributary land, according to the late Rev. George Aberle of Dickinson, who wrote extensively about Germanic people in North Dakota. They turned the Banat into some of the best farmland in the Austro-Hungarian Empire.

But their own success contributed to their emigration, according to Aberle. They filled up the land quickly, and farms grew smaller and smaller. Also, they became apprehensive about military draft for wars in eastern Europe.

They began to leave for North America and South America during the 1880s and they were attracted to North Dakota by advertisements of railroads and land companies.

According to one newspaper account, the first German-Hungarian immigrants in North Dakota went to an area near Lefor in 1891. They built sod homes and were squatters for a time — the land hadn't even been surveyed. That area became the St. Stephen's Catholic parish.

They were surprised to find their new land better than they had expected. When the Northern Pacific Railroad opened the land southeast of Dickinson for sale, the settlers were able to buy it for about $1 to $1.50 an acre; the price went up as years went by.

Near St. Stephen's, the community that is now Lefor was begun when a number of families from the Banat, including the Lefor family, arrived in 1892 or 1893. They homesteaded along Black Creek in south central Stark County.

A son, Frank Lefor, established at his homestead a post office, which he called Hungary, after his homeland. That post office didn't last long, but another one did. Adam Lefor started a post office in 1911, a town grew up around it and it came to be known as Lefor.

Catholic missionaries established St. Elizabeth's parish at Lefor in 1898 to serve the German-Hungarians. The congregation built the first church out of sod.

When weather wore down that structure, they built a second one out of prairie rock, straw and gumbo. A brick church was constructed to replace it in 1929.

German-Hungarians also settled around Richardton. Another belt of homesteads extended from Lefor to New England in Hettinger County.

A larger contingent came during the early 1890s and they expanded through the Hirschville region of Dunn County.

Also during the 1890s, German-Hungarians settled north of Glen Ullin and near Hebron in western Morton County and southeast of Mott in Hettinger County.

Some of the German-Hungarians in North Dakota had worked first for a time in cities such as Chicago to save up money. There were "Burgenlanders," who came in 1887 from Ohio to settle at St. Anthony in southern Morton County. In 1896, they changed the name of their community from Littleheart to St. Anthony, in honor of their church.

Most of the German-Hungarians settled southwest of the Missouri River, except for some from the Burgenland — another part of the Austro-Hungarian Empire — who went to Fingal. Fingal is a small community in southern Barnes County.

Many of the German-Hungarians were very poor. A motto of the settlers at Lefor was "Schnell Reich," meaning "get rich quick," says Phyllis Feser, secretary of the Germans From Russia Heritage Society at Bismarck. Her husband, Adrian, had a number of German-Hungarian forebears who settled in the Lefor and Glen Ullin areas.

Most of the German-Hungarians were farmers and tradesmen, the Fesers said, but several of them were well-educated. Feser notes that one of Adrian's grandfathers, Stephen Thiel, who homesteaded in 1906 at Russian Flats near Almont, could speak four languages: English, Rumanian, German and Hungarian.

Although just 26 years old when he arrived, Thiel already had worked as a farmer, shoemaker, postal and liquor inspector and army cavalryman back in Austria-Hungary. Thiel become a successful homesteader and a coal miner at Russian Flats.

He also obtained a job as a dispatcher with the Northern Pacific Railway and had a shoe and harness

German-Hungarian Lodge began as benefit society and social club, became place to have "a good time."

repair shop, and his clerical and linguistic skills enabled him to hold positions as Glen Ullin city assessor, state liquor stamp inspector and page in the state Senate.

Feser also notes that Stephen's wife, Mathilda, who he married in the Banat just before they emigrated, had worked in a cigarette factory and had sung in a nightclub.

The German-Hungarians in North Dakota have, for the most part, adjusted to society more quickly and easily than the Germans from Russia, according to Feser. She says the German-Hungarians were more outgoing than the Germans from Russia, in part because they were accepted more by the Austro-Hungarian government and native peoples than those who went to Russia.

"A little bit of the (Hungarian) gypsy rubbed off on them," she says. They liked more stylish, colorful clothing, especially reds and purples. They loved Hungarian goulash, she added, and one of her grandmothers would "eat hot peppers like candy."

Both Feser and the Rev. William Sherman, a Grand Forks sociologist, note that intermarriage between German-Hungarians and other North Dakota peoples, especially the Germans from Russia, began to occur after the first generation.

According to Sherman, German-Hungarians still make up a large part of the population at Fingal, but elsewhere there has been so much assimilation that few pure German-Hungarians are left.

John Pearson

German-Russian

Most North Dakota Germans came from Russia

Germans went to Russia largely to obtain free land.

They left Russia largely to avoid becoming Russians.

But once they came to the United States, they encountered even stronger pressures that worked against their intense desire to maintain their German identity.

How much German identity has been maintained is a topic of debate.

Tim Kloberdanz, assistant professor of sociology at NDSU, maintains that while German-Russians speak English and have assumed the trappings of American culture (acculturation), they still perceive of themselves as being different.

Kloberdanz says he believes the German-Russian ethnic consciousness will grow stronger in future generations.

A different view is offered by Armand Bauer, editor of the Heritage Review, a publication of the Germans from Russia Heritage Society.

"The German-Russians, I would say, have been essentially assimilated into the American mainstream," says Bauer, the grandson of German-Russian immigrants to south central North Dakota.

Bauer says the cultural barriers against intermarriage with other people and between German-Russians of different religions are virtually gone.

Tangible signs of German-Russian culture, such as language, seem to be eroding at a faster rate with each generation, as time puts distance between today's youth and the immigrants.

Unlike some immigrant groups who willingly became Americans, the German-Russian settlers who came to North Dakota wanted to preserve their German culture, just as they had done for 100 years in Russia.

How important was cultural identity to the German-Russian immigrants?

Bauer recalls translating a text a few years ago: "When the German blood was mixed with the Slavic blood, they were lost to their kin forever."

When the German-Russians came to North Dakota, they were thrown into a mix of other newcomers and into a new structure of government and commerce.

Individual homesteads replaced the colonial communities of the Volga and Black Sea regions in Russia, where German-Russians of various religious faiths had lived separately in villages and worked the surrounding farmland.

In North Dakota, compulsory schools were conducted in English.

Social pressure, during two world wars that pitted Americans against Germans, also forced German-Russians to identify with the United States.

There were instances during wartime of German-Russians being forced to carry the American flag and of being forbidden to speak German. A recent example of similar pressure, says Kloberdanz, was the distrust and scorn sometimes heaped on Americans of Iranian descent after the seizure of Americans in Iran in 1980.

Economic and cultural privileges that had helped the German-Russians maintain their culture in Russia stemmed from promises Catherine the Great and Alexander I gave to attract German farmers to Russia to settle new land and boost agricultural output.

In the late 1800s, however, the privileges were revoked when new, nationalist russification policies were instituted.

Changes in policy in Russia included the institution of universal military service, which meant German youths would have to leave their ethnic communities for a harsh life in a culturally mixed army.

Russian language was made mandatory in schools.

A new administrative structure also put Russians in charge of the German colonies.

Bauer says he recalls his wife's grandmother saying one of the reasons people left Russia was that the Germans were being "stolen blind" by impoverished Russians, who went unpunished by Russian administrators.

In addition, life in Russia was sometimes harsh, and Russians grew increasingly jealous of the higher standard of living enjoyed by the German settlers.

Beginning around 1870, many of the Germans, who had immigrated to the Volga and Black Sea regions of Russia from southwestern Germany from 1766 to 1865 to obtain land, felt it was time to move on again.

Homestead acts in the United States and Canada offered new land and escape from problems in Russia.

German-Russians from the Black Sea region settled mostly in the Dakotas, says Kloberdanz.

German-Russians from the Volga region settled mostly in Kansas, Colorado, Nebraska and southeastern Wyoming, he says.

Some German-Russians from both groups also settled in other areas such as California and the Pacific Northwest, he adds.

Bauer, however, says many of the German-Russian emigrants didn't know where they were headed until they were aboard ships, whose captains sometimes had quotas of settlers for other countries such as Brazil and Argentina.

Immigrants also were diverted to South America when U.S. officials turned them away for various reasons. For instance, some German-Russians were refused entry to the United States because they suffered from an eye ailment called trachoma, to which many were susceptible.

By 1885-1905, when most of the 28,000 German-Russians who immigrated to North Dakota arrived, either from Russia or from other settlements in America, much of the better homestead land in the river valleys, particularly in eastern North Dakota, had been taken.

The homestead area that remained included prairie similar to the steppes of Russia.

Kloberdanz says some people look at North Dakota's lack of trees and call it empty and desolate. "North Dakota German-Russians will say it is free, open," without trees that have to be cleared for farming, he says. "Hills, indeed, were thorns in the eye."

The German-Russian immigrants settled and tended to dominate the central region of the state, which Elwyn B. Robinson called "the German-Russian triangle" in his history of North Dakota.

The triangle had its base along the southern border from Dickey County to Hettinger County and its apex in Pierce and McHenry counties.

German-Russians built homes mostly of sun-dried bricks, a cheap available material they had become accustomed to in Russia.

Life had been hard in Russia, where the German-Russians had developed a reputation for resilience and willingness to stick to the land.

That reputation was tested in North Dakota. They were basically wheat farmers, which made them vulnerable to drought, other natural disasters and the Depression of the 1930s, when many lost their land and many moved to California.

In North Dakota, they also experienced a revolution in status, according to historians. They went from being at the top of society in rural Russia to the bottom in North Dakota.

Gordon Iseminger, professor of history at the University of North Dakota, says the initial generations of German-Russian immigrants have been stereotyped as disinterested in politics and higher education, and as having an aversion to war and military service.

"I'm not so sure they were anti-war, anti-military, as they were anti-Russian military," says Iseminger, whose view coincides with that of Armand Bauer.

Bauer says the German-Russians may have been viewed as being at the bottom of the social scale partly because of their lack of involvement in business or political office, which stemmed from their background and preference for agriculture.

Bauer says language also may have been a primary reason German-Russians were looked down upon by some other immigrants.

But he says German-Russians were good farmers and their greatest contributions to the development of North Dakota probably were in the field of agriculture. He notes that modern winter wheats have been developed in part from grain brought to the United States by German-Russian immigrants.

Bauer says that, through the years, the barriers against cultural and religious interaction with other immigrants and even other German-Russians have fallen by the wayside.

The German-Russians tried and failed to preserve their language as common usage in North Dakota, although many descendants can speak the language today. The religious barriers between Catholics and protestants are virtually gone, according to Bauer.

Bauer says the German language and ethnic identity seems to fade with each successive generation.

He says that perhaps one factor

Count Maximillian von Bismarck and his sister Countess Gunilla von Bismarck, great-grandchildren of the "iron chancellor" for which the capital city was named, were feted at North Dakota Germans from Russia centennial celebration in Bismarck. Lower photo of exhibits shows a Back Schissel, covered bread-rising pan.

that worked against German-Russian cultural preservation in North Dakota was individual homestead land, as opposed to Russia, where the Germans lived together in villages and worked the surrounding land.

The legacy of the German-Russians today includes some traits of the early immigrants.

One notable example is the work ethic, in which North Dakotans take pride.

The German-Russians also may

Germans from Russia float in centennial parade transmits a swinging German sound.

show a preference for "meaty" disciplines in higher education, such as medicine and engineering.

Ted Pedeliski, associate professor of political science at UND, recalls teaching at Napoleon High School in the 1950s. He says his students at Napoleon were some of the highest achievers he's ever encountered as a teacher.

German-Russians rank second to Norwegians in percentage of the state's rural population, according to the Rev. William Sherman, Grand Forks, who studied ethnic distributions in rural North Dakota in 1965.

Sherman found that 30 percent of rural households were Norwegian and about 20 percent were German-Russian.

North Dakota has the highest concentration of German-Russians of any state in the United States, according to Iseminger, and McIntosh County has the highest concentration of German-Russians of any county in the United States.

Robert Wilkins, a UND historian who wrote a history of North Dakota about five years ago, says he believes that although people of various ethnic backgrounds helped settle the state and new people continue to move into the state, the overall population will always be mostly of Norwegian and German-Russian stock.

Larry Johnson

Wishek observes frugal habits, customs of McIntosh County pioneers

The German people came into the west by the thousand from southern Russia, took up free land here and from the virgin soil built their homes, have developed the county and endured privations with the rest of us. (In the early times, because the foreign-born settlers came from Russia, they were called Russians, but later we learned that they were not Russian but of pure German extraction.)

They suffered hunger and cold and passed through those years of heat, drought and poor prices. They lived on bread and chicory, and their thirft and stoic fortitutude saved the day and helped to establish McIntosh as one of the richest counties in North Dakota. Gladly and honestly do we give to those immigrant settlers their just due.

We American pioneers thought we sacrificed, lived cheaply and enjoyed no luxuries, but I doubt if we could or would have lived the simple frugal life that was theirs.

Being frugal, these German people never used cream or butter, but saved all dairy produce to take to the nearest town in exchange for groceries. They used chicory instead of expensive coffee. I rather liked it, and, diluted with hot milk, surely it was a natural and healthful drink. As they used no butter, they ate their bread dry with the chicory drink, "segora", and for days at a time this bread and drink would compose all their meals. In those times they knew nothing of pie or cake, but for a sweet taste they did make "kuchen" from bread dough. I often wondered if they did not crave oranges or fruits, but the acid touch in their diet was supplied by the natural fermentation of preserved cabbage, sauerkraut and dilled cucumbers and melons. For fats, in place of cream or butter, they had their fat pork, meats and gravies. They even ate fat salted pork raw; the children often brought a piece of it to school to eat with their dry bread. But, taken all in all, it seemed a fairly healthful and satisfying living. In its simplicity it still supplied the right vitamins to build up a sturdy and hardy people.

Their homes, so crudely and economically built, were to me a very interesting feature of imported Russian ways and means. Never before had I seen or heard of a house so unique, so cheaply and warmly constructed. Cut from the virgin prairie soil, laid up in tiers and then plastered without and within with a natural clay product (probably part gumbo) these houses were warm in the winter and cool in summer. Many were composed of two rooms, but I have seen them, when the family was small and poor, with but one large room. There was always an outer storm shed or entry, which was used chiefly as a storage place for the hay or straw for fuel and as the site from which the oven was fired. The houses all had the natural dirt floor, so hard and dry that it could be swept like board floor. The housewife would sprinkle the dusty floor before sweeping. The interior walls of yellowish clay plaster were often decorated in bright colors or with a border-like frieze in reds, blues, greens or yellow. These colors were never modified or softened. The outer doors might be painted in a gay yellow, with blue panels or some other additional color.

To me, one of the strangest ways of the foreigner was the custom of women working in the field. In later years I became accustomed to it and even came to realize that the girls and women enjoyed the freedom of outdoor life. Many girls preferred working outside. Of course this outside work was made possible because the home life was so simplified and because the children all shared in the work.

The women bore large families, and in busy times like seeding or harvest it seemed they could hardly spare the time for a confinement. Many unbelievable stories I have heard. For instance, there was the mother, who came in from the field, gave birth to a child and cared for it alone, and then prepared the meal in time for workers when they came. They seldom employed a doctor. Each community supported a midwife or two who felt amply competent to care for such cases at a charge from $2 to $5. While mother and child mortality was far too great, it is surprising that it was not greater.

When the children were very young, they were taught to do chores about the house and barn, and at an early age began the heavier work of an adult. With all of this unpaid farm help and with their simple inexpensive provision for living, these pioneers of a new undeveloped land rapidly accumulated money, bought more land, put up good frame houses to replace the old sod homes, and prospered generally.

I asked Mr. Christian Becker, an old pioneer resident, "Do you regret leaving Russia, or are you contented here in America?" "Ach, Gott, yes, I wish I was back in Russia." Then he went on to tell of his home in Russia near Odessa. The houses of stone had been built by the order of Catharine the Great, for the German people imigrating into Russia from Germany. He told of all the comforts they enjoyed and said that most of them wished they were back. But Mr. Becker's statement may result from the nostalgic memory of those glamorous days of youth, for certainly the few Russian Germans who have returned to their homeland have always come back within the year to America.

Nina Farley Wishek
Along the Trails of Yesterday

Making 'Russian lignite' fuel

Wall of mischt was built three to four feet wide at base and about eight feet high, drawn in at top and ends to shed rain and snow.

Mischt, or Russian lignite as it was commonly called, furnished heat in many German-Russian homes. Similar to the buffalo and cow chips burned by many pioneers, the mischt was, however, carefully prepared.

The circle of manure was begun in winter when cattle were brought into the barn, according to Edmund Schnabel of Bismarck. Every day as barns were cleaned, manure was hauled out in the wheelbarrow and dumped at the edge, making a broad area about 12-18 inches thick. Throughout winter and spring the circle grew. Moisture from snow and rain helped to pack it.

After spring thaw the pile was tramped, says Schnabel. As it dried more, horses could be used with one or two being driven around and around on lines. Sometimes a team was hitched to a heavy packer. Or, if the area was fenced, several horses might be turned in with a small boy posted to keep them moving. As the manure dried, it was packed several times until it was about six inches thick.

When dry, foot-square blocks were cut. These were turned over to dry, then set on edge for further drying, alternating one block lengthwise and the next crosswise in long rows.

All summer the blocks dried. In the fall they were stacked near the house, but not too near, notes Schnabel.

Building the wall of mischt was also an art. Good blocks were stacked in two parallel rows, making a base about three to four feet wide. In between were piled the uneven sizes and broken pieces. As the wall was built higher, it was drawn in slightly until it was about eight feet high and narrow on the top. The ends sloped in also.

To best protect the mischt from winter moisture and snow storms, it was then plastered over with fresh manure. "Not everyone did this, but we did," recalls Schnabel. Cattle were held in the corral overnight; in the morning fresh manure was collected in the wheelbarrow. It was taken to the wall and "plastered on till it was smooth and tight." This kept the snow from blowing between the blocks, keeping it dry for burning.

When used the mischt was taken from the south end of the wall. In the house it was broken with hammer or hatchet to fit into the cookstove, or could be used full size in the early clay ovens. A twist of hay started the fire; mischt added to the top meant a fire would be hot in "no time." Mischt burned with a hot quick fire and left plenty of ashes. So when people could afford it they burned coal in the heating stoves instead.

F.B.

Thrifty pioneer wore shoes for church, town only

Much could be said here of the simple and frugal living of the early pioneers on the prairies and their few needs. They never bought what they could not pay for. They tried to get along with the most necessary and essential things. Already in their colonies of the Ukraine and in the Banat of Austria-Hungary they were trained and became used to live thrifty. Their demands were small and their needs few. When settling on the wide and vast prairies they started out with little or practically nothing. They learned to live sparingly and simply. Later, when by their thrift, zeal, hard work and the blessing of God they reached a certain degree of well doing, remembering their former hardships and trials, they nevertheless lived frugally. They believed in thrift as a long-proved virtue and lived by the same. No wonder that those simple pioneers, who had few earthly goods, had often more credit in the stores and banks than many opulent people. Their word of honor was accepted in financial transactions as readily as the best promissory note.

But no one is expected to carry the virtue of thrift to the length as is told of one of those staunch pioneers. The good man was wearing one and the same pair of Sunday shoes for five years. In going to Church, which he never missed on Sundays, he usually walked barefoot during the warmer months of the year carrying his shoes on his back to within an eighth of a mile from the church, where he stopped and put them on. On his return walk he took them off at the same place walking barefooted home. Whenever he was driving to town he had his shoes in the wagon, putting them on before entering the town. On his return trip the shoes were off as soon as he was out of the town limits. This was supposed to have been a practice with him for many years.

Msgr. George Aberle
From the Steppes to the Prairies

Beata and Joseph Greff were married in 1915, raised 18 children. They are, back row, left to right: Pauline Galles, Sturgis, South Dakota; Beata Moses, Gresham, Oregon; Sam, Regent; Ann Demick, Reno, Nevada; Mike, deceased; Margareta Nagel, Hettinger; Vincent, deceased; Ida Heidt, Hettinger; Tillie Friedt, deceased; Sally Frank, Bismarck. Front row: Joe, Spokane, Washington; Kay Severson, Mandan; Val, Regent; Joseph, deceased; Cecilia Kullman, Portland, Oregon; Beata, Bismarck; Albert, Huff; Frank, Berlin, Wisconsin; Rose Caliento, Croton-on-Hudson, New York; Kasper, Almont. In her wedding photo, Beata, at age 15, looks much like and scarcely older than her daughter Rose, seated second from right.

Large family knew sacrifice and fun

At 15 Beata Jahner was known as one of the best dancers in Stark County. With her brother she performed the striking Russian dances. A popular routine included a leap from floor to chair, from chair onto a table, a dance on the table and back to floor, never missing a beat.

Then Beata's sister died, leaving three young children, and Beata dutifully obeyed her parents' wishes to accept her brother-in-law's proposal of marriage. Hardly more than a child herself, she married Joseph Gref and took on the endless task of mothering his children.

She never danced again, except for a turn now and again at a wedding dance. She had no time or energy for the pleasures of youth. Her own babies began coming, one after the other. Altogether there were 21 children, three of which died in infancy. Beata raised them all, counting each a blessing and never voicing any misgivings or complaints she may have had.

Joe Greff had come from Russia (where his family lived 50 years) at the age of five. He lived on the family homestead near Richardton, then took his own homestead near Mott in 1907. The next year he married Celestina Jahner. In 1915 he and Beata married; he was 29, she was 15.

Joe Greff — like other German-Russian husbands and fathers — made the decisions and gave the orders. Beata did not argue. As one of her daughters, Ida Heidt, Hettinger recalls, "If she was eight months pregnant, with two little ones hanging onto her skirts, and he said to go out and pitch bundles, that's just what she did, with never a word of protest."

Beata stacked thistles for the year's meager crop on the day before her third child was born. She was alone for the birth of another child, her husband gone off working for wages and only the younger children at home. These small children she sent off on errands when she knew the birth was near. They returned an hour or so later to find the new baby brother wrapped snugly in his cradle.

Times were hard and life is recalled by the family as full of sacrifice and continuous struggle. Beata did all her washing for more than ten years on a washboard, using handmade soap.

Joe loved a party, his children recall, and "mother was stuck with the work." He provided guests with plenty of homemade brew and "all the men would get drunk." Weddings and other celebrations in the German-Russian communities are remembered for the good times had by the men and younger people. Women had their liquor or wine, too, but the get-together invariably included much work for them, caring for younger children and helping with food preparation. The hostess was busy baking for many days in advance.

Ann Greff Demick recalls the wordless toasts of her parents which helped them "become and remain the greatest family ever.

"Before breakfast each day Dad would pour himself a shot of Schnapps, lift up the glass (or bottle) to the family and drink it. Then he would pour for Mother and she would do the same."

The Greffs lived in a 4-room stone house, painted a "rainbow of colors" on the outside. Three rooms were used for living, with always a bed and baby bed in the living room, with the fourth — which had a dirt floor — used for storing coal and as a summer kitchen. As the family grew this was made into a bedroom for the girls. Later a small bedroom was made in the attic, where the boys slept several in a bed. The beds were pushed close to the chimney and a small floor register brought up some warm air in winter.

The oldest daughter, Margaret Nagel, quit school when she was old enough and worked full time on the farm. She recalls that she could harness and hitch seven horses to a two-bottom plow in 15 minutes. She would plow, seed, drag, cut and rake hay, haul in hay and straw, drive header boxes, stack wheat, load and pitch budle wagons at threshing time. The next daughters helped both outside and inside with the younger children. When old enough, they took outside jobs, sending most of the money home. Ida remembers earning $18 one month and spending most of it to help her mother buy a new washing machine.

The Greffs worked hard but remember enjoyable times, too. Evening entertainment usually began in the kitchen while the girls were doing the dishes, recalls a son, Mike. It would get pretty noisy then, "when Dad yelled at us it would get quiet for awhile. If it didn't we had to stand up in a long line and say our night prayers which we knew well enough to just rattle off. Once in a while, though, we would start to giggle. So we'd have to start all over again. If we were lucky, somebody knew at which point in the prayers we had stopped and we would start from there. We always had to say our prayers in German. We said them aloud and usually one or two of us had to lead the Rosary. After the prayers during Lent, an Epistle and Gospel were read in German with Dad sitting beside us to help us.

"Dad would often sit and read us stories and news from the two German papers that we got once a week. The stories were interesting if we listened, and sometimes even made us cry. Sometimes we could hardly wait until the next paper came and was read to us — during the winter it didn't come every week."

Sacrifice was a way of life in this family, as in many other pioneer homes. Success was completing each day and being able to face the next. Fear and disaster, when they came, were taken in stride. Dignity and pride were cherished in a good meal, clean clothes and hard work.

As the Greff children married and prepared to leave home, each knelt with his or her spouse for a final blessing from both sets of parents. They confessed their sins and asked forgiveness. The parents in turn asked forgiveness for any wrongs done to the child and gave their blessing to the marriage.

In this family many home and religious traditions are kept into the third generation. A daughter keeps holy water and a blessed candle in her home. In a bad lightning storm she lights the candle, and the holy water is sprinkled throughout the house as they leave on a trip to protect the home till their return. In moving to a new home, family members have their house and farm buildings blessed by the priest.

Joe Greff died in 1956. Beata now lives in Bismarck and at the age of 83, still keeps up her own apartment.

F.B.

English and Celtic influence great but now intangible

The influence of people of English and Celtic stock in the making of North Dakota history and society is probably greater than that of any other ethnic group.

The English language, civil laws based on English antecedents and a form of government founded by people who had considered themselves English until 1776 all are part of a heritage North Dakotans share with other Americans.

Yet, tracing the English/Celtic influence in North Dakota is difficult, because the more tangible evidence of ethnic groups — customs, foods, folklore, crafts and the like — is sadly lacking. Few, if any, North Dakotans enjoy the ritual of tea and scones at 4 p.m.; the sounds of Scottish bagpipes and Welsh choirs are conspicuously absent; and St. Patrick's Day is noted only by wearing green.

Even a generic name for these people presents difficulty, since there are four ethnic groups — the English, the Scots, the Welsh and the Irish — under consideration. The term Anglo-Saxon would apply at least in part to the English, but not to the Scots or Irish, who are Gaelic Celts, or to the Welsh, who are Brythonic Celts. "English/Celtic" will have to suffice.

These people arrived in what is now North Dakota in three groups.

There were those who immigrated to North Dakota directly from the British Isles, those who came from Canada and those who were native-born Americans of English/Celtic stock.

The examples of immigration directly from the British Isles are mostly scattered, since there was apparently little recruitment of British settlers.

In a paper entitled "Nineteenth Century Immigration from England to Dakota Territory: The Example of Wensleydale," Frederick C. Tring describes the attempted recruitment of unemployed laborers and displaced farmers in England's industrial Midlands, but he notes that it is not known if any of them came to Dakota Territory.

In fact, Dakota Territory — indeed the entire United States— would have been less attractive to people in Great Britain than Canada or Australia, which still were part of the British Empire.

Yet, there were substantial numbers of settlers from the British Isles. In his "History of North Dakota," Elwyn Robinson writes that in 1890, there were 81,461 foreign-born residents of North Dakota, who together with their children made up 69 percent of the state's population. Of those foreign-born, 8,174 came from the British Isles.

The fact that these immigrants did not settle in groups, as did those from other countries, is not surprising. That they already spoke the common language gave them a mobility that immigrants from Scandinavian countries and western and central Europe could only gradually acquire. They found familiar economic and legal systems and thus had much fewer problems adjusting to the new country.

There are interesting stories connected with the immigrants from Great Britain.

Marie Downing gave up a position as maid-in-waiting to Queen Victoria to join her husband, a former butler in the royal household, on a homestead near Rolla. When Mrs. Downing left Windsor Castle, the queen and Empress Eugenie of France saw to it that she was well-supplied with expensive linens, court gowns, jewels and silver. The items may have been somewhat out of place on the prairies, but they provided the Downings with capital to buy more farmland.

Unlike the Marquis deMores, whose ranching operations in western North Dakota failed, John Sutherland Sinclair, seventh Earl of Caithness, ran a successful dairy farm near Lakota in the 1880s before he returned to Scotland. Few of his neighbors knew that he was a Scottish peer with a castle and a seat in the House of Lords.

There was William Budge, a rough Scottish-born land entrepreneur and

The Scottish Caledonian Society of Cavalier County during the late 1800s or early 1900s. Note the ethnic change —these men wore trousers under their kilts.

politician, who became a close friend with the erudite Webster Merrifield, president of the University of North Dakota. When the school's appropriations were vetoed in 1895, Budge led a campaign to privately raise the funds, possibly saving the school.

In the 1870s and '80s, there were a number of Scots in southern Burleigh County and northern Emmons County. In particular, a family named Campbell established a huge cattle and sheep ranch, as well as the town of Kintyre, which was named Campbell before being renamed in honor of the family's Scottish home. Today, about the only reminder of these people is the Glencoe-Sloan Presbyterian Church, about 12 miles southeast of Bismarck. In the cemetery there, a headstone marks the grave of Alexander Campbell, who was born in 1840 in Kintyre, Scotland, and died in 1910 in Kintyre, N.D..

English visitor Mike Casswell and host Bert Berg enjoy dinner of roast beef with Yorkshire pudding.

Perhaps the most colorful of these immigrants was Dennis Hannifin, the "Squatter Governor" of North Dakota, who hailed from County Kerry, Ireland. Hannifin was, to put it mildly, an unusual person.

After distinguished service in the Civil War, Hannifin arrived in Dakota Territory, supporting himself by gambling. Once Bismarck was founded, he opened a saloon, although he was a teetotaler and ardent supporter of prohibition. A caustic wit, Hannifin's commentaries on local and state politics included the following:

"It's all right to have the farmers control the constitutional convention; they controlled the last Legislature, and spent more money than any other Legislature that has ever been held in North Dakota. It is a mistaken idea that people have that farmers are in favor of economy. They want money put in circulation. They are right. Keep it hoarded up and it benefits only one person — the treasurer. Spend it, and all receive the benefits. By gad, sir, the farmers are the philanthropists and the philosophers. Throw the money to the four winds of heaven if you want to do good."

The second group of English/Celtic settlers under consideration are those who came from Canada.

By far, the biggest concentration of what might be termed Anglo-Canadian settlement in North Dakota was in the Red River Valley. The centennial book of the Cass County Historical Society shows a large number of early settlers to be from Canada. Not all, of course, were English/Celtic; many were Scandinavian. Moreover, not all were born in Canada; some had been born in the British Isles and had settled in Canada before coming to this country.

UND history professor Robert Wilkins believes the Scots are the forgotten people of North Dakota. "They were terribly ambitious people with a great feel for business," says Wilkins, adding that from early territorial days to statehood, the influence of the Scots, many of whom came from Canada, could be felt everywhere.

Among the immigrants from Canada was Alexander McKenzie.

Born in 1851 in Ontario, McKenzie arrived in Bismarck in 1873 as a railroad laborer. The next year, he was elected sheriff — the only office he ever held — and engineered the removal of the territorial capital from Yankton, S.D., to Bismarck.

It was only a start for McKenzie. Despite being almost illiterate, he became the political agent for the Northern Pacific and Republican national committeeman for North Dakota. With his power base established, McKenzie went on to almost completely dominate state politics for the next 30 years.

The third group of English/Celtic settlers to come to North Dakota were really Anglo/Americans — native-born Americans of English/Celtic stock.

In 1870, there were 14,181 white inhabitants of Dakota Territory of whom 9,336 were native-born Americans, 1,218 were British and 1,178 were Norwegian. Although it cannot be said conclusively that the majority of those native-born were of English/Celtic stock, it can be supposed such was the case because the majority of Americans at that time were of such background.

Less than a decade later, the first annual directory of Bismarck shows a preponderance of British and Celtic surnames, including many, if not most, of the early community leaders. People such as physician B.F. Slaughter, Tribune publishers Clement Lounsberry and Marshall Jewell, railroad agent Walter Burleigh, attorney Erastus Williams and druggist J.P. Dunn provided a measure of stability in the town's wild youth.

Even Bismarck's best-known prostitute, Little Casino, used the surnames Lewis and McClelland, one of which may have been real.

Early churches provide another indication of Anglo/American settlement. The three oldest Protestant churches in Bismarck were Presbyterian, Episcopal and Methodist — three denominations associated with Great Britain. And St. Mary's Catholic church, now attended largely by people of German descent, originally was almost exclusively Irish. In fact, St. Mary's originally was located at about 200 W. Main Ave., in an area known as "Kerry Patch" because of all the Irish in that particular area.

Because of the Anglo/Americans, North Dakota became more or less similar to the rest of the nation. As UND history professor Playford Thorson put it: "after all, we do speak English."

The effect of the Anglo/Americans continues even today, as traces of other languages and folkways gradually disappear. A generation ago, overhearing a conversation in German or Norwegian in Bismarck was not unusual; now, it is considered an oddity.

Ted Quanrud

Pools and formal gardens of the Peace Gardens reveal British and Canadian influence. Canada had early ties with state through English, Scotch, Welsh, Irish and French settlers.

Joyce Halliwell, Ivy Erhardt and Barbara Grady of Bismarck area British Friendship Club help serve English luncheon including, left to right, butterfly cakes, trifle, scones, sandwiches and pork pies.

French explorers, trappers brought first European culture

The French were the very first to bring European culture to North Dakota. French traditions remain today, but in a diminished fashion.

Oui, it is true that onion soup and pea soup pose no great threat to the popularity of borsch and fleisch kuchla. And lefse is more common here on the plains than croissant. But one must admit that onion soup was here before all the rest.

Recognized as the first white man to visit North Dakota was Pierre Gaultier de Varennes, Sieur de La Verendrye, who had grown up in the

French nobelman Marquis de Mores built this mansion, the Chateau de Mores, in 1883. The same year he established the town of Medora, naming it in honor of his wife.

Three Rivers area of Quebec. He had been given a monopoly on the fur trade in the new country by the king of France, and profits were to support western exploration.

In the early 1730s, La Verendrye and his sons, Francis and Louis, had several trading encampments from Lake Superior to Lake Winnipeg and the Red River. In 1738 he pushed farther west, visiting the Mandan Indians.

There followed in Dakota a long list of French explorers and fur trappers, probably several hundred before the Americans came. We know, for example, that a French man, "Old Man" Menard, lived on the Missouri for over thirty years before Lewis and Clark arrived at the Mandan villages.

But the early French adventurers did not stay.

Thomas Howard, associate professor of history at the University of North Dakota, suggests that the French culture didn't stick because those explorers and trappers were men who came without wives or families.

"This shortage of women meant a shortage of families. And it is the family, above all, that is the greater preserver and transmitter of culture," he says.

Yet the French influence continued in two different ways. The first was the heritage of the numerous French trappers and voyageurs who traveled through Canada and the northern part of the United States in the late 1700s and the early 1800s.

These French men married Indian women who passed on both the native culture and also the culture of their French husbands. Their descendants, primarily in the northern part of the state, are known as the Metis. This blend of Chippewa, Cree and French is the heritage of over ten thousand present-day North Dakotans. The language, food, religion, dances and festivals of the Metis still echo the ways of the Quebec French.

The culture of France persists in a second way. French agriculturalists came from Quebec to homestead in North Dakota in the later half of the 1800s. They were preceeded by missionaries who came to serve the Metis, but also assisted the French families in their first days on the plains.

The missionaries, Thomas Howard suggests, were successful in preserving two aspects of French culture—the French language and the Catholic Church.

Leading the parade of French missionaries was the Rev. George A. Belcourt, a Quebec priest who came in 1848 to the mission of Pembina. He later established churches at St. Joseph (Walhalla) and Leroy. The largest house in the St. Joseph settlement served as a chapel, school and home of the Sisters of the Propagation of the Faith, a religious community of Metis.

Today, French settlements can be found in Cass County (Wild Rice), in Walsh County (Oakwood), in Pembina and Cavalier Counties (Walhalla and Olga), and in the Turtle Mountain area (St. John, Thorne, Willow City).

The best known group, and also the earliest of the farming colonies, began late in the 1860s when French Canadians from the Three Rivers area began to settle at the junction of the Wild Rice and Red rivers, a few miles south of Fargo.

The Holy Cross Mission was founded near that junction in 1870 by the Rev. Jean Baptiste Genin, a Catholic missionary who was born in France and immigrated to Canada in 1860.

Marie Flore Cossette on March 21, 1870, became the first white child born in Cass County. Her parents, Ulphie and Zoe Cossette, had settled in the Holy Cross area about eight months earlier.

Ulphie Cossette had been employed by Hudson's Bay Co. of Winnipeg and made several trips down the Red River as a guide with missionaries before he decided to homestead.

Helping found the settlement were two French-Canadian brothers, Charles and Joseph Sauvageau, who arrived in 1871. There are many descendants of the Cossettes, the Sauvageaus and the other early French-Canadian settlers in the Fargo area.

French Canadians came early to homestead.

Georgiana Denis Rivard was a young girl when she came to the area in 1871. She married at age 15 and told about pioneer hardships in a March 1957 interview with the Fargo Forum.

Her husband had built a small shack to comply with provisions of the Homestead Act. But after taking a bride, he needed a more substantial shelter and she helped with the building of a log cabin.

Rivard recalled filling cracks with a plaster made from buffalo manure gathered from the prairie. "I made our bed," she said. "I took pieces of wood and fastened it together, and I got hay from the prairie and put it over the wood. That was our first mattress."

The couple couldn't afford oxen and farm equipment, and it was two years before they were able to sow and harvest a crop.

Holy Cross Mission became St. Benedict's Parish in 1883, the same year the community of Wild Rice was founded nearby.

St. Benedict's in 1903 came to include St. Joseph's Catholic School and a convent for nuns from the Sister of St. Mary Presentation, a French order. St. Joseph's remained a grade school until the Depression years, when the nuns began offering a high school curriculum for farm youths who could not afford to go elsewhere to school.

In 1964 the high school closed, and the final eighth-grade class graduated two years later. The school building has since been torn down.

Well known also is the Oakwood settlement, which began when a French Canadian group of homesteaders stopped just east of what is now Grafton in Walsh County. The site was later to be named Oakwood.

Joseph Charpentier, who was born in Canada, became the first white settler there in 1874. A mission, later the Sacred Heart Catholic parish, was started in 1880, and by 1906 the Presentation sisters had opened the St. Aloysius Academy, a school operated at Oakwood until 1965.

The Park River furnished good water and the oak trees provided wood for wagon parts and ox yokes. But early times there were also hard, notes Mrs. Frank Byzewski, whose maiden name was Gourde.

Writing for a Walsh County history book, she recalled that the pioneer children were usually barefoot. About adult wearing apparel, she noted that for the men, "overalls were bought but seldom washed as that was to hard on them and a washboard was a difficult job."

The French, she wrote, made use of everything when butchering a hog. "Not a thing was wasted, as the tails and ears were placed in the oven and kids enjoyed chewing on them and they were nice and crisp."

The French in North Dakota have been a quiet people, yet they have every reason to be proud. It was their people who "opened up" the frontier; all the others came later. Their colorful ways still brighten the lives of North Dakota's Turtle Mountain Metis residents. Their humble onion soup may not have the popularity of lefse, but it was the delicacy of the first pioneers.

Holland Dakota land company brought Dutch settlers

Sometimes one wonders why the Dutch, a sea-neighboring people, came to North Dakota, the geographical center of the North American continent.

After all, there were other places to go.

Perhaps it was to get as far away as possible from their battle with the sea.

In any event, 10-year-old John Kuylen was part of the wave of Dutch immigration when he arrived in North Dakota in 1929 with his dad, Alfonse, his mom, Johanna, and his 4-year-old brother, Andy.

For young John, now 63 and living in South Heart with his wife Mary (she's formerly a Kostelecky, of Czech descent), the move was "an adventure."

For his dad, who had grown up on a farm, it was an opportunity to return to farming, leaving behind the non-prescription pharmacy business he had been running in the seaport of Middleburg, Holland.

Perhaps John's most vivid memory of moving to the United States is the boat trip from Holland to Ellis Island.

"It took us seven days, and I was sicker 'n hell the whole way," he recalls.

John and Andy returned to Holland for three months in 1973. That time they flew.

John recalls that his dad's brother, Casey, who lives near Dickinson, had come to North Dakota in 1920.

An enterprise called the Holland Dakota Land Co. owned a lot of land in North Dakota. It in 1908 started convincing young Dutch people to immigrate and farm the company's land.

"These guys, they worked for wages until right about 1935, then they (the company) went broke, and all these individuals got a chance to buy the land, which they did, like my dad," says John.

Casey originally came out to North Dakota through the land company. By the time he talked his brother Alfonse into coming over in 1929, he already owned land.

Casey wrote a letter to Alfonse. "He said you can make here in dollars what you can make there in guilders," John recalls.

At that time, there were about 3/ guilders to the dollar.

So, the Alfonse Kuylen family packed their bags and moved to America.

Immigrant children wear typical Dutch attire of early 1900s. In lower photo, sisters Nellie Stuit and Greta LeFebre of Hettinger drink tea from a Thee Lichtje, tea server with alcohol burner, and delft china brought from Holland, where both sisters were born.

They all lived with Casey in Dickinson for a year, then moved out to the South Heart area in 1930 when Casey got married.

America took a little adjusting to.

"I had a hard time in school at first," John recalls.

Was English difficult to learn?

"You bet it was," he says. "When I first started, I was in the first grade in my English and the fifth grade in my arithmetic, but by my second year it all evened out."

After that, John assimilated pretty well.

Now, the Dutch language is about all he's retained of the old country culture, and he says he's "pretty Americanized."

His mom, who lives nearby, made some Dutch foods, but not a lot of them. Mary, who he married about three years ago, doesn't cook any Dutch specialties.

Greg Turosak

Hot dry '30s not like Holland

There was a time, Gerritt Van Boven says, when he considered leaving the prairies of south central North Dakota. That was in the drought years of the 1930s.

In fact, many people did move off the parched land.

"We didn't have any rain for about 10 years," recalls Van Boven, sitting in his small home in the tiny Dutch community of Hull in southern Emmons County. "We didn't have any harvest in '33 or '34. Then we had a fair crop in 1935 ... we thought it (the drought) was over."

"But in 1936 to 1938, it was drier than ever," he says. For many people, Van Boven says, that meant getting rid of their cattle and moving their horses some 75 miles north for pasturing near Steele.

"Hollanders are noted," says Van Boven, "to never say die. They plug on. They never quit."

That's how they hung on in the '30s, acknowledges Van Boven, the son of a Dutch pioneering family.

At 88, Van Boven sometimes has to lean forward to hear things. He is fragilely thin, but as he speaks, he reveals a mind that nimbly recalls the past.

Van Boven lives in what has been termed the most significant Dutch settlement in North Dakota. According to church records, there were about 500 people of Dutch descent in Emmons and Campbell counties by 1890.

However, the hot, dry prairie was not the ideal spot for people who were accustomed to the more humid climes of Holland. Most Hollanders immigrating to the United States chose locations more akin to the homeland, such as Michigan, New York, Illinois, New Jersey or Iowa.

So it was that John Van Boven, Gerritt's father, went to Michigan when he came to the United States in 1883. But within a year, he headed west, settling in Nebraska.

Led by the promise of land via homesteading, the elder Van Boven came by covered wagon with a group of Hollanders into Dakota Territory in 1886, staying in the Hull area. It was there he met and married Tena Haak, who had come with her parents from Nebraska to Ipswich, in what now is South Dakota.

The couple homesteaded in what is southern Emmons County today, about 10 miles northwest of what became Hull.

However, in 1892 a fire swept over much of the southern county. The Van Bovens lost everything, and they spent that winter with her parents, the Gerritt Haaks.

The Van Bovens hadn't lived on their homestead for the five years required in order to "prove" the claim. And because water was nearly impossible to find on their original site, they decided to establish a new homestead.

What they finally settled on was a parcel about 1½ miles southeast of the Hull community. There John Van Boven built a small wooden shack, put up a sod barn and granary and started breaking the land.

Gerritt Van Boven was born at the homestead Aug. 13, 1893, the second of six children. There were no doctors in the area until about 1912, says Van Boven, so he was born with the help of a midwife.

The first home was a small, two-room shanty, he says. Mattresses were stuffed with straw or corn husks.

But in 1903, the elder Van Boven built a two-story home. "It was a decent home for those days," according to Gerritt.

He started school at age 5. The Dutch pioneers emphasized "schooling," says Van Boven, noting that most immigrants were well-educated. So Van Boven, like other youngsters in the Dutch community, went to school for about six years until he got through his fifth "reader," equivalent to about the eighth-grade level. That was considered a good education in those days, he noted.

Back then, children went to school for six months each year — three months in the fall and three months in the spring, he recalls. For about two years, he and about 15 other children attended school 1½ miles southeast of the homestead.

Later, he went to a school built at Hull, which once boasted a post office, general store and, later, a filling station.

Few traditions were carried over from the old country, according to Van Boven. The pioneers wanted to adopt the ways of the country they were becoming citizens of, he says. His mother, who was born in the United States, always spoke English and his father talked "Yankee-Dutch." Although the children could speak the Hollander language, "we always talked English," says Van Boven.

His father raised flax on the newly broken land and later wheat, corn and other grain. For many years, people hauled their grain to Eureka, S.D., which was a two-day trip with a team of two horses hauling perhaps 50 bushels of wheat, he says. Later, those trips were made to Herreid, S.D., as the railroad was extended closer.

In those early years, some Hollanders grew disillusioned with the area and decided to move to a more humid climate such as Washington state, says Van Boven. "There was a lot of land for sale when I was a boy," he recalls.

Life centered around the family, visiting neighbors and the church. The first church to serve that Dutch community, Hope Reformed, was built in Westfield about 1886, followed shortly by the Christian Reformed at Hull. The major denominations, Dutch Reformed or Christian Reformed, are Calvinist and, thus, tended to be conservative about dancing, card playing, drinking, working on Sunday and other similar matters.

Ministers were available only occasionally during the early years, says Van Boven. Often, people within the community would lead services.

The Hollanders didn't arrange marriages, as the Germans did, Van Boven told an interviewer with the State Historical Society. "My grandfather said that in Holland you couldn't marry out of a class," he said. "One of the great things in America is you could find your own girl."

Hollanders in America "saw that freedom," he chuckled, "and enjoyed that freedom." As wedding presents, the girl's parents usually gave a milk cow and some chickens, while the man's parents generally donated a team of horses and some machinery.

Although weddings were a big social event, wedding dances were not, probably because of the religious restrictions.

Van Boven moved off the home farm when he was 22 and married Anna Dornbush, whose parents lived just southwest of Hull. Their wedding was simple, says Van Boven. The couple moved to a farm outside Hull, farming there and raising five children, two of whom died.

His son, Dennis, took over the family farm in 1954 when Van Boven and his wife moved into Hull. Anna Von Boven died in 1973.

Stan Stelter

Neat, well-kept farms

South of Strasburg the route passes through territory settled by Hollanders, and the landscape is dotted with their neat, well-kept farms. Although many of them are American-born, the native tongue is retained in their homes. The Dutch Reformed Church forms the focal point in their communities; many of their children attend college at Holland, Michigan, and members of the settlement annually go to Michigan for the Holland Tulip Festival. Hague, named for The Hague in the Netherlands, is one of the market towns for the Dutch settlements, although its population is principally Russo-German.

North Dakota Federal Writers' Project, 1938

Ukrainians started out simply

Pete Basaraba was 7 years old when his parents escaped from under the thumb of the Austrian Empire in the western Ukraine.

The year was 1902.

When Basaraba's parents arrived in Belfield, the family of seven stayed with friends for two weeks — 10 people in a two-room house — until their host needed more room for members of his own family who soon would arrive from the old country.

So, the Basarabas walked 10 miles each day to their homestead, where they cut 2-foot-square chunks out of the prairie to build a sod house. Each night as they walked back to Belfield, they kept an eye on a hill with a rough log cross on top, which served as a landmark for early settlers so they wouldn't become lost among the endless hills and gullies of Billings County.

When they were building their sod house, Basaraba relates in a heavy accent, "everything was open and there were wild longhorn cattle roaming (near) the big springs north of there. We built the house about 2 feet high in one day and when we came back the next day, we saw the cattle had tore it out."

To prevent damage, the Basarabas began to live in the sod house before it was finished. One night while his father was in Belfield, the cattle came back. "My mother drove them off with her coat by flapping it on the ground. We chased those cattle about a mile when they turned around and started chasing us. I ran away, and my mother was frightened. She kept yelling, 'Don't leave me; don't leave me.'"

They survived that incident and many others, like "mosquitoes so bad if you opened your mouth, you got it plumb filled up."

All the Basarabas had to use in their farming operation was a plow, a wagon and a horse. To help make ends meet, his father, like many others, gathered firewood from the Badlands and hauled it 50 miles to Dickinson. Three days' work netted $1.50.

Basaraba had to quit school at 12 to help out on the farm. During the ensuing years he experienced drought, black rust that killed the wheat crop and a bout with the Spanish Flu epidemic of 1918-1919 that killed 2,971 North Dakotans.

Basaraba's story is repeated again and again by other Ukrainian pioneers — like John and Catherine Fedora, who started out their married life by living in a hole that John had dug in the ground and covered with brush. Or by John Struchynski, who took over the family farm at the age of 14 when his father died of pneumonia.

Basaraba, at 87, half laughs: "We came from the bad and came to the worse. If you ever have it as bad as we did, then you'll know something."

But Basaraba survived and prospered as did some 10,000 Ukrainians who eventually populated the state.

The first group of Ukrainians came to western North Dakota in 1896, to farm and ranch in Billings and Stark counties. There they founded the towns of Ukraina and Gorham and moved into Belfield. They also lived in Grassy Butte and Mary in McKenzie County and Oakdale in Dunn County and in Sheridan County.

In 1897, a group came to Wilton along the Missouri River to mine lignite coal, work they still carry out for "coal country's" electric generating plants.

In 1899, a third group founded Ruso, Kief and Kongsberg, to raise crops along the Soo Line tracks of central North Dakota. They also settled in the towns of Drake, Harvey, Benedict, Max, Douglas, Ryder, Makoti and Balfour in McLean, McHenry, Wells and Ward counties.

Individual Ukrainian farmers also migrated north from Fargo to Pembina along the Northern Pacific tracks to farm the rich loam of the Red River Valley of the North.

Economic problems, land shortages and religious and cultural persecution figured prominently in the migration of Ukrainians to North Dakota.

Agnes Palanuk, executive director of the Ukrainian Cultural Institute, in "The Ukrainians in North Dakota," based on her interviews of early settlers, wrote that the Russian czar was determined to stamp out the culture of Ukrainians in the eastern or Great Ukraine.

He attempted to end the Ukrainian Catholic and Ukrainian Orthodox Churches — the hub of Ukrainian cultural and social life — and absorb them into the Russian Orthodox church.

He forbade the publication and writing of books and materials in the Ukrainian language and ordered Russian taught in the schools.

In 1876, a "ukaze," or proclamation, issued by the czar pronounced that, "There never was, there is not and there never will be a Ukrainian language."

Other immigrants, like Basaraba, came from the Western Ukraine, part of the Austrian Empire. They saw their culture suffer because Austrians and Poles attempted to deny them schooling.

Most of the land was owned by aristocrats. In Struchynski's case, his father was a serf to a "pananier" — a Polish aristocrat who paid him $20 a year and gave him "a little grain, wood and wheat."

Basaraba recalls that his father did own some land. "My dad had 20 morga. Each morga was about 1 acre. He had 10 kids, too — no one would have had anything when he gave it to the kids."

Despite — or because of — the hardships they left behind and then overcame in their new home in North Dakota, the Ukrainian community is one of the most culturally intact in North Dakota.

Because of its rural nature, Belfield and those Ukrainians who moved to Dickinson from the Belfield area have retained many of their customs and traditions, Palanuk believes.

Ted Pedeliski, a Belfield Ukrainian and an associate professor of political science at the University of North Dakota, says, "Religion plays a tremendous role in maintaining their uniqueness in all of these Slavic communities. The Ukrainians have survived the most intact," because of their strong ties to their Ukrainian Catholic and Ukrainian Orthodox churches, Pedeliski says.

He notes that churches are a strong link to retaining the customs of a people. When the Ukrainians north of Bismarck went to the Baptist and Seventh-day Adventist churches, they began blending with the general population, according to

Pedeliski, and lost some of their cultural traditions.

There have been many successful attempts by the Ukrainian Cultural Institute, formed less than two years ago, to inform and to sponsor classes in dance, Easter egg decorating, woodcarving, embroidery and language to perpetuate the traditions.

Additionally, a children's dance group in Belfield, the Veselka (Rainbow) Dancers, was formed two years ago to replace a similar dance group that was disbanded.

The advances in Ukrainian cultural activities have been helped by a turn-around among Ukrainians, who, after three generations of shaking off the effects of discrimination and russification, are exhibiting a strong pride in their culture, Palanuk says.

The Ukrainians who came to North Dakota between 1890 and 1912 in the first of three waves ripped up their roots completely, Pedeliski says.

They left a country of beautiful villages and fruit trees to settle into a difficult life of taming the marginal lands that earlier settlers had avoided. Many began to blend into the American scene immediately. Present-day Ukrainians recall that many of the immigrants tried to leave the vestiges of the old country behind.

Many Ukrainians eventually left the soil and raised their children to become professional people, according to Wasyl Halich, who wrote "Ukrainians in North Dakota" for North Dakota History in 1951.

After World War I, there was a second wave of immigrants escaping the collapse of Russia. Immigrants after World War II were mostly professionals and few came to the farm communities of North Dakota.

Those Ukrainians who kept the traditions — the farm families — began to see some erosion of the culture after World War II. "(It) kind of broke the parochialism of a lot of these communities because the boys went out and saw the world," Pedeliski says. After the war, there was more intermarriage with people outside the community.

And many of the settlers began to retire from the farms in the late 1940s. That led to the end of Ukraina, Gorham, Mary and Oakdale, whose settlers moved to Belfield and Dickinson, and to the end of Kongsberg in McHenry County.

Mark Kinders

George and Julia keep lifestyle despite oil wells

It was a little more than 70 years ago that George Hurinenko's parents sat huddled around their fire within a semicircle of grain sacks on the land they had just come to settle.

George's dad — Artem — had the seeds and assorted tools so he could get the first crop in during the late spring of 1910.

At the time, George's mother, Irene, was pregnant with George, their third child.

Together, Artem and Irene, Ukrainian immigrants from the Kiev area, would build their sod house during the next two weeks.

"It was a one-room sod house," recalls George, a rotund person like his wife, Julia.

George grins as he relaxes in his kitchen chair to tell the story; he likes to talk.

"That's the only place they had to live. It was one room at first, and they built some more on later."

Soon the family had a home, but all was not cushy.

"The buffalo were here banging into the sod house with their horns," says George, "trying to get rid of the house."

"And the coyotes and wolves; there were hordes of them here.

"I got up one morning — on that hill east of our place, and there was about 500 wolves there waiting to eat," says George.

"Well, maybe not that many," corrects Julia, an equally jovial person who speaks with a distinct Ukrainian accent, like Natasha of Boris and Natasha in the Rocky and Bullwinkle cartoons. "But they roamed in packs."

George appears not to mind being interrupted or contradicted.

George and Julia have really started talking now, and it'll be a while before the visitor will be able to wind down the conversation.

They'll talk expressively and openly about almost anything — their lives, their farm, their family, their Ukrainian culture.

Julia, a "Romanyshyn" by birth, married George in 1936. Julia's folks farmed about nine miles south of the Hurinenko homestead. Her ancestors also are from the Ukraine, but from farther west than George's ancestors.

George returns the conversation to the early days.

"When I was 5 years old, I was dragging the horses over the field. We had oxen at first, two oxen."

That's what they used to break land on the homestead, the two oxen.

"They could pull a gangplow like nothin', those boys."

Farming was hard work.

"Oh, the people worked hard then. Oh, they worked hard," doing everything they could to improve the land. "They worked it over and over again to get something out of it.

"I work the Ukrainian way. I work for two men all the time ... twice as hard, and it don't bother me."

George bought out his dad's farm in the 1940s. Over the years they've had a diversified farming operation — cattle, pigs, turkeys, horses, hay, wheat, oats, corn, flax, "just whatever we could raise, you know, to make something out of it."

George and Julia now have 1,500 acres.

Did they live well?

"Oh, yes, we thought we did," says George. "We couldn't complain in the '30s. People were eating cats in St. Paul and Chicago, and we were eating beefsteak here. We had plenty to eat."

The couple pretty much retired from farming in the mid-1970s and were enjoying the peace and quiet when the oil industry moved in during 1976 and 1977.

The farm now sits in the middle of the prolific Little Knife Oil Field; they have nine wells on their land.

They've gotten plenty of royalty money, but they really didn't need it.

However, they had no choice about oil development.

"We couldn't help it," says George. "We had it leased years before," for a dime an acre.

"It spoils the farmland," says Julia.

All around their farmstead are wells, roads and activity. A couple miles southwest, over a ridge of hills, lies Western's natural gas processing plant.

"Four years ago, there was nothing but pasture there, cattle. Now it's like a city," says Julia.

Greg Turosak

Away from the army and into the mines

Nick Sologuk was ready to go back to the Ukraine after the first day he worked in Wilton Mine No. 1 in 1911.

Sologuk, who was 19 at the time, had immigrated to the United States to avoid being drafted into the army of the Austro-Hungarian Empire, which occupied his homeland of the western Ukraine.

Now, at the age of 90, he, along with his wife, Anna, 82, can lean back and laugh about the rougher days of their early life, and their luck in riding out the storms.

They are "Americanized" in a comfortable retirement in their neat, three-bedroom frame house in Wilton.

But there is a sense of regret at the good things that were sacrificed to hard times: lost relationships between friends and family, lost ties to cultural traditions.

Unlike the modern strip mines, these mines had shafts through which lignite was harvested.

It was darker than night working under the ground in a vein so thick that the shaft was large enough to stand up in.

Sologuk and the 450 other Ukrainians who manned two 10-hour shifts six days a week found their way around by the light of a carbide lamp attached to a hatband. "All you could see was what was in front of you. Everything else was black," Sologuk says.

The clinging filth of coal dust was ever present, he recalls. There was a room for washing at the mine, where the miners would switch from street clothes to the dust-crusted clothing they wore during their work.

The conditions left their impression on Sologuk the very first day: no additional pay for working in water, the brute manual labor, frequent injuries and continuous pressure to keep working. He began to think that barracks life in the army might not have been so bad after all.

"Boy, I wished I was back in the old country. Did we ever get dirty, yi, yi, yi," he says with a laugh as he shakes his head.

The pay was 20 cents an hour for a 10-hour shift. The scale in 1911 was more than his father-in-law, John

Irena Iwaniw, an immigrant from the Ukraine, lights a votive candle before shrine in the Ukrainian Catholic church in Wilton.

Young Ukrainians in Belfield-Dickinson area learn folk dancing. Traditionally beginners wore a single flower with ribbons in the hair; teenage girls wore full flower headpieces.

Babnick, got when he started work in 1901 — 50 cents a day.

But the Sologuks recall that things got better in 1918 when John L. Lewis arrived to enroll the miners in the ranks of the United Mine Workers. The pay went up and an eight-hour, five-day week was instituted. Miners who had to work in water got extra pay, too.

Sologuk loaded coal and operated a cutting machine for 19 years before the mine was sold to Traux-Traer Coal Co. in 1931.

Like almost 200 other miners, he lost his job when the new owners converted the shaft mine into a strip-mining operation.

There were hard feelings about the switch. According to historical accounts, some of those who were involved in making the equipment switchover were waylaid and beaten at night in an alley.

The death of the shaft operations signaled the beginning of the end of the Ukrainian community in Wilton.

The Sologuks went into a farming operation about 4½ miles northwest of Wilton, near the Missouri River. It was a small operation of about 300 acres.

It wasn't like the early days, when Anna's parents first homesteaded with other Ukrainians north of town.

Back in 1897 they didn't have anything, "just the clothes on our backs." But there were kind neighbors who would give them a horse or a cow to be paid for when they could manage, Anna says.

The Dirty '30s were a different story. "In 1931 we didn't have a crop," Sologuk recalls. "It was a real hard time. For seven years we got nothing."

"We made a living," Anna says. But because they had only three children — Harry, Alice and Stephanie — they didn't receive the government commodities given other families.

Until the '30s, there was a vibrant Ukrainian community at Wilton, Anna says. There were regular church services in both the Ukrainian Catholic and Ukrainian Orthodox churches. There was a Ukrainian newspaper, a dance group of adults and children and Ukrainian language plays.

Family traditions were kept, too. For instance, many bachelors in Wilton traveled to the Ukrainian community of Belfield, some 150 miles away, to find a wife.

"Back then they married their own," Sologuk says. "Everything had to be Ukrainian."

Anna adds that "a lot of them just barely learned to talk English."

When the loss of mining jobs and the Depression caused the economy to collapse in Wilton, things changed, Anna says.

"Some went to farm, but a lot of others moved away. The years were so hard, you couldn't do nothing, and the kids couldn't do nothing. There weren't any jobs."

The Sologuks weathered the 1930s and stayed on their farmstead for 29 years before retiring.

Their children left for Fargo, Bismarck and California, though, because there wasn't enough work to keep them in Wilton, Anna adds.

Saint Peter and Paul Ukrainian Catholic church still conducts weekly services attended by about 40 people. The pastor, the Rev. George Pruys, also serves congregations in Bismarck and Minot.

There is only a handful of Orthodox Ukrainians in the town and their church is used only for weddings and funerals, although it is kept in good shape, Anna says.

The Sologuks still keep many of the Ukrainian traditions. They display pysanky — decorative Easter eggs — in their living room. Among the family portraits on the wall is a print of St. Nicholas, the Santa Claus of Ukrainians. Newsletters from the Ukrainian Cultural Institute, operated out of Dickinson State College, are kept on a living room end table.

And Sologuk still corresponds with his cousins in the Ukraine.

But there are few cultural activities organized within the community on a continuing basis.

"You have to have somebody push it," Anna says. "It has to be the younger ones who want to push it. Out in Belfield they have a lot more Ukrainians to keep up the traditions. A lot of them stay because they have oil wells. They're rich when they get that oil, so the sons can stay and help their fathers ranch."

Mark Kinders

Czechs commonly termed Bohemian in North Dakota

For those who wonder who Bohemians are, it first is necessary to explain who they aren't.

They aren't bohemians.

The bohemians, spelled with a small "b," are thought of as gypsies or vagabonds. Further, says the dictionary, they often are followers of art or literature who have unconventional, easygoing and sometimes eccentric lifestyles.

The Bohemians, on the other hand, are natives of the land of Bohemia or descendants of natives of Bohemia.

"Maybe I am a gypsy," jokes the Rev. Ladislaus Brydl (pronounced "briddle"), 78, a full-blooded Bohemian from New Hradec. However, Brydl has lived in New Hradec, and has been priest of his hometown Saints Peter and Paul Catholic Church for 48 years. He's hardly a gypsy.

Folks he knows don't usually mistake Bohemians for bohemians, he says. "They don't connect the two," he notes.

"It's really not fair," being mistaken for a bohemian when you're a Bohemian, says Albert Ficek (pronounced "FEE-tcheck"), also of New Hradec. "I don't know where they came up with that," he adds. "Gypsies were mostly from Hungary," he says. "Of course, they traveled through Czechoslovakia ..."

Nowadays, to avoid confusion between Bohemians and bohemians, Bohemians usually are called "Czechoslovaks" or "Czechs," according to reference books. However, the term "Bohemian" still is commonly used in North Dakota.

Most of the Bohemians in the state live in the New Hradec-Dickinson area of the southwest and in the Pisek ("PEA-zek") and Lankin area of the northeast.

Brydl, Ficek and other southwestern North Dakota Bohemians are descendants of Bohemians who lived in the Crimea of Russia for about 20 years before coming to American. Brydl was even born in Russia.

Ancestors of the northeastern Bohemians, however, came directly to America from Bohemia or from Moravia, according to Agnes Jelinek ("yeh-LEE-nek"), rural Pisek.

Some of the Pisek area Czechs are Moravians, including her husband's family, Jelinek notes, but folks of Czech descent in that area are usually called Bohemians whether their forefathers came from Bohemia or Moravia, she says.

Moravia is Bohemia's sister province in Czechoslovakia today.

Folks familiar with the Fargo area also may be familiar with the six Moravian churches in Cass County, but the religion is not to be confused with the ethnic group, says the Rev. Jim Hicks, pastor of Fargo Moravian Church.

"(Our) Moravians aren't in any way an ethnic group," says Hicks. "We're a mainline protestant church," which originated in Moravia and Bohemia as a breakaway from the Roman Catholic Church, he adds. "Most of our people are of German descent," he says.

Many older Bohemians in the state still speak their native language.

"If you were poor —in Bohemia—you stayed poor."

Like other Slavic languages, the Czech language is noted for its rolled r's. The letter "c" is pronounced "ch." And there are no q's, x's or w's in the Czech alphabet, according to R.F. "Pete" Matejcek ("MAT-a-check"), Lankin. If those three letters are used in Czech names or words today, he says, it's because someone added them in America.

Walsh County, home of Pisek and Lankin, is easily the Bohemian capital of North Dakota. Walsh County has hundreds more Bohemians than any other county, and Bohemians outnumber all other nationalities in that county.

Stark County, which contains Dickinson, and Dunn County, where New Hradec is located, follow Walsh in numbers of Bohemians. There are smaller groups of people of Bohemian descent south of Mandan and in Mountrail, Nelson, and Richland counties.

The first Czechs to sail to America during the late 1800s fled crowded localities and poor farming conditions in Europe to pursue lives of freedom in the land of plenty.

"Conditions were bad under the Austro-Hungarian Empire (which dominated Bohemia and neighboring lands) until World War I," says Ficek. The poor had little chance of ever owning their own land in their country. In addition to the crowding and poor farming conditions, many of the Bohemians who left their homeland "had to work for the barons and elite ... those that owned a lot of land," Ficek notes.

Charles Kottsick, Mandan, notes, "If you were poor there, you stayed poor."

And, "There was a time during the Hapsburg Dynasty when they weren't allowed to talk the Czech language," Ficek says. Those who spoke Czech were punished.

After arriving in America, they soon discovered that a life of freedom isn't necessarily a life of leisure. Far from it.

Prairie fires were a major concern, and many lives were lost battling them. Walsh Heritage, a four-volume history of Walsh County, tells of a young Bohemian woman with two small children who died fighting to save the family farm while her husband was in Grand Forks signing homestead claims on the property.

Large families were the norm — and another common worry on the prairie was the small children getting lost in tall grass. While those in the family old enough to work worked, small children sometimes wandered away from the house, only to fall asleep somewhere in the grass at naptime. A search party then had to be formed to comb the area.

"Those were lean years," says Joe Kolar, 93. "Wheat was 25 cents a bushel. Nobody had money to buy anything. Everything was on credit." Kolar managed his Pisek butcher shop's bookkeeping even though, like many of the early pioneers whose education was limited, he never went beyond first grade in school.

"I learned by myself from reading the papers," he says.

Those were the days, says Kolar, when folks lived on the many Bohemian foods that have become delicacies today, including kolache ("Ko-LAW-cheh"), which is bun dough filled with prunes, poppy seed or apricots; rohleky ("RRROH-lee-kee"), or crescent rolls; knedleky ("KNED-lee-kee"), dumplings; vomacka ("vo-MOCH-ka"), gravy; and jiternice ("YEE-therrr-nye-tse"), sausage made from pig head meat.

Jelinek notes, "You have to grow up with them" to fully appreciate the taste of Bohemian foods.

Most of these recipes brought from Czechoslovakia include simple ingredients, for in those days exotic ingredients were not available for cooking.

Bohemian dishes take much longer to prepare than today's convenience foods, according to one Bohemian. Thus they are treats popular when relatives gather for holidays.

Bohemians who moved to America didn't forget their religious faith, as is evidenced by several Catholic churches dotting the countrysides of Bohemian settlements. Mass was said in people's homes by visiting priests until the first churches were built.

St. Luke's Catholic Church, the first Catholic Church in Walsh County, was built in 1881 by a group of Bohemians from Spillville, Iowa. The church is located at Veseleyville, a tiny community a few miles east of Pisek. Veseleyville, like Pisek and New Hradec, is named after a town in Czechoslovakia.

Similar Bohemian parishes were established elsewhere, including Saints. Peter and Paul Catholic Church, New Hradec, and Saints. Peter and Paul Catholic Church, Bechyne. Bechyne, named after a pilgrimage in Bohemia, is near Lankin.

Another Bohemian parish, St. John Nepomucene Catholic Church, Pisek, received national recognition in the 1960s when an old painting found in the church was discovered to be worth $25,000.

The painting of Saints Cyril and Methodius was painted by Alphons Mucha ("MOO-ka"), a now-famous Czechoslovakian artist. Mucha's cousin, Frank P. Rumreich, one of the first Pisek settlers, commissioned Mucha to do the painting in the 1880s.

When Czechoslovakia became a nation after World War I, Mucha designed its first currency and stamps, according to a booklet about the Pisek painting written by Faith Chyle Knutsen, George Chyle's daughter. And after his death in 1939, Mucha was widely acclaimed for his works of art nouveau.

Then in the '60s, a visiting priest discovered the Pisek painting (which, incidentally, is not painted in the art nouveau style) and recognized it to be the work of Mucha.

Celebrations, consisting of Mass, dinner and dancing in honor of the church patron saints were popular in the Bohemian churches and still are well-attended in some areas, according to several Bohemians.

In recent years, the church at Bechyne has celebrated a "polka Mass" on June 29, the feast day of Saints Peter and Paul. During the Mass, instead of singing traditional church hymns, the congregation sings religious words to the tunes of familiar songs. The songs, accompanied by accordion music played in polka and waltz tempos.

Dances, with music provided by

Czech-language plays were frequently presented in New Hradec hall, as this one, "Vesnicka Pod Lipama," was in 1942.

Father Brydl burns leaves by Saints Peter and Paul Catholic Church in New Hradec. At left, a church alcove.

the popular Bohemian orchestras, commonly are held at Catholic Workman (Katolicky Delnik) and ZCBJ (Zapadni Cesko-Bratske Jednoty or Western Bohemian Fraternal Association) halls located near the churches.

Not all of the Bohemians who arrived in America were Catholics.

"A lot of free thinkers came over," says Matejcek. Those who moved to areas like Lankin and Bechyne who were not Catholic established their own ZCBJ lodges, including their own dance halls and cemeteries, that were not affiliated with a church.

Kosobud Hall, located a few miles from Bechyne, is an example of such a lodge.

Another lodge of this type is located south of Mandan. The ZCBJ Lodge and cemetery there were begun by a group of about 25 Bohemian families in that area, according to Kottsick, a Bohemian who once farmed south of Mandan.

"We had some rough parties there," Kottsick recalls with a chuckle. During Prohibition days, many a dance at the hall was highlighted by moonshine, Kottsick says. Moonshine stills, though well-hidden, were common on several farms and "many of the poorer neighbors made their living that way" for a time, he says.

Matejcek says Bohemian dances at Lankin and Bechyne lasted longer than they do now.

"It used to be they danced till the bride's dress wore out," he jokes.

Much has changed in the lives of North Dakota's older-generation Bohemians.

The small Bohemian towns like New Hradec, Pisek and Lankin — "retirement towns," as Matejcek calls them — continue to shrink, and younger generations keep marrying people of other nationalities, says Kottsick.

"We have seven children and only one of them married a Bohemian," he notes, with a touch of regret in his voice.

The old Bohemian traditions, the customs, "a lot of that is passing away with the younger generations," says Bob Bezdicek ("BEZ-dgi-check"), a New Hradec area Bohemian.

Young generations cannot speak the language and Czech probably never will be among foreign language courses offered in colleges and universities because "we're such a minority as far as population goes," says Swartz.

Many Bohemians feel their children, stirred into the potpourri of Americanism, are missing out on something.

"We're not doing enough to preserve our heritage," says Swartz.

Patricia Fix

Farming part of his Bohemian heritage

His hands are gnarled from 40 years of tilling the soil.

One finger is twisted at the knuckle, a testimony to a past injury; blood-blackened fingernails attest to more recent mishaps.

They are the hands of a farmer, Albert Ficek, who, with his wife Lillian, works 1,600 acres of land three miles southeast of New Hradec, in Stark County.

Ficek is a man of average build. His hair is silver and thinning, and he walks with a stooped gait. But his handshake is firm and strong at 71, the legacy of working long, rough hours tending cattle and raising grain.

Ficek was born to be a farmer. He says farming is his heritage as a Czechoslovakian whose ancestors plowed the plains of Bohemia.

He proudly adds that Czechs were always meant to be farmers. Now his son, Delmar, a graduate of Dickinson State College, is taking over the family operation. "He's the fourth generation" on this chunk of land 12 miles north of Dickinson, Ficek says with a grin.

Ficek's ancestors grew up in the plains south of the Carpathian mountains, in towns named Chruden, Hradec, Oesha, and Trebova Svitavy.

Some began to migrate to the United States in the 1860s because of "hard times" and settled in Minnesota, Texas and Missouri.

Ficek's grandparents headed in

Lillian and Albert Ficek stand on step where Albert used to sit as a child with his grandfather. Farmhouse was built in 1909.

another direction — they walked 800 miles through the mountains and into the plains of Crimea to settle land promised them by the Russian czar, who recently had won it from the Turks.

Most of the land was already occupied by Germans and the Czechs stayed only 20 or 30 years.

The Czechs weren't persecuted for their Catholic religion, as were those of other denominations.

But, "They were quite dissatisfied because of hard winters, and the crops weren't good," Ficek says.

"And they were disappointed in the Russian culture. The Czechs left partly because they were afraid they were losing their intelligence as a whole, because Russia was backward and isolated."

The first group traveled back to Czechoslovakia and then east to the Atlantic. They eventually ended up in Aberdeen, S.D., in 1886. Some of them followed the Missouri River north until they reached Bismarck, where they were told of free land near Dickinson.

Agents for the Northern Pacific railroad took the farmers around by buggy and showed them an area that reminded them of the terrain around the town of Hradec — Castle — in the old country.

The next year, the railroad extended through most of the state, and more Czechs arrived to stay with the first four or five families until they could build homes of their own.

Mrs. Ficek's grandparents, the Urbanecs, came to New Hradec from South Dakota in 1886 in the first batch of settlers and were sheep ranchers.

Ficek's grandfather and family came here in 1891.

In 1898, the Bohemians built their first church at New Hradec, and at its peak, New Hradec boasted about 300 residents.

At one time there were many traditional activities in the town. Ficek recalls that in the 1920s Czech plays were put on regularly in the town. And in 1948, when the church celebrated its 50th anniversary, a commemorative publication outlining the history of the church and the town was written and printed in the Czechoslovakian language.

Now there are about 100 residents, Ficek says, because farms are getting bigger, some residents have died and some left during the Depression.

Ficek notes that most Czechs disappeared into the great American melting pot and few customs are left in the New Hradec area, although many of the older farmers still speak Czech, he adds.

"Some of the customs were kept. But we were so glad we were American we didn't try to preserve as much as we could have. Some of the early settlers didn't even want to talk about their lives in the old country. That's why so much has been lost."

Ficek recalls that when he was a boy, he would be disciplined by his teacher at the one-room schoolhouse near New Hradec if he spoke Czech. "My Dad never talked English, so we spoke Czech at home. My mother thought it was great that I was punished for not speaking English because she wanted us to get ahead."

Ficek notes the younger generation is beginning to show a greater interest in the Czech culture. He believes it tied to a national resurgence and interest in all ethnic cultures.

Czech members of Saints Peter and Paul Catholic Church in New Hradec still sing traditional Christmas carols, he notes. Traditional songs are used at Easter and for funerals, as well. There was a Czech singing group in the town, but it recently disbanded, Ficek notes.

These days, "We're trying to preserve as much as we can and it's an uphill fight. No one wants to be the leader. Czechs are an independent people and we are hard to organize.

"But I hope it will be a little better from now on," he adds.

Mark Kinders

Warsaw centered on church

St. Stanislaus Catholic Church, Warsaw, is often called the "cathedral of the prairie."

"Have you seen the church?"

That's what the folks of Warsaw, a small Polish village north of Grand Forks, always ask visitors.

They're referring to St. Stanislaus Catholic Church, a majestic brick structure that's been keeping pious vigil over Warsaw and the surrounding Walsh County countryside for more than 80 years. Its steeple is visible for miles.

The 80-some citizens of Warsaw and all of the predominantly Polish St. Stanislaus parishioners are understandably proud of their church.

It's an ever-present symbol of the deep religious convictions and determination of the Polish people who settled the area, say the townspeople.

Often called "the cathedral of the prairie," St. Stanislaus once seated 1,100 people and is one of the largest rural churches in the state.

It's listed in the National Register of Historic Places. And the church is still "the center of everything," in the community, says Walter Gerszewski, Warsaw, whose grandfather first broke ground on the Gerszewski homestead near Warsaw in 1878.

Warsaw itself never incorporated as a city and is not on the map. The town was first called Pulaski in honor of Casimir Pulaski, a famous Polish patriot and hero of the American Revolution. But its name was changed to New Warsaw and then to Warsaw after a post office was established in 1894, according to Ed Gudajtes, Minto, whose father, Anton Gudajtes, was one of Warsaw's founding fathers.

The deeply religious Roman Catholics first built a small church in the area, but in 1896 a priest named Gawlowicz arrived with the dream of building "a church that the people would be proud of and that would be an inspiration to them," according to Walsh Heritage, a four-volume history of Walsh County. So the present-day St. Stanislaus Church — named for the Polish bishop and martyr — was built in 1900.

"It cost $50,000 and was completely paid for when it was dedicated in July of 1901," says the Rev. Stanislaus Duda, a full-blooded Pole who has been priest there since 1976. Church dedication ceremonies drew 50 priests to take part in the festivities and 4,000 spectators.

Duda notes that, monetarily, the church, with its huge pillars, paintings and stained glass windows, today is worth more than 20 times what it cost to build.

But, more importantly, the church is worth more than any money in the hearts of the people who learned their catechisms there, who were married there, and who have prayed there all of their lives.

Their devotion was evidenced in 1978, when an October fire caused considerable damage to the church's interior and roof, says Duda. While men of the parish helped firemen put out the blaze, women gathered around an outdoor altar and prayed, sang hymns and wept.

The fire damage exceeded $400,000, but the church has since been rebuilt to its former splendor.

The history of the Polish people is a lesson in political and religious oppression.

Poland ceased to exist as a country for about 100 years after Austria, Prussia and Russia partitioned it at the end of the 18th century. After unsuccessful Polish revolutions against the powers in the mid-1800s, anti-Polish and anti-Catholic policies were invoked. The use of the Polish language and the establishment of Polish societies were prohibited.

And Polish lads of military age were at one time required to serve four years in German armies, according to Gerszewski, 71, whose grandfather and many others like him came to America to avoid service in a foreign army.

"About that time the U.S. government passed the Homestead Act," says Gerszewski. "That was a great deal for them."

Thus began a mass migration of about 3 million Poles to the United States.

In North Dakota, most of the Polish immigrants settled in and around Warsaw, which is five miles east of Minto, a town of 600 people today.

A smaller group of Polish families established themselves at Geneseo, today a town of about 70 people near Lidgerwood and Hankinson in southeastern North Dakota.

Some of the ancestors of the Geneseo Poles lived in Pittsburgh, Pa., before moving to the Geneseo area, says Tom Kaczynski, rural Geneseo, who farms the land his grandfather did.

Louis Siemienieski, rural Geneseo, like many of the people in his area, is part Polish and part German. A number of Germans also live in the Geneseo area.

Warsaw folks, however, tended to intermarry with Bohemians, since many Bohemians settled in Walsh County.

Full-blooded Poles may be fewer and fewer, but Polish traditions have not fallen by the wayside.

For instance, St. Stanislaus Church's Polish choir, which still sings Polish hymns, is going strong at Warsaw, says Gudajtes.

"People that have settled in neighboring towns come back home to hear the singing," he says.

And Warsaw has an active Polish National Alliance group that's keeping alive Polish dancing and other traditions.

Of course, one of the best ways to keep abreast of history is to talk to the senior citizens.

Katie Misialek, 104, Grafton, a Polish wife and mother, spent 63 years on the farm in Walsh County. She'll say it wasn't easy raising her 11 children; that life in the old days was "mostly hard work and no money."

Stephanie Prepiora, Minto, reminisces that her mother and another pioneer woman in the Minto area proved a homestead claim all by themselves, before her mother and father were married.

"She was really something else," she says. Prepiora's mother, a first cousin of the priest involved in the building of St. Stanislaus Church, came to America to be the priest's housekeeper.

The family name used to be Przepiora.

"My name had a 'z' in it, but I dropped it," she says. "It's hard enough without hauling that 'z' around."

Prepiora, curator of the Walsh County Historical Museum, Minto, says the museum annually holds "Museum Alive Day," with live demonstrations and exhibits of old-time ways. During the event, Polish women make and distribute samples of noodles and other ethnic fare.

"There's a tremendous amount of history here," she says of the museum.

Warsaw was saddened in 1969 by the closing of St. Anthony Academy, a grade school where nuns taught Polish customs, Polish language and Catholic religion in addition to the three R's.

"I remember when the sisters first came to Warsaw in 1919," says Gudajtes, a St. Anthony's graduate. He says the parents of the community were "all smiles, because (the nuns) would be teaching religion and preserving the Polish tradition."

The four-story academy was built in 1920 and run by the Sisters of Resurrection. It was a boarding school for a time.

The Polish and religious classes at St. Anthony's were so well-taught, says Gudajtes, that even children from the Minto school attended them.

The school closed when problems arose over school-district reorganization, busing and finding teachers for the academy.

"They still had plenty of pupils," says Gudajtes, "but the problem was, they couldn't get the nuns to live in a rural area."

Gudajtes, like many of the Warsaw area's older citizens, learned his prayers in Polish at the academy. He still says them in Polish.

"God understands me better that way, I think," he says.

Recent events in Poland have worried people like Gudajtes and Gerszewski, who have cousins living in Poland.

Gerszewski says treatment of striking Poles is "sad, of course, but there isn't a thing we can do about it over here." The Poles eventually will have unions, freedom of speech and freedom of the press "little by little," he believes.

"They're not going to quit until they do get them all," he adds.

Patricia Fix

Pioneers came by ox cart

In about 1877, among tall grass and weedy wilderness of southeast Walsh County, migration of Polish immigrants was started, by ox carts and wagons settling on the vast prairie 30 miles north of Grand Forks in the townships of Walshville, Ardoch, Harriston, Acton and Pulaski. They were staking claims, breaking and plowing land and seeding to wheat, oats, potatoes and rutabagas. They were building sod and log houses and shelters for their oxen.

Along the Forest River and to the west of the Red River was choice land and these pioneers recognized it as such. They passed the word on to their friends and relatives in Winona and Perham, Minnesota, and Pine Creek, Wisconsin, who were already working there, and they, too, rushed to this new opportunity.

By 1880 there were over 100 people in this area and more were coming until all available land was taken up. Some of the names were Tandecki, Kiedrowski, Kamrowski, Rogalla, Szarkowski, Maszk, Wysocki, Slominski, Pelowski, Grzeskowisk, Hefta, Gornowicz, Lizakowski, Grzadzielewski, Gerszewski, Moga, Galewski, Babinski, Czapiewski, Perkerewicz, Worczak, Gudajtes, Glinski, Bazia and many others.

The community was prospering and soon lumber and building supplies were arriving by river boat to an established town of Acton on the Red River. There they could sell their produce and purchase their needs and many were building new homes from lumber.

All of these immigrants from Poland were deeply religious Roman Catholics, and were concerned about Sunday worship. There was more and more talk about a church and parish in the area. A temporary cemetery was established. The burials there were a Hefta boy, a Koehmstedt boy, a Blazek child and Mrs. Gornowicz, mother of Jozef Gornowicz, who froze in a blizzard and was found in a field in the spring.

The early settlers were Polish, German, Irish, Scottish and other nationalities. Most of these became discouraged by the floods from the Red River causing many of them to drop their claims or selling to the already settled and established Polish pioneers.

Poland was built shortly after the Soo Line junction or spur was built in the years 1903-1905 connecting Oslo, Minnesota and Ardoch. It was about four miles west of the Red River. A group of railroad men met to decide on the name; Frank Nice and Joe Michalski suggested Poland and all agreed. Many benefit dances and basket socials were held in the Poland dance hall for the Red Cross benefits during World War I. Also, because most of the settlers were of Polish descent, benefit dances were held for financial aid for the country of Poland, so they could gain their freedom from German control.

St. Stanislaus Centennial Book, 1983
Walsh Heritage

Syrians arrived by peddling, homesteading

Imagine it's about the year 1900, and you're part of a jostling throng of immigrants at Ellis Island, New York.

You speak only Arabic and you're wearing strange Western clothes that Mrs. Trabulsi, a Parisian benefactor of Middle Easterners, arranged for you to obtain en route.

Through the strange smells, languages and sights of Ellis Island, you know one basic thing about America: you're looking for McClusky, North Dakota.

"They would literally get off the boat with a note pinned on their coat that would say, 'McClusky, North Dakota,'" says Bismarcker Mike Saba, who has done considerable research on North Dakota's Arab-American population.

"They would wander around and say, 'How do I get to McClusky, North Dakota, from here?'"

Most of the Arab-Americans who migrated to North Dakota were from Lebanon, although others came from Syria proper, Jordan and Palestine.

However, all generally were called Syrians, because at that time, present-day Lebanon was part of what was known as Syria.

Their route to North Dakota was basically the same — by horseback over the Levant mountains to Beirut, by steamship to Marseilles by way of Alexandria and other Mediterranean ports, by train across France to either Cherbourg or Le Havre, by boat again to New York, then by train to the Midwest.

Because of problems with immigration officials, some had to enter the country through Canada or Mexico.

Those Arab immigrants with notes pinned to their clothes had the smoothest path to North Dakota. The notes meant they probably already had friends or relatives in North Dakota who had homesteaded in the McClusky-Denhoff area.

Others of Middle Eastern descent were peddlers, and made it to North Dakota in a more roundabout way.

Ninety percent or more of the Arab immigrants were Christians, many from the village of Ain Arab in Lebanon.

A main reason they left was because they felt oppressed by the Turkish Ottoman Empire.

These Christians settled mainly around McClusky or Denhoff.

But there were some Moslems, who settled mostly in the Ross-Stanley area.

In fact, by Saba's reckoning, the first mosque in the United States was built at Ross.

Although it may be impossible to establish for sure this status, a magazine published by Arab-Americans — The Link — says, "The earliest recorded group who organized for communal (Moslem) prayer in private homes was in Ross, North Dakota, in 1900. By 1920 they had built a mosque."

Charlie Juma Sr., 78, formerly of Ross, is one of those who remembers well the old worship services.

"There wasn't too many Moslems out here," recalls Juma, formerly a Moslem. Juma now lives in Stanley.

His dad was a Moslem and a peddler who moved to Ross in about the first decade of the 1900s.

"They kept up the religion in their homes, as best they could."

He says it was in 1929 that they formed a congregation, dug a basement, put a roof over it and called it a mosque.

The intention was to add onto it, but no one had any money in the 1930s. By the time the Depression was over, a lot of Moslem families had moved, says Juma.

The mosque never was anything so fancy as to have domes and minarets.

Its potential significance went unknown for many years.

However, a few years ago, the North Dakota Historical Society began some research into the mosque, intending to submit it for inclusion on the National Register of Historic Places, in order to preserve it.

Researchers soon were disappointed to find out the building had been torn down a year or two earlier.

Juma says worship took place at the mosque into the 1960s, but usage fell as the older people died off. Juma now attends a Lutheran church and his children are Lutherans.

Juma regrets the demise of the mosque. "It doesn't feel good, because it was a good congregation."

It's not a lot different being a Lutheran, he says. "The only thing is that there is a little different beliefs, but we're all humans."

Elsewhere in North Dakota, Moslems lived in the Glenfield area of Foster County.

In the Middle East, the Lebanese and the inhabitants of the eastern Mediterranean before them, the Phoenicians, had always had reputations as shrewd merchants.

Saba and Floyd Boutrous, a Bismarck businessman, believe it's important not to underestimate the significance of the Arab immigrants' commercial activities.

As Boutrous understands the history, many Arab immigrants set up small businesses as railroad towns popped up beside the newly laid tracks all across the plains.

"I'll bet you had one Lebanese business in every one of those towns," says Boutrous.

Saba agrees: "They just really filled that merchant kind of void."

Old-time residents of Bismarck will remember some of the old Lebanese merchants.

Boutrous' dad, Attas, ran a grocery store where the Town Crier now is located and also the Corner Grocery at Avenue A and Third Street, which Floyd Boutrous Realty now occupies.

Decades ago, the Corner Grocery was where the kids from the west side of Bismarck would get their candy, while kids from the east side would go to the old OK Confectionary at Seventh Street and Thayer Avenue.

Saba's grandfather, Michael, ran a restaurant on what is now the Parkade block in downtown Bismarck.

There, according to Saba, his grandfather employed a black cook from Driscoll, who used to have his kids by to eat. One of those kids was Era Bell Thompson, an international editor of Ebony magazine before her retirement.

There were other Arab businesses, too, such as the fruit market and bowling alley the Nicola family used to run on the block at Sixth and Broadway.

As for the peddlers, Saba says they were an important part of the social fabric in the early homestead days.

"Here you had homesteaders that were 10 miles away from the nearest neighbors," says Saba. "The peddlers were really the link with those farmers to the outside.

"They were friendly, they had great stories, they were from the

**includes all Arabic-speaking immigrants: Lebanese, Syrians, Palestinians, etc.*

Syrians engage in traditional wrestling match on Mountrail County homestead. In lower photo, Charlie Juma of Stanley, standing at left, hauled livestock for White Earth ranchers in early 40s.

Holy Land, they had the news.

"They (the isolated homesteaders) really looked forward to these guys."

Not only the Arab men, but the Arab women, too, would peddle.

"They would peddle lacework, thread, go out on their own. They were extremely independent in those days," says Saba.

Others earned their living however they could, employing a little resourcefulness.

Both Saba and Juma remember Joe Albert, another Arab-American. Albert used to wrestle bears.

"He wasn't a very big man," says Juma, "five-six or five-seven and 160 or 170 pounds, but he used to wrestle a bear, and he had monkeys, and he traveled around.

"That's the way he made his living. He didn't care if he made any money, he just wanted to show his skills. He was a strong guy."

Albert had a stunt, Juma recalls, in which he'd somehow knot or loop a thick rope around his neck and have three other ropes trailing. Volunteers from the audience would pull on the ends of the rope, but Albert's neck was strong enough or he was clever enough with his knots, that he didn't get hurt.

Albert traveled around North Dakota in the late 1930s and early 1940s. He lived in Belcourt, was married to an Indian and had four children.

From their peddling and homesteading days, most North Dakotans of Arab heritage have settled into jobs as independent businessmen and professionals.

Some still are involved in agriculture, but by and large, they live in urban areas like Williston, Bismarck and Fargo.

This relatively small ethnic group in North Dakota now numbers perhaps up to 1,000 including mixed bloods, according to Evelyn Barkie, who immigrated to this country from Lebanon in 1952 at the age of 19.

The largest number of Arab-Americans live in the Bismarck and Williston areas.

There are smaller communities in Fargo, Glenfield, Stanley, Rubgy, Ross, Belcourt, Rolla, Cando and Dickinson, and a scattering elsewhere.

She and her husband, Robert, also of Lebanese descent, farm near Williston.

She says about half the Arab-American families in North Dakota are full-bloods, and about half mixed.

She estimates about 195 Lebanese/Syrians are living in Bismarck and about 190 in Williston. After that, the numbers per community drop rapidly.

As an ethnic group, the Arab-Americans appear to have retained their culture in just a few ways — food, language and music — much like other ethnic groups.

A lot of Arab families still cook Arabic food, and not just around holiday time — foods like kibbeh, tabouli, schawarma, baklava, lehem, yebruk and shiskebob.

Barkie and her daughter bake Arabic bread for the thrift shop in Williston. They also have, on occasion, made the communion bread for St. Peters Episcopal Church.

Many Arab-Americans keep in touch with relatives in the old country; some even have visited there. The older people still know the language, but it is dying out.

As for music, there still are some fans of the plaintive, mysterious Arab style of music.

A driver stopped in Bismarck on a nice day, hearing the wailing of Arabic music through rolled-down windows, may be in the vicinity of someone like Eli Nemer, a painter who enjoys hearing old country music behind the wheel.

Arabic music is also big in the Barkie family, and Barkie says even her children have taken to it.

"We have tapes in the cars," she says. "The kids love it; I'm proud of them."

Greg Turosak

Arab businesses followed tradition of world trade

Like their countrymen throughout the nation, many Arab Americans here got their start by peddling. Or they went into peddling when crops failed on the homestead, or times were hard. It wasn't usually considered long-term work, but rather a way to gain capital in order to go into a more permanent business. Through peddling many moved into family businesses such as groceries, dry goods or clothing stores through the state.

Peddling was an ideal trade for these immigrants who could speak little or no English but had a natural business ability.

His efforts to communicate are described by Mike Abdalla of Ross to a WPA interviewer.

"I couldn't talk or understand the American language and when I was peddling I had to talk to people by motions. When I wanted to tell anyone the price, I would take money from my pocket and show them the amount. When I wanted to ask for a place to sleep, I had to lay down on the floor and play that I was asleep; then they knew what I wanted.

"Nearly everyone felt sorry for me because I couldn't talk their language," said Abialla. "I remember one time when a bunch of people wanted to know what nationality I was so a man asked me if I was Jewish. I shook my head, no, so he asked me if I was a sheeny. It sounded enough like "Syrian" so I nodded, yes. Everyone laughed very hard. It took me about two years to learn enough English to get along good. Many times I felt like I wanted to go back to the old country."

Shaker Nassif struck out west on foot from New York after working long enough at a packing plant to outfit a peddler's bag. His grandson, George Skaff relates his story:

"The only way he could make it was to take merchandise which he bought for pennies — like thread, scissors and small notions that people would buy readily. He put them in a big bundle on his back and walked all the way from New York, stopping at villages and farms along the way. It took him nearly two years before he reached St. Paul. There he got more merchandise and trekked westward into the Dakotas because he had heard that there was free land. He kept selling merchandise which he carried on his back and made a few dollars."

Nassif had left his wife and four children in Lebanon, promising to return after making enough money to make life easier there. After working four years on his homestead at McClusky he did return and built a new stone house for his family. He then decided to go once more to America and earn enough to live in luxury for the rest of his life. This time he brought a son and a daughter with him. But, though he lived to be 94, he never did return to Lebanon.

Skaff recalls that his own father, Ferris Skaff, did not like farming, so he decided to go into the Watkins business, selling medicine, spices and extracts farm to farm. "He bought a team of horses and an old buggy. He'd stay out a month or two months at a time, traveling about 10 miles a day, stopping at all the farms along the way, staying all night at the last farm — probably about six or seven at night. He'd start out again the next morning. Winter and summer he hardly stopped. My mother and we children were alone on that farm (near McClusky) for months at a time."

Peddling was a hard life. But for wives, alone with small children, often speaking little or no English, life was also hard.

Mary Farris, age 72, was interviewed in Williston during the depression by a WPA field worker. In halting English she told of leaving her two children with her parents in Lebanon, of her loneliness for them and her efforts in producing needlework for her husband to take on his rounds.

Ferris Skaff, McClusky, delivered Watkins products with team and wagon in 1912; later he used the car in photo at right.

"We thought we come here, make some money, stay couple year, then go back," said Farris. "Lots people come like that — leave children. My husband, he travel, he sell men goods, some lady goods. When my son John born, I sick four months. I stay home alone, my husband he gone all week, sometime two week. I cry and cry. I crochet all time. I get three-four Syrian women live in other room. We come together and crochet. I get up six o'clock, stay up twelve. My husband come home, he see big pile crochet. He take it 'long, sell it. Oh, dat's hard times; now it's easy for everybody."

When interviewed on the farm many expressed surprise when asked about recreation. Replies were painfully similar, "We don't have any recreation, we only work. Sometimes friends stop in to talk."

Arab Americans found farming in North Dakota difficult, and very different from what they'd known. Even harnessing a team of horses was a perplexing task for which, at first, many needed the help of neighbors. Skaff says his father offered many a "God bless" for the help his neighbors gave when he was getting started on the homestead.

Many left their farms and went into business. The Lebanese came from long traditions of world trade. From ancient times their land had been a crossroads for the civilized world — for 4000 years a transportation and trade center. Many Arabs in North Dakota traced their ancestry to the times when Alexander the Great crossed the land. As an Attiyeh family reunion booklet states, "(Our ancestors) were there when the famed Phoenicians, first ship builders of the world, launched their craft from the ports of 'cedared Lebanon,' as the Bible puts it; they saw the armored legions of the Roman armies, the Turks and many other invading forces, cross the borders of their nation."

These roots are treasured, but the Lebanese also recall a continual fear of war. They came from a land rich in tragedy, overrun many times by conquering armies.

In North Dakota they felt safe from war. Another reason so many came here, descendants suggest, is that it was a long way from New York immigration authorities. In the United States they had often met prejudice and were never quite sure of their immigrant status. They were barred from citizenship until 1909. They feared being sent back before they had made their stake.

Many North Dakota Lebanese are descendants of a Christian Arab tribe of nomads which ruled southern Syrian deserts in the 8th century. In the 800's, as Islam spread through the area, many tribesmen were converted. Christians left the deserts and moved into more settled areas. The patriarch of the Attiyeh family was one who settled at this time in a Lebanese village called Ain Arab.

Descendants here cherish their ties with the town of Ain Arab. They contributed money for water, electric and telephone services for the town and for improvements to the road and school. In the 1940's, during a crop failure, they shipped 200 bushels of North Dakota wheat to the people of Ain Arab.

In addition to Christian Arab settlements focused in the McClusky-Denhoff area, three Moslem settlements grew up in North Dakota. These were in the vicinity of Stanley-Ross, Rolla-Dunseith and Glenfield-Binford. At Ross the Moslems built a basement mosque for worship. The Greek Orthodox Christians had difficulty finding a church or priest of their denomination. For baptisms and weddings they would wait a year or two till a traveling priest came through from California or Chicago.

Though a vast gulf separated their religions, these Arab Americans had a common heritage in both language and culture. Mike Saba of Bismarck says, while growing up, he was never aware of religious or political differences among these people.

"All I understood clearly was that they spoke Arabic and seemed to enjoy speaking Arabic," says Saba. "They did the same kinds of dances and ate the same kind of food and enjoyed each other's company so very well. Also the houses were all so similar. The living room (was) the center of activity with couches lining the periphery so that literally scores of people could sit in that living room and visit with one another. I recall that I wondered, in non-Arabic friends' living rooms, often with only one or two chairs, where can people sit?"

Saba recalls stopping at the homes of other Arabs when traveling through the state as a child. "We would never use hotels or motels or any public eating place. We would always go to the next town or the next street where there was an Arab. Even if it were four in the morning, we'd knock on the door and we'd go in and stay and they would welcome us with the great Arabic term 'Ahlan wa Sahlan' — welcome!" *F.B.*

"Even at four in the morning they welcomed us."

Della Boutrous of Bismarck was among the first Lebanese immigrants to this area.

Jewish settlements sapped by harsh climate

Norman Kamins knows why Jewish settlers had difficulty farming in North Dakota a century ago.

As early as 1882, two Jewish farming colonies were established, at Painted Woods north of Wilton and about 15 miles northeast of Devils Lake near Garske.

"They couldn't communicate and they lived like they did in their home countries," says Kamins of the settlers, who mostly emigrated from Russia.

"The Jews who came here had three strikes against them: One, they weren't farmers; two, the language; and three, poor land. There aren't any (Jews) farming now (in North Dakota) and there used to be two or three Jewish families in every town."

Kamins, a Bismarck resident and a partner in Western Steel and Plumbing, knows of what he speaks.

His grandfather, Phillip Kamins, homesteaded near Regan in 1902. Unlike many of the Jewish settlers who quit farming after a few years to either leave the state or start new businesses, he operated his farm for 14 years before turning to new enterprises.

In 1916, he opened a general store in Heaton, then moved to Zap, opening a store named P. Kamins and Son, which the family operated until 1931, when his son, Abe, established the Kamins Coal Co. at Zap.

Norman Kamins, born in Zap in 1919, worked in the mine as a youth.

"But they had to close down the mine because they couldn't get the men to operate it."

He also remembers his first contact with anti-Semitism.

"There was a lot of anti-Semitism in that area. It wasn't out in the open, but you could feel it."

Finding a better way to make a living was perhaps what all Jewish settlers in North Dakota sought. And for most, that meant not farming.

When Rabbi Judah Wechsler of St. Paul, Minn., obtained a land grant and settled 11 Jewish families at Painted Woods 100 years ago, the immigrants had little idea of what to expect and were hardly prepared for the rugged farm life.

Originally, Wechsler apparently had been moved by the spirit of the immigrants. "Nothing but land could satisfy them, and we finally yielded to their requests," he wrote.

But harsh winters, crop failures and other calamities quickly sapped the spirits of some. In 1884, the colony's best year, there were 54 families, each owning one quarter-section of land. But when the crops failed the next year, some settlers began moving away.

The drought of 1886 was virtually the end of the colony, although Wechsler encouraged other American Jews to come to the aid of those in North Dakota. The St. Paul Jewish community had spent about $30,000 — a substantial sum in those days — to help Wechsler's dream colony. Even after Wechsler moved to Mississippi he continued to plead for the colony, which had been considered a major test in communal effort.

However, an account by Rabbi Dr. W. Gunther Plaut lists only three farmers remaining at Painted Woods in 1901.

The Garske colony near Devils Lake also was started in the early 1880s. It suffered through some horrendous years, but was reported to be a success in 1901. An account stated, "All of the farmers threshed in good season. This is the first time that the crop of the Jewish farmers has been threshed before November since they have been here."

The settlement, sometimes call Iola, was considered the northwest's oldest Jewish settlement in 1912, but it had melted away by the mid-1920s.

One of the Devils Lake settlement children, Lottie Kaufman, later became the wife of famed movie producer Adolf Zukor.

Many Jewish immigrants settled in other areas of the state, including Wing, where a list of students in 1912-13 included at least nine Jewish children among the 48 pupils.

Jewish people established businesses in Wing — the first ice cream shop was owned by a Mr. Palonski and the first harness and shoe shop by Issador Shanno.

There were other settlements in the Dakotas, including a large colony near Ashley, but the colonies near Painted Woods and Devils Lake were ones most familiar to Jews around the country, particularly in the Twin Cities.

Farming wasn't the only interest of the early Jewish settlers.

When a Fargo merchant placed a "help wanted" ad in an Ohio newspaper, Isaac Herbst responded in 1884. He is remembered as a pioneer in merchandising techniques who later opened the Herbst Department Store in 1892.

Other early Fargo businesses operated by Jewish people included fur and women's ready-to-wear stores, and a feed store owned by Isadore Goldberg that grew into a thriving enterprise. The firm, in the 1930s, was said to be the largest handler, processor and distributor of sweet clover, legume and grass seed in the nation.

Currently, an estimated 140 Jewish families live in the Fargo area. The city's Temple Beth El also serves members throughout eastern North Dakota and western Minnesota.

In Grand Forks, the Panovitz Furniture and Carpet Co. was founded in 1891 by Samuel Panovitz.

And Silverman's Men's and Boys' Wear continues to be a leading clothing store in Grand Forks.

Its roots go back to 1908, when Herman Silverman started the business from the back of his automobile. He had immigrated to the United States, worked first in the New York garment industry and later as a dock worker in Duluth, Minn., before moving to Grand Forks.

"I don't know what he did in Russia," says Sam Silverman of his father. "He just came to the land of milk and honey, and I think he wanted to avoid the military (in Russia) like a lot of others."

There also were peddlers named Silverman in the area who weren't related to Herman and his family. Orville Bakken of Northwood recalls a Jewish peddler named Silverman who often visited his farm with a wagonload of goods.

Sam Silverman remembers his family bringing "a lot of relatives from Russia" to the United States. He also has memories of the two world wars.

"The Jews here were well thought of during the war," he says of World War I. "I was just a little boy, but we remember it well."

In World War II, he says, "a lot of (Jewish) people went into the service and two of our young men (from Grand Forks) were killed."

Many of the Grand Forks pioneers originally came from the Garske settlement.

The first Jewish settler in Bismarck, and probably the first in what is now North Dakota, was Dan Eisenberg, who opened a trading post south of Bismarck in 1869.

Abe Winter

Other immigrant groups

There were Chinese, Armenians, others too

Anglo-Americans, Scandinavians and people of various German backgrounds make up much of North Dakota's ethnic heritage.

But there were some pioneers from other countries.

An example is Lem Heen, a Chinese homesteader near Williston.

According to information gathered by interviewers working for the federal Works Projects Administration, Heen came to San Francisco from China in 1872 at age 10.

In 1887 Heen, a cook, was in Glendive, Mont., when the Great Northern Railroad was pushing through. "Believing that good cooks could find employment along the railroad route, Lem Heen arrived in Williston just about the time the railroad did, and quickly found work there," wrote the WPA interviewer, Donald Graner.

But Heen didn't like confined quarters and took a job as a sheepherder. In 1893 he married Nellie Mayo, a local woman, and they settled on a homestead in Williston Township that came to be known as Chinaman's Coulee.

But, it was learned that a federal Chinese Exclusion Act prohibited the Secretary of Interior from approving homestead land for Chinese who had not become naturalized American citizens. The Catch-22 was that it also prohibited Chinese nationals from becoming naturalized citizens, and Heen had neglected to become one before the law was enacted.

Influential citizens of the Williston area circulated petitions attesting to Heen's character and honesty of purpose. Congress passed and the president signed a special law that allowed the Interior secretary to issue the homestead patent to Heen's wife, Nellie.

Heen died in 1909 when he was run over by a horse, and is buried in a Williston cemetery.

There are and always have been a scattering of oriental people in Noth Dakota.

Information compiled for the 1961 Dakota Centennial Edition of The Bismarck Tribune notes that Chinese operated a big share of Bismarck's restaurants and laundries around the turn of the century.

Jamestown became the new home for Armenian immigrants in the early 1920s.

Viola Reimers, who lives on a farm near Courtney, recalls that four Armenian families lived in one neighborhood of northwest Jamestown, where they all attended a Presbyterian church and sent their children to the same grade school.

There were other Armenian families at Eldridge and near Tappen. All of the Armenian men worked for the Northern Pacific Railroad.

Reimers' father, Melkon Abrahamian, had come to the United States in 1911 at age 19 and toiled in a Virginia lumberyard for a time before moving west.

Reimers notes that in those days there were lots of single men, from various ethnic groups, working for the railroad and living in boxcars.

Those who came to North Dakota probably found that railroad labor was a job they could get with their limited knowledge of English. "I think they did whatever they could do, like immigrants nowadays," Reimers says.

She recalls that there also were Italian and Bulgarian immigrants living in Jamestown and working for the railroad.

Jack Hagerty of the Grand Forks Herald recently unearthed old news items detailing the settlement in 1905 of a group of Gypsies north of Spiritwood Lake in eastern Stutsman County.

The Gypsy "king" was a man named Zek Marks. The group, immigrants from Eastern Europe, was reported to have come from other states like Indiana, Ohio and Oklahoma. They bought 1,000 acres of land and farmed for about 10 years, successfully raising sheep, cattle and horses.

"Cold weather, however, proved too much for them and they gradually drifted back to their former homes," the report indicated.

According to Hagerty, nomad bands of Gypsies were frequent visitors to North Dakota. They first traveled in caravans of horses and wagons, later switching to big and expensive touring cars.

Often when a band of Gypsies visited a community, there were rumors that they were on the lookout for children to kidnap in order to build their population.

Research by the Rev. William Sherman, a Grand Forks sociologist, indicates that immigrants from Belgium settled in a small pocket near Joliette and Bowesmont in Pembina County.

The opening of the Washburn Lignite Coal Co. mine at Wilton attracted small groups of immigrants to the area, including a few Bulgarians and Romanians.

Among other ethnic groups, there were immigrants from Luxembourg who settled near LaMoure, Casselton, New Rockford and Grenora, and Swiss around Wimbledon.

Bob Jansen

New immigrants still come

New people are still arriving in North Dakota. Many come as refugees.

War has always meant refugees. The second world war brought displaced persons from Europe, including many Latvians. Cubans came later, and today Eastern Europeans are again arriving.

Since 1975, about 1,200 Southeast Asians have come to North Dakota; about half remain in the state. The first wave of these were Vietnamese and included a cross section of farmers, fishermen, professionals and wealthy businessmen. Recently, most refugees have come from Cambodia, Laos or Thailand. Major difficulties have been learning English and finding jobs. And, like immigrants from the past, these people think often of home.

More Hispanic-speaking people are settling in North Dakota, too. In early days, Mexican cowboys came up the trail and, for decades, Mexican Americans have come as migrant workers to the Red River Valley and the irrigated sugar beet lands of western North Dakota. Some have elected to stay. Usually these people come from the sunbelt states such as California and New Mexico, not directly from south of the border, although many have relatives there.

Immigrants who come singly are often professionals, such as doctors and college teachers. Of 956 physicians licensed and practicing in the state, 232 were born in foreign countries, nearly one-fifth in Canada. Like other immigrants, some have fled political or social oppression; others come for the opportunities available here. *F.B.*

Early boomtowns, such as Bismarck, shown here in 1880, were largely settled by older stock Americans: civil war patriots, miners, lawyers, preachers, promoters. Invariably they, too, claimed homesteads when land was available.

Old stock Americans provided early leadership

The striking ethnic mosaic which is North Dakota is underscored by the statistic, given in Elwyn B. Robinson's "History of North Dakota," that in 1910 foreign born people with their children made up 71% of the state's population.

Yet we should not lose sight of the fact that nearly 30% of the population was not foreign born; nor were these people the children of immigrants.

They were older stock Americans and they came here from every state in the Union: from Ohio, Missouri and the New England states, from Flordia, Oregon and Kansas.

Some were third generation Americans from ethnic communities in eastern cities or rural areas; others were descendants of Revolutionary War patriots. During the 1860's Civil War veterans, granted special homestead privileges, flocked in from both north and south, representing every national heritage. Soldiers fighting Indian wars in the Dakotas and Montana stayed on after discharge. Cowboys rode up the Texas trail with longhorn cattle; prospectors drifted in from the gold fields of Montana and the Black Hills.

Perhaps traditional early American stock predominated: Irish, Scotch, English, Welsh, German and Dutch. But certainly, too, they included a heritage from every European country and many continents: Spanish, Italian, Swiss, Greek, black, Chinese, Polish and Mexican.

They came, like the others, for opportunity and free land. They came to build railroads, to establish towns, to work in the harvest fields. Many settled in the new boomtowns and became business people or the state's earliest professionals — doctors, lawyers, teachers and ministers. From their ranks came the early politicians and land promoters.

They had an advantage over first generation immigrants in that they were skilled in language and customs of the country. Yet virtually all of them took up homesteads where open land was available. In ranch country they predominated. Many have continued to be farmers and ranchers in every area of the state.

A problem with identifying these old stock Americans is that so many intermarried into strong ethnic communities. Their offspring tend to identify with the prevailing ethnic culture. Even today this makes ethnic statistics deceptive. In the 1980 census, for example, people were asked to give their ancestry. Many identified themselves with what they felt to be their strongest and most recent heritage even though it might be less than half, the other nationality lines being smaller and more distant.

But old stock Americans are a vital factor in the state. They were early leaders in bringing a diverse people together, in teaching and inspiring generations of youth, in helping to mold a strong Dakota state and character. Everywhere they have intermarried, mellowing ethnic customs — helping to preserve what they saw as good, working to change what they felt needed changing.

In a sense, these old stock Americans have been the blending agent which helps the mosaic work so well.

F.B.

Most blacks chose not to stay

There are black people in North Dakota.

There have been black people in North Dakota nearly as long as there have been white people in North Dakota.

Like other ethnic groups, blacks were homesteaders, cowboys, soldiers, drifters and steamboat hands.

Like other ethnic groups, they came in search of the promises of the American West: adventure, wide-open spaces, free land and a chance at a better life.

Today there are 2,568 blacks in the state out of a total population of 652,695, according to the 1980 census.

In most cases, blacks are in North Dakota to attend school or are with the Air Force. Most live on or near the air bases at Minot and Grand Forks.

A few stay on, but most do not.

In a sense, they fit an old pattern: blacks have always come to this state, but with few exceptions, have not settled permanently.

According to one historian, "the steamboat industry was the first to introduce Negroes in numbers to Bismarck, since the Northern Pacific did not hire them for laying its track."

During the 1890s, about 200 black soldiers were stationed along the Missouri River to protect the early railroad workers from Indians.

They were called "buffalo soldiers" by the Indians, because of their kinky hair.

The steamboat hands came and went.

The soldiers came and went.

The occasional black cowboy, drifter and handyman came and went.

And even the black homesteader came and went.

Thomas Newgard and Rev. William Sherman, Grand Forks, are researching the ethnic origins of North Dakota's people and has determined that there were 50 to 100 black farmers in the state between 1890 and 1915.

They came mainly from Indiana, Illinois or Missouri. Most were scattered across the state, but there were two fairly large settlements, near Larimore and Alexander.

Their reasons for leaving, says Sherman, were not connected to racial intolerance.

"There was a minimum of hostility or prejudice toward blacks. The blacks weren't threatening to whites because there weren't many of them.

"Also, in a sense, they had an advantage over their immigrant neighbors because they were true Americans. Many had fought in the Civil War, they understood American customs and they spoke English," Sherman says.

He says there was some hostility toward blacks who were transient field hands, arriving in boxcars each harvest season. But this transient population, white or black, tended to be looked upon as outsiders and troublemakers, which they frequently were, Sherman says.

By World War I, the harsh conditions of prairie life drove most blacks from the farms.

They joined relatives in cities outside the state or moved to North Dakota's towns and became businessmen, shopkeepers and barbers. Or they joined the Army.

"Blacks didn't stay on the land because, knowing America, they knew there were better opportunities elsewhere. The European immigrants stayed in North Dakota because they simply didn't know enough to leave," Newgard says.

Black homesteaders had another reason for leaving the farms.

The likelihood of interracial marriage was great because there were so few black families. As their children reached adolescence, the black homesteaders left the farms. They wanted to avoid the problems of interracial marriages and wanted to preserve their culture.

Newgard and Sherman's study of the black homesteaders in North Dakota matches the experience of Era Bell Thompson, a black woman who in 1917 moved as a child with her family from Des Moines, Iowa, to a small farm near Driscoll.

Thompson, who went on to become an author and international editor of Ebony Magazine, now is retired and living in Chicago.

"I think it's true about immigrants being more accepting," Thompson says.

She recalls Norwegian and German neighbors helping her family during their first difficult winter on the farm.

"These people would stop and stare at first, but they didn't know anything about black people. But neither did I," she says.

Thompson says she has no regrets about being raised in North Dakota. But Thompson, who never married, says if she had had children, she would have wanted them to grow up with other blacks, at least for part of their lives.

"Had I attended a black school or a black college, I would have associated with people of my age and color. I think we all need that. Otherwise, you're kind of lost out there.

"I never really adjusted to black life in Chicago. I've found as much prejudice among blacks as among whites. If it came to a division of the races in this country, and I had to make a choice, I couldn't. I would just leave," she says.

"The people in Chicago didn't talk my language. I had an accent. And they had different interests. They liked cabarets, I liked to go hiking."

Avoiding interracial marriages for their children was definitely a reason for some blacks leaving the state, according to Thompson. One of her childhood friends, Helen Johnson, left for that reason.

Thompson says her upbringing might have had something to do with her remaining single.

She grew up among whites but says her father would have disapproved if she had married a white man.

"My uncle married a white woman and my father resented it. Because my father didn't believe in interracial marriage, I thought I didn't either," she says.

And young black men in Chicago during the 1930s had little in common with a black woman who had a degree, was career-oriented and hailed from North Dakota.

Thompson attended the University of North Dakota for two years and in 1933 received a bachelor's degree from Morningside College, Sioux City, Iowa. She later did graduate work at the Medill School of Journalism, Northwestern University, Evanston, Ill., and received honorary doctorates from Morningside College and UND.

"Education put me ahead of most black people at that time. And I was

The Gospel Choir of Minot Air Force Base brings southern spiritual music to North Dakota.

too involved in my career," she says.

The Thompson family moved to Bismarck after Era Bell's mother died.

Her father, Tony, became a messenger to the state's first Non-Partisan League governor, Lynn J. Frazier. He later ran a second-hand store and then a cafe.

The pattern of black families coming to the state for short periods of time and for very specific reasons, then moving on, has continued into modern times.

In 1918, several black laborers were brought from the south to work at the Hebron brick factory, where laborers were scarce because of the war.

Walter Klick, a Hebron resident whose family owned the Hebron general store, was about 15 years old at the time.

"The brick company built a large building east of town and the black families lived there. They all seemed to get along all right."

Marcia Harris

An 'American daughter' arrives through snow

All day long we rode through the silent fields of snow, a cold depression spreading over us. Here and there was a tiny cluster of buildings, a windmill or silo towering above the snow-covered roofs; strawstacks sheltering thick-coated horses and cows that had eaten their way deep into the sides of the stacks away from the wind and the snow. Occasionally we passed through tiny country towns with their inevitable grain elevators, one-room dull red depots and companion section houses.

I looked at Mother. She tried to smile, but there were new tears in her eyes. She was thinking of the green hills of Virginia, thinking, too, of the lush valleys of Iowa. All these things, these friendly things that she knew and loved, were far behind her now. I think she knew then that she would never come that way again.

Weary and hungry, we arrived at last at Driscoll. I tumbled down the steps of the train into the outstretched arms of my father, hidden in the collar of a huge sheepskin coat, his face buried in the folds of a wool muffler, only the merry eyes visible. Pop was beside himself with joy. He and Uncle John loaded us into the straw-covered bed of a big sled and covered us with horse blankets. I was so thoroughly bundled and so firmly lodged between my mother and father that I could see very little, but I could smell the clean, fresh odor of straw and feel the sideways jolt of the runners as they bumped into rocks underneath the snow. The steady, rhythmic beat of horses' hoofs sounded pleasantly beneath my uncle's constant chatter.

"But aren't there any colored people here?" asked Mother incredulously.

"Lord, no!" said Father.

Uncle John laughed. "There's a couple of colored families over north of Steele, about thirty miles from here — Williams brothers, Ted and Mack. Both of 'em got kids; got right nice farms, too. A little gal there about your age, too, Dick." Uncle John looked at my brother and winked.

Era Bell Thompson
American Daughter

Cowboys who trailed cattle up the Texas trail often stayed on to homestead. This roundup scene in western North Dakota shows chuck wagon at left with its canvas tent-like shelter from wind and rain.

Cowboys came prepared for vigorous life

Of the many different groups of settlers who populated North Dakota, perhaps none was so well-prepared for the rigors of life on the northern plains as the cowboys.

Starting in the years immediately after the Civil War, the great cattle drives out of Texas extended farther and farther north. Finally, the drives reached what is now North Dakota and, in particular, the badlands of the Little Missouri surrounding Medora.

The arrival of the cowherds was made possible by the nearly simultaneous elimination of the buffalo herds and the subjugation of the Indians and reduction of their reservations. And with the cowherds came the cowboys.

While most of the cowboys brought the herds to North Dakota and then returned to the Southern Plains, there were a number who stayed in the area to start their own operations or to work for the large cattle companies that were setting up in the early and middle 1880s.

Some like Bill Follis started their own ranches and spent the rest of their lives here. A Texan, Follis first arrived in the badlands in the 1870s, working for and later managing the huge 777 brand operation of the Berry-Boice Cattle Co., which was headquartered along the Little Missouri near the confluence of Deer and Horse creeks.

When the Kansas City-based operation closed in about 1900, Follis started his own ranch on the Little Missouri, later moving to Bullion Butte south of Medora. Selling out in 1942, Follis died in Dickinson in 1954.

Another of the well-known cowboys was Billy Timmons, who started his career as a wrangler on the famous Ben Goodnight Ranch in Texas. In 1896, Timmons was sent to deliver a consignment of buffalo to Yellowstone Lake. After finishing the job, he wound up in North Dakota, where he worked with the 777 operation and other ranches. He then settled in Dickinson with a livery and feed business, but shortly thereafter returned to ranch work.

Well-known rancher and political figure Brooks Keogh of Keene remembers Timmons well — "He helped bring me up," says Keogh, himself the grandson of a pioneer cattleman.

Timmons and Keogh's father, Frank, became partners after both had worked on J.E. Phelan's "75" outfit, probably the biggest locally owned cattle operation in the state's history. Keogh recalls Timmons as a short, stocky man with a pronounced limp, the result of a horse-breaking incident when Timmons was a youth.

"He was one of those easygoing Texans," says Keogh, recalling how Timmons, without consulting Keogh's father, traded in a string of horses for a car for Mrs. Keogh, who had just moved onto the ranch, located in what is now the southern half of the Fort Berthold Reservation.

Perhaps the most famous (or infamous) of the Texas cowboys was "Turkey Track" Bill Molash, who has been portrayed by Larry Sprunk of Mandan in a series of monologues.

Sprunk, who is working on a biography of Turkey Track Bill, says he was born in Michigan, but raised in South Dakota. Moving to Texas, he earned his nickname from working on the Turkey Track outfit, and apparently came to North Dakota with the cattle drives in the early 1890s.

The late Frank Keogh recalled Turkey Track Bill as being a man of dubious integrity, but "one hell of a good cowboy".

Ted Quanrud

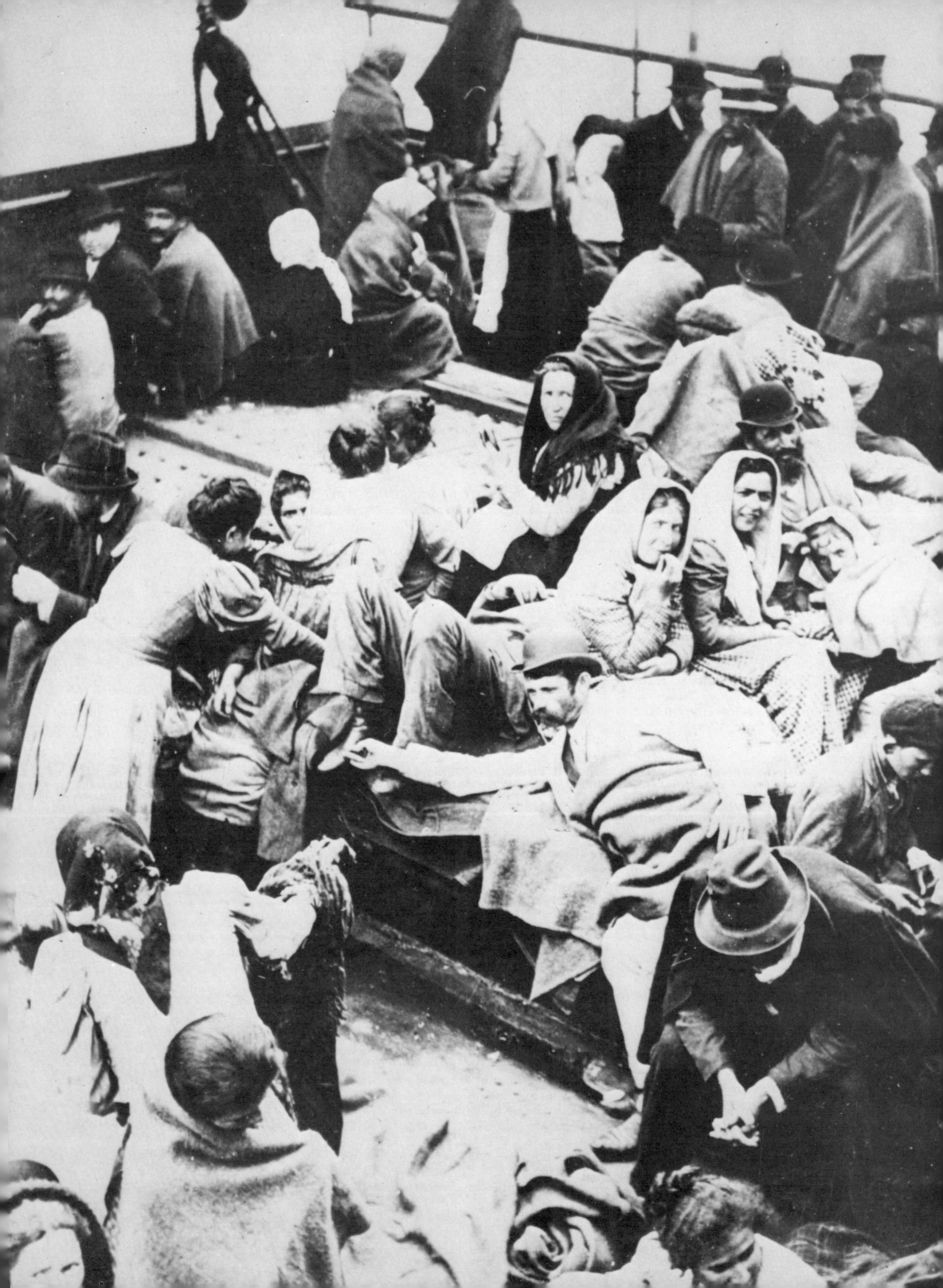

The immigrant experience

The immigrant experience began, often enough, with a vague rumor about a far-off place called America. It grew to an obsession that led to farewells for loved ones and a small farming village forever-after remembered as home.

The experience included an anxious journey by ship; the uncertainties of Ellis Island loomed ahead. "Tranen Insel," Island of Tears, as the Germans called it, was a place where families could be separated, some members refused admittance, others accepted and reluctant to give up this new chance in life.

Once safely through immigration, many newcomers did not hesitate, but caught the first train west. Or they walked, rode horseback, came by wagon or stage. They had heard tell of open land in Dakota, homestead land free for the asking.

Their personal stories tell of problems adjusting, of settling in, and finally, of looking back in wonder: How could I do this enormous thing? Why did I? And — was it such a good idea after all?

Immigrants arriving in New York in 1902: more than one million entered the United States in 1907. Many came west to claim homestead land.

Czech bids farewell to 'this beautiful village'

When I was about 20 years old, my father began to talk about America. My brother-in-law who left Russia for America the year before, insisted my father should go, that it is very good living in America. I did not like the idea of leaving. Some people claimed that only those went to America who didn't have any other place to go. And it was considered that America is a desert like Siberia, and that God did not create America, but the Indians did. And when someone goes to America he gets lost like falling to the bottom of the ocean, and nobody hears about him anymore. My friends tried to persuade me not to go, that I could make a good life for myself even in Czehohrad, better than among the Indians.

On the day of my departure, all my friends came to wish me a safe journey and lots of luck in America, many gave me presents or sent greetings and presents to friends from Czehohrad. It was very sad as I took a last look on the houses as we passed by. The school, where I spent time as a small boy, the church where I always liked to go and where the sound of the organ where I played was so touching. I wanted to imprint the picture of this beautiful village in my mind, for I would never see it again. I kept looking back until it was lost beyond the horizon....

So I am in America. What a strange country. Much different than I imagined. The train traveling so fast, I wondered why they are in such a hurry. As I looked out the window I saw hills and forests, which I never saw before. Then the conductor came in and I shivered all over. He was a black man — I never saw a Negro before.

My first experience in America was hunger. I did not buy any food thinking that I can buy something on the way at any station. But the train kept going without stopping, and when it did stop I didn't see any food. Now and then a porter came carrying apples or oranges. I stopped him and asked "Brod," that much I knew in German. He shook his head and said, "no bread."

I finally arrived at my destination, Dickinson, North Dakota. Many people were waiting there for me. My old boyhood friend, who came

Norwegian immigrants Andrew Berg, Maddock, and friend collect their baggage, including homemade wood trunk, and prepare to leave ship for relatives' homes in North Dakota.

here three years ago took me to the saloon and ordered, "Two glass beer."

"Aha," I thought, "he can speak English."

My brother took me then to a store and bought me a hat, so as not to embarrass him with my Russian cap. After awhile we got into the one-horse buggy and sped over hills and valleys. I hung on for dear life and begged my brother to go slower, that we would surely tip over, but he only laughed and said, "Wait till you see the badlands, then you will see big hills."

As we were riding, there appeared a big object in front of us and I asked my brother, "What is it?"

He replied, "That's our hill, beyond that is our farm."

It seemed to me that we are just next to the hill, and I asked him, "Are we going over it?"

"Oh no," he replied, "first we have to cross the river." So there are even rivers here. I was anxious to see it, as I never saw one. There were no rivers where I came from.

The horse shot out of the river. We went around the big hill and were at my parents' farm. So now we are home, says my brother. By the door stood a shovel. My brother set it aside and said, "This is our American lock for the door."

I was surprised and said, "What if somebody breaks in?"

"So what, if he is hungry he will eat, and then leave."

I did not want to say anything, but I surely was not too happy about this region.

Frank Nadvorik, Dickinson
"My Experiences", 1936

Syrian lands in New York with only $1

I couldn't speak a bit of English and everyone left the boat and went ashore and I was left there all alone. I didn't know what to do; I had but one dollar in my pocket.

Pretty soon a girl came over, probably an immigration employee, and tried to talk to me, but I couldn't understand her and she couldn't understand me. She and others took me to a hotel. They knew I was Syrian from my passport and that I was American born. So I was confronted by a Syrian lad whom they had summoned and he asked me where I was going. I told him I was going to Cedar Rapids, Iowa, that my father and brother lived there. They then asked me if I had any money, and of course I could only tell them that I had the dollar.The boat ticket had been paid by my father.

The girl said that if I didn't have any money they would give me some.

I was afraid they were going to send me back to Syria because they left me in the hotel room for two days. Finally I went downstairs to get something to eat. When I had finished eating the girl came.

She took me to the bus. My father had sent some money to pay my fare to Cedar Rapids, but I did not know this at the time. She gave me my ticket, five dollars in silver and $30 in bills, which she put in my pocket and pinned it shut with a safety pin so that I would not lose it. I tried to tell her that she was giving me too much money. I thought it must be pretty good country when they gave you money for nothing. Afterwards I found out that the girl had wired my father and he had sent them $75.00.

George Saba

Finn is called for Russian army

I went home for a visit to Finland from Stockholm where I worked in a jewelry store. And while I was home I received this card. Do you know what it is? It is a notice for me to report for duty in the Russian army for Siberian duty. I had heard about the treatment of Finns in the Russian army. I had heard just a little about the United States, that it was a free country and if a fellow wanted to work, he could get along.

I decided to sneak out of the country instead of serving in the Russian army...I had to leave in such a hurry. As it was I missed the firing squad by only about three days. I left home in March 1903 and landed in New York in April. The trip took about 16 days.

When I landed in New York I had only six dollars — twenty-nine dollars short of the required thirty-five dollars to enter this country. I was held at Ellis Island for nine days before they took me to New York and turned me loose. Had they kept me three days more, I would have been returned to Finland to face the Russian firing squad. I do not know to this day what made the immigration officers decide to let me into the U.S.A.

I believe what impressed me most in this country, was the freedom of the people. In the old country we had to notify the police every time we changed our place of residence. While in this country I could move every day and not notify anyone. I stayed in New York for only a very short time. A popular saying at that time was "Go west young man and grow up with the country." That was my only reason for deciding to leave New York and go west.

Frithiof Kinnoin, jeweler
Stanley, 1940

A Great Northern Railroad colonization effort brought 350 German Baptist Brethern from Indiana to Cando in 1894. The train of more than 40 cars, festooned with banners, traveled only in daylight to encourage "land fever."

Letters told tale of 'life fighting for existence'

Ole Lima painted pictures of pioneer life on the North Dakota prairie.

He used neither brush nor canvas. The portraits created by this Norwegian immigrant were the letters he wrote to his parents and others back in the old country.

"The country hereabout is quite monotonous, with flat prairie, and a hill here and there, and deep valleys with woods and rivers at the bottom.

"The houses are for the most part small and plain, but their dwellers often show great good will and sympathy, as well as a degree of warmth toward their fellow countrymen — that is when the spirit of Christ rules their hearts," he wrote in November 1886.

Lima, who was born on a farm near Stavanger in southwestern Norway, had come to the Cooperstown area in April 1886 and stayed until 1890 when he returned to Norway for a time. In 1893 he came back to Cooperstown, married his Norwegian sweetheart and, after working a short time for others, acquired his own farm and lived there until his death in 1931.

About four months after his initial arrival in North Dakota, Lima had some thoughts for a Norwegian friend who was considering emigration from the homeland. He warned that his friend's book bindery trade probably would have to be given up in favor of farming.

"If you should at any time decide to come, you must be prepared to find your well-known friends either in sod huts or in small wooden houses like the peat shelter at home. However, one grows accustomed to such things.

"But this I will say, that if you would avoid being disappointed, you must not expect to discover much that is glorious to the eye. No, in that respect Norway is a thousand times richer than Dakota."

During his first summer in North Dakota, Lima worked for other farmers, earning 75 cents per day during spring planting, $1 during haying season and $1.75 daily in harvest-time.

That winter, he observed that "it has been white with snow everywhere for a month, and on many days so bitterly cold that one can scarcely walk 500 yards with bare face and hands without freezing them."

But, he also noted in a letter to his sister, Malena, that he and other pioneers were eating well. "Coffee at every meal is quite possible, as well as wheat bread, butter, pork and beef. ... But I can't deny that I sometimes think of the home fare — potato flat-bread with milk, oatmeal, etc."

He also told of frequent dining on nourishing wild game like rabbit, prairie chicken or goose.

"In this connection I will not conceal that there seems to be a trace of hunter in me, for yesterday noon I took the gun and going out immediately saw a rabbit which I stalked and shot with the result that it died. Perhaps I was overproud of my skill in this line, but not without reason as it was the first time I aimed and shot at a living creature."

In the spring of 1887 he had some advice for Malena. "All who have good prospects of getting along in Norway, and who are not plagued by too violent an America fever, they will not attain any great advantage by emigrating," he wrote. "It is different with poor, oppressed, working people — they can here, by working diligently, earn three or four times as much as in Norway in the same amount of time."

He tended to look at life from the brighter side. "This last summer has been especially favorable for trees here on the prairie. The tops have shot three, four, five feet into the air, and my 5-year-old woods is now visible for miles on the prairie," he wrote in 1904.

Schooling was important, to both Lima and his children. "David and Ruth learn easily and make good progress in school. They are so eager about reading and numbers that as soon as they have come home and eaten, they take their book or pencil and paper again, and I must act as teacher."

Even while living with relatives during his first, temporary stay in Dakota, Lima was concerned about his own education.

In 1889, he wrote his father: "I should like to be able to use a part of next winter also for going to school. During the three winters I have stayed here I have used, respectively, eight, four and eight weeks for learning English.

"It is a somewhat slow matter for me to learn English, as I am thus far advanced in age, but I believe that the knowledge is useful, and when the instruction costs no more than time and food, it must be regarded as cheap schooling."

Also that winter he suggested that perhaps education was more important in the new world than back in Norway. "Many a penniless young boy here in America has by working in summer and going to school in winter for several years, procured for himself education and training sufficient to hold high and remunerative positions in society."

Religion was an important part of Lima's life, and he wrote extensively about the varied Norwegian Lutheran congregations being organized.

"There is now considerable discussion in the papers about that the Norwegian Lutheran synods in America ought to join together into one. It is, however, to be feared that those who hold this view form but a small minority, especially among the ministers and professors," he advised his parents in 1905.

Four years later, he contrasted the religious differences in America with those in Norway: "Rationalism has not yet appeared in the Lutheran synods as undisguised as it has in Norway, and for that reason the battle is not fought in just the same way here as at home. Yes, it even occurs to me that here it is life itself that fights for its existence, while in Norway they deal chiefly with its forms."

In the fall of 1889, he told his father of North Dakota's impending statehood and the vote to approve or reject a constitution. He pointed out with apparent pleasure that the constitution, as drafted, contained a clause that "forbids all manufacture, sale and transfer of intoxicating liquor."

Bob Jansen

Wild oats is stacked for hay on Sam Juma farm near Stanley in about 1927. During settlement of most of western North Dakota only one quarter homestead land was allowed; much came without mineral rights.

Homesteading, land promotion brought thousands of immigrants

The Homestead Act with its promise of free land brought great numbers of immigrants into North Dakota. In crowded European countries where the "seventh son of a seventh son" had no chance of land and little opportunity to make a living, 160 acres seemed like a kingdom.

Vigorous promotion by land companies, railroads, states and territories fed the land hunger. Great Northern and Northern Pacific railroads opened promotional offices in Britain, Norway, Sweden, Denmark, Holland, Switzerland, Germany and Canada. At first the immigrants came mainly from Canada and Scandinavian countries; later there were big German-Russian migrations.

The Homestead Act granted one quarter of land, 160 acres, to anyone over 21 (or head of household) who would live there five years during at least seven months of each year, and make certain improvements.

To speed the process, homesteads could be commuted or purchased for $1.25 an acre after six months residence. In later years this was changed to 14 months. (This cost was $2.50 per acre within Northern Pacific grant lands which encompassed most of the southern half of the state.) Many who wished to sell took this route and commuted their homesteads. Immigrant homesteaders making a permanent home usually preferred to wait out the five years, or even seven, and thus delay paying taxes on their land.

Non-citizens who filed homesteads had to declare their intention to become American citizens.

In the eastern half of North Dakota, largely settled before 1890, many settlers obtained three quarters of land under homestead, pre-emption and tree claim provisions. To do this the homesteader would select and try to hold three quarters while he pre-empted the first by living there six months, then paying $1.25 per acre for the land. Then he homsteaded the second quarter and took the third as a tree claim — planting 40 acres of trees, later lowered to 10. (The trees were not necessarily required to grow.)

Because of much land fraud both the pre-emption and tree claim laws were repealed in 1890. From that date until 1909 homesteaders were only allowed one quarter of land.

It was during these years, between 1890 to 1909, that most of western North Dakota was settled, with homesteaders obtaining only one quarter. In 1909 when two quarters were at last permitted, due to the obviously lower productivity of the land, Congress reserved all mineral rights. Hence many families in coal and oil rich areas, such as near Amidon, have never owned mineral rights to their land. Northern Pacific railroad lands purchased in this area also came without mineral rights. Although it was the intention of Congress for mineral rights to be sold with grant lands, the railroad was, by this time, obscuring transactions by using holding companies to buy and sell the grant lands.

In 1912 the five-year residence requirement was dropped to three years. In 1916 four-quarter grazing homesteads on low quality grazing land were permitted, without mineral rights.

More homesteads were granted in North Dakota than in any other state except Montana. (Outside the

Sod houses were built on the open plains by pioneers from many countries; know-how may have come from the steppes of eastern Europe. This 1910 photo shows sod home of the W. E. Klingler family, a mile west of Werner.

Peak year for North Dakota homesteads granted was 1908

Homesteads granted in North Dakota

Dakota Territory

1868	29
1871	33
1874	371
1877	563
1880	1,147
1883	1,735
1886	3,117
1889	5,814

North Dakota

1890	1,863
1893	1,464
1896	883
1899	1,929
1902	2,270
1905	7,314
1908	14,287
1911	6,753
1914	4,190
1917	2,348
1920	1,302

Bureau of Land Management

Dakota Territory includes both states. Herbert Schell notes in "History of South Dakota" that the majority of Dakota Territory filings were in the southern half every year but 1884.

Great Plains, less homesteading land was available.) An early peak of finalized homesteads was reached in 1889 — and many believe that date to be the all time high.

But North Dakota homesteading had only just begun. This was easily surpassed in 1903 and multiplied five times in 1908, the real peak year for homesteads in North Dakota. In 1889 North Dakota's share of the Dakota Territory homestead totals was probably less than 3000. In 1908, 14,287 homesteads were finalized in the state. By 1915 the totals were still above 3000, but by then most available land was gone and numbers dropped again.

In addition to a high number of homesteads, North Dakota had one of the largest railroad grants. The Northern Pacific grant, plus another small grant in the Red River Valley, took over ten million acres — 24% of the land in the state, the largest percentage taken from any state. These lands lay in a checkerboard strip 120 miles wide across southern North Dakota.

Northern Pacific advertised lands east of the Missouri River at prices of $3.00 to $6.00 per acre and those west of the Missouri at $2.00 to $4.50. Many of the first grant lands went to big investors and speculators, thus beginning the bonanza farming era in eastern North Dakota. Later the railroad decided to sell directly to small farmers, viewing them as more likely to develop communities and make heavy use of the railroad.

The state's two major railroads competed with each other and with promoters from other areas at immigration centers, and even with ship companies, to bring immigrants into the lands they served.

Foreign immigrants were considered choice colonists — they tended to work hard and stay on the land. A Northern Pacific land commissioner toured settlements and reported the people he saw would be good prospects for the Mott-Carson area.

"We saw colonies of Russian-Germans and Hungarians doing well on lands similar to those in the Cannonball district," he said.

"Being frugal and industrious and not afraid of hardship, people of these natonalities, who have had some agricultural training in their old homes, make excellent pioneers."

Low excursion rates were advertised, and special trains dispatched. Max Bass of Great Northern brought a trainload of 350 German Baptist Bretheren colonists from Indiana to Cando in 1894. The special train, with 38 freight cars and 9 passenger cars, traveled only in daylight so people all along the line could read the large banners, "From Indiana to the Rich, Free Government Lands in North Dakota, via the Famous Red River Valley, the Bread Basket of America!"

Much credit for bringing German-Russians into southeastern North Dakota is given the enterprising real estate agent John Wishek of Ashley, who is said to have helped locate 10,000 people in McIntosh, Logan and Emmons counties as well as an adjoining South Dakota county.

An item in the Bismarck Tribune in November 1886 noted that Wishek "will go to Odessa, Russia, during the winter and organize a colony for McIntosh County, which already has been favored by the location of several colonies. Mr. Wishek is a genuine Dakota hustler and has done much for this promosing young town and if successful in his winter venture, expects to bring back 1000 families in the spring."

In the all-time record year, 1907, more than a million new immigrants entered the United States. Many of them came to North Dakota and claimed homestead land. *F.B.*

Rammed earth house of "Russian settler" near Kief. Both house and barn have a type of thatched straw roof, half-completed in this photo.

Architecture reflects pioneer culture

This side of diaries and journals, architecture leaves perhaps the most vivid trail to a people's values, energy, creativity and perseverance.

It is even more revealing when a people moves to a new land, using an alchemy of tradition laced with new necessities. To move, for example, from forest land to great plains of grassland demands a cultural adjustment that is deeper than architecture, but architecture often is the only remaining key to the past.

In developing America, the log cabin seemed to be the most prevalent type of house. But the supply of lumber in the Dakotas was limited, requiring some settlers to look around them for building materials.

Norwegian immigrants were accustomed to using wood in the old country, and most who homesteaded in the Red River Valley continued to do so.

If they happened to settle farther from a railroad or wooded area along a stream, some of those first Norwegian immigrants lived in a home made of sod before putting up what was usually a simple, wood-frame dwelling.

In the open plains of Dakota, sod houses were one of the most typical for first homes.

The following is an account of Hans Westley, who recalled being 12 when his family moved from Norway to the Cooperstown area of Dakota Territory in 1881:

"The first thing we discovered about our sod hut was ants, found here and there; and not only that but once in a while we found lizards crawling about.

"But a hut such as ours, dug into the hillside, was cold in summer and warm in winter. In order to make it more homelike inside, and instead of having only the black sod walls and floor, we began making clay from gumbo and slamming it into the wall, fistful by fistful.

"One had to throw hard to make it stick. We then smoothed it out to resemble a plastered wall, and having finished this process we procured some lime and washed the walls with it, making them as pretty as plastered housewalls.

"For the floor we had to get lumber and lay it down. Aside from the long rafters inside holding up the roof, the room was open to the very top. The brush and hay laid over the supports was, of course, timber-dry, and from our stove the smoke-pipe went up through the roof, with the tinder nearby."

About 85 percent of the Germans from Russia who homesteaded in North Dakota built their first homes of sod or a straw-and-clay brick, according to John Hudson, a Northwestern University geographer who has studied records of about 1,000 of this state's early settlers.

Hudson, in the article "Frontier Housing in North Dakota," suggests that the German-Russians were the only pioneers who came from a physical background similar to that of this state.

He says they "were thus largely pre-adapted to the ways of life on the plains. They had the least need to modify their traditions. They were also the most likely group to construct sod houses."

In addition to the sod houses these pioneers used four basic construction methods, according to Rev. William Sherman of Grand Forks. All were borrowed from Russian housing methods: "puddled clay with occasional mixture of rock rubble, the adobe type of clay brick, the stone house with clay mortar and the rammed earth style."

"A fifth and less frequent variation was used by some early German settlers, a type of wattle and daub which is upright poles interspersed laterally with sticks and saplings in a latticework kind of structure. Clay was daubed onto the framework until the walls reached a desired thickness."

He advises: "As it is difficult to

Sun-baked bricks mixed of clay, straw

These clay bricks, displayed by Alvina Schnabel of Bismarck, were taken from houses near Ashley and Selby, South Dakota. Stick was inserted into brick on right, probably as support.

Sun-baked bricks for German-Russian homes were made by first digging a large shallow hole in the ground, then mixing local clay, straw and water in it, says Edmund Schnabel of Bismarck. "Lots of people mixed this with their feet. Or they would lead a horse around in it," recalls Schnabel.

When the clay, straw and water were well blended, the mixture was packed tightly in forms. These were long wooden troughs with two-by-four dividers to form bricks about six by six inches and ten to fourteen inches long. They dried until solid enough to hold together. Then they were removed to bake hard in the sun and the forms used for the next batch.

All summer the bricks dried. By fall they were usually ready for building, and were put together with a mortar of wet clay of the same type.

Also made of these clay and straw bricks were the big heating ovens which were a unique feature of the German-Russian homes. Nina Farley Wishek describes these ovens in "Along the Trails of Yesterday." About five feet in each direction, they were built into the partition between two rooms, she says, often projecting into the living room. These big ovens were used primarily for heat, but also for baking bread through an iron door facing into the kitchen. The door for firing was nearly level with the floor in an outer room or storm shed.

For summer use a similar oven was built outside. This was rounded, with only one large opening at the end. To bake bread the bricks were first heated thoroughly with a big fire inside the oven. When hot, the ashes were raked out, the oven was cleaned and bread placed inside. Ten or twelve "monstrous" loaves were baked at one time, says Wishek. Baking took two hours since the loaves were so large.

Bread was unquestionably the staff of life for these big German-Russian families, according to Wishek who gives a typical size as "six, eight, ten and even fifteen children — and I have known of families with twenty and twenty-four."

The big loaves of bread, baked in these homemade clay-brick ovens by an experienced hand, she says, were "invariably light and sweet and perfectly baked, with a faintly nutty flavor coming from the manner of baking and the flour used." *F.B.*

Inside view of the Holler house east of Ashley on Highway 10. Note deep window sills and cement-like plaster covering brick interior.

Outdoor ovens were built in a similar manner. Ukrainians Dan and Marian Letvin, Kief, built this oven of clay and flax straw for baking bread at Butte Jubilee.

separate the 'German' from the 'Russian' in the study of German-Russian housing forms, so also it is difficult at this distance in time to distinguish the 'Russian-German' from the early American. The question 'who borrowed from whom?' must be approached with caution, and the investigator must be satisfied at times with some very tentative conclusions."

Tim Kloberdanz, assistant professor of sociology at North Dakota State University, says the clay brick homes were more durable than sod houses and didn't wash as much in the rain. Clay brick also allowed better control of architecture since windows could be set and walls stuccoed and whitewashed.

With an eye toward functional usage rather than ethnic individuality, the German-Russian rammed earth dwellings are still being studied for their energy efficiency in natural cooling and heating, Hafermehl says.

The Johannes Goldade house at rural Linton is a particularly well-preserved example of the German-Russian form, says Jackie Sluss, formerly an architectural historian with the State Historical Society.

The house is constructed of handmade clay bricks on a sandstone slab foundation. Mortar throughout the house is a mixture of native clay, straw and water. Bricks were made by ramming a similar mixture into a wood mold.

Wet bricks were sun-dried for several months, Sluss explains. When dried, the bricks were hard enough to spark a flint and insulate against extreme heat and cold.

The house, built in 1890, has been lived in continuously and currently is occupied by the Gerard Goldade family.

"There's quite a bit of cold air that comes in, especially by the windows, but we keep our heaters going," says Linda Goldade in an interview. "There isn't anything that's really wrong with it. We just don't have enough money now to get another house."

She says she, her husband and their son, also named Gerard, stay in the kitchen and bedroom and use the third room for storage since one of the walls is caving in.

It's a 19-by-50-foot, one-story house, with gabled roof and the "vorhausel," or entryway, characteristic of early German-Russian housing, Sluss says.

Nominating the Goldade house to the National Register of Historic Places Sluss wrote: "The existence of these houses on the North Dakota prairie symbolizes the continuity of highly stable German-Russian communities: rural and village communities bound by common church affiliations, language, customs, family and history."

Stone houses were built in many German-Russian settlements. Where available, flat rocks were often used without mortar.

The Hutmacher complex at Manning is the best-known example of the stone slab construction technique in North Dakota, according to the Historical Society.

This method was brought to North Dakota from eastern Europe by Ukrainian and German-Russian immigrants and was used most in the late settlement of the state's southwest corner, says Kurt Schweigert of Bismarck, who prepared the Historical Society's nomination of the Hutmacher complex to the National Register of Historic Places.

The Valentine Hutmacher farmstead was built at the complex in 1911 by an immigrant from South Russia. "And although in ruins, it established the ethnic-cultural continuity of the building method," Schweigert says.

"The Frank Hutmacher farm (built in 1928) is a very late utilization of the stone slab building technique," he says. It was abandoned in the summer of 1979.

"All of the Hutmacher farmstead buildings are made of sandstone slabs quarried from nearby hilltops and erected crib-like with a clay-straw composition mortar," notes Schweigert.

Alexander Hutmacher, now of Dickinson, lived in the Frank Hutmacher residence until 1979, when he was 29. Frank was his father. "It was warm in the winter, and cool in the summer," Alexander said in an interview, pointing out that the rock walls are two feet thick. "I considered myself lucky to be living in a house that old."

Another typical first home on the claim was the tar paper shack, though it was notoriously ill-suited to withstand either the heat of summer or the cold of winter.

Where immigrants settled, they also built churches.

Carpenters John Krivatski and John Schowchuk supervised construction on the Ukrainian Greek Orthodox Church at Wilton and carved out the icon screen and handmade tabernacle, says Nick Kassian of Wilton, who looks after the church property.

"They didn't have blueprints," Kassian recalls. "They had a picture in their minds from the old country."

The Grassy Butte post office is the last known remaining example of Ukrainian-type log and clay plaster construction in North Dakota.

Built in 1914, the post office served the area until 1963. It is maintained by the McKenzie County Historical Society as a museum.

Sandy Paraskeva

Ukrainian mud and wattle home of Dan and Polly Cerkoney was built near Gorham in 1909. Construction is of wood, cedar poles and clay mixed with horse dung and straw, with four-sided roof.

Pioneers tell memories

As the 1930s and the Great Depression came to an end, some of North Dakota's immigrant pioneers were given an opportunity to record some of the history in which they had participated.

Their memories and thoughts about the old country and establishing new homes in America were collected by traveling interviewers employed under the federal Works Projects Administration.

Most said they were happy with their new lives. However, some might have done things a little differently if they had had another chance.

"Well, if I could live my life over, I don't think I'd come to North Dakota. The homestead made an old man out of me before my time," said Adolph J. Stuth, Williston.

Stuth was born in Franzburg, Germany. He immigrated to the United States as a youngster and worked in Chicago factories for a time before breaking North Dakota sod in 1903.

"I had a good steady job in Chicago, but I was anxious to get out and see what there was to be had somewhere else," he said.

"Things have been so different out here. In Illinois I would have been ashamed to live in a tar-papered shack, but out here I didn't care. Everybody was doing the same thing just to get a little start."

First impressions of America differed.

"When we landed in New York I was so disappointed in America that if I would have had the money to return to Sweden I would have gone right back again," said Andrew Gustafson, Langdon, who left the old country at age 21.

"My first impression of America was not very good when I first came here, as we felt that we were lost all the time. Especially when we came to Bismarck and Mandan, which were very small towns at the time," said Martin Graner, Huff.

Graner was born in Austria-Hungary and came to the Mandan area as a youngster.

Karolina Anderson, Ludden, left her home in a small Finnish village for America in 1902.

Upon her arrival, she was disappointed.

"There was always white bread and so much light eats, and such poor houses I never saw; and I would have gone right back if I had the money. I never saw people burning cow chips (before) and it didn't look good to me," she said.

Lina A. Haugen, Esmond, left Norway in 1928. "We did not see much of the country in America

Homes were plain inside, many held only bare necessities as in the log house below. Note unfinished sod wall at right. But a few treasured items brought from a far-off land were likely to be stored carefully somewhere in a trunk. At right are such articles: a photo of the old home in Holland, tea server and china. Small silver box in center foreground is a "snuif doos," sniff box, which held a sponge with a drop of perfume. In church it was passed down the pew for sniffing as people in Dutch communities today pass peppermints or lemon drops.

until we got into the Middle West. There we thought the whole thing was turned around," she said.

"There we saw cows feeding out on flat fields, while in Norway the fields were almost sacred and no cattle were allowed there."

The prairies, she recalled, "seemed like big oceans."

Swan Peterson told of a "religious wave" that was rolling over his native Sweden in 1876. "We had revival meetings, and if anyone sat down to the table without a prayer he was a hog."

Peterson was in his 20s when he came to America. He remembered arriving in New York with 11 cents in his pocket, and spending that the next day for popcorn.

In 1903, he started a shoe repair shop at Pembina. There were no other Swedes there; in fact Scandinavians of any kind were scarce.

"There was only one Norwegian in Pembina, and he didn't want anybody to know it," Peterson said.

Peterson homesteaded in Williams County in 1908 and 13 years later opened a shoe shop in Williston.

His children, he recalled, weren't allowed to speak English until they started school. That was because, Peterson said, he wanted his son to "learn English right."

It was the availability of land that attracted most immigrants to North Dakota. But some had other reasons for leaving the old country.

Nestor Halonen of Dickey County emigrated from Finland in 1910. "I attended a political meeting as the Russians were trying to get control of the locality in which I lived. I, with others, opposed (Russian control), and the other two were arrested and I was given 24 hours to change my mind; and I left on that account."

Anterm Domaskin, who farmed near Ross, came to America from Russia in 1913, with the encouragement of two brothers who had gone before him.

He had unpleasant memories about serving in the Russian army and said he should have emigrated sooner to avoid military service.

"There they (the army) taught me what they called engineering. It was how to kill people. We were treated terrible, never had enough clothes nor enough to eat."

Domaskin's views about the government in his homeland had not changed over the years. "I think Russia has no business fighting Finland. That Stalin is a terrible skunk.

"The men in the army didn't know that the people at home are suffering because Stalin takes everything, the bum."

Many of the early settlers lost their farms when banks foreclosed on mortgages in the 1920s or '30s. Some then left North Dakota but others, like Nels P. Larsen, Williston, stayed.

"If I had my life to live over again, I would sell everything and keep the money," said Larsen, who was born in Denmark.

He also blamed economic hardship for his lack of attendance at church. "I would go to the Lutheran, but I can't give them any money and they expect some of it if you go."

Hard times were on the minds of many of the immigrant Americans.

William Abentko of Butte, a Ukrainian, recalled losing most of his 1903 crop during a September snowstorm. "Most of that winter all we had to eat was some cornmeal mush and soup with milk. Once a week we would have a potato for each of us. We considered ourselves lucky to have a cow, as a good many of our friends did not have one."

For others, religious convictions may have influenced the way they pursued a livelihood.

Gerrit Van Beek of Westfield was born in Holland and homesteaded in North Dakota after living for a time in Michigan and Iowa. "I didn't farm with oxen because they said if you farm with oxen you won't go to heaven and I want to get there," he related.

Emile Foussard of St. John had left his native France for a Rolette County homestead in 1882. He didn't believe in borrowing money, and that philosophy caused problems after he was elected to the local school board.

"I don't like mortgage on farm and I don't want school to be in debt," he said, telling of how he resigned immediately from the board when he learned that the other members didn't share his viewpoint.

Christine Sorenson, a Williston Dane, recalled having some regrets upon her 1904 arrival in North Dakota. "I just couldn't understand how anybody could live in such a country. The main street here was nothing but a dust bed," she said.

Sorenson's fiance had filed a claim on land 12 miles east of Williston. She told of attending a religious meeting and seeing "homesteaders there wearing overalls, and some had no socks inside their shoes."

A few of the immigrants shared anecdotes about adjusting to a new country and way of life.

Daniel Nickisch came to the Wishek area from Germany in 1881. Although unable to speak English, he got a job working on the railroad under an Irish foreman for 65 cents a day.

"Some of the fellows who could already speak English to some extent called me aside and told me that if the boss said anything, for me to say 'You big overgrown pig, don't tell me what to do.' Well, the boss happened to hear this conversation and he called me to the side and told me not to say that and, well, I didn't know so I said what the fellows told me to say. He didn't get angry because he knew the cause and its source."

Nickisch also told of the time he needed a chicken, but couldn't get one except from an English farmer. "Well, I went over to buy it but I couldn't make him understand what I wanted. So I put out my hands as wings and flapped them, as if I was flying.

"Well, he still didn't know what I wanted and I suppose he thought I was crazy. But finally I got a better idea and started jumping around and crowed like a rooster. Well, that did the trick and I got the rooster."

Some shared memories of social life on the prairie.

"There were quite a few Frenchmen who lived around (us) and every week we would gather at one house during the winter for a party and dance," recalled Emile Foussard.

He noted that there was usually "a lot to eat and a jug or two of liquor to drink" at those gatherings.

Asked to compare North Dakota with the country of their birth, some of the pioneers had mixed emotions. One of them was John O. Haugen, Maddock, who came from Norway in 1898.

He recalled that although it was difficult to make a living, there was no strife back among the green hills and mountains of Norway. But he had been stricken with America fever.

"I know that after I began thinking about going to America, I would dream about it both at day and night. I saw myself over here as a 'gaardsman' or farmer.

"I could see that beautiful place along a small river, the many windows in the magnificent building reflecting the glow of the setting sun, the well-fed herd grazing down the slope — in fact, not much different than this farm now looks with its location on the Sheyenne Coulee banks. I could see my contented family going and coming with cheerful expressions on their faces.

"Yes, I had dreams; and many of them nearly became facts for me. If the Depression had not come, many of them would be facts today."

Bob Jansen

Tracing Norwegian ancestry is eased with help of Colleen Oihus and 450 Bygdeboks at University of North Dakota library.

Tradition is savored through foods like these Swedish sand bakkelse served by Esther Asplund of Bismarck.

Back to the roots in a time of uncertainties, mass culture and high living standards. Throughout North Dakota and across the nation people are reclaiming their heritage—in foods, music, crafts, pageantry, genealogy and in travel.

Ethnic fun and pride mix as Icelandic Viking ship leads a parade through streets of Mountain, and teenager of Ukrainian ancestry sports her heritage.

Travel brings poignancy as a North Dakota son of Lebanese descent discovers this small village of Ain Arab and a relative in fez playing Arabic music.

Youth find inspiration and sense of belonging in ethnic celebrations. These boys in fancy dress contest show pleasure and excitement found at powwow.

Bibliography

Aberle, George P. *Anecdotes of the Prairies.* Printed by Quality Printing, Bismarck. *From the Steppes to the Prairies.* Printed by Bismarck Tribune, 1963.

Adams County Record. Hettinger.

Art of Cooking Ukrainian Style. Lesia Ukrainka Branch of the Ukrainian Women's Assoc. of Canada, Vancouver, B.C., 1965.

Berg, Francie M. *North Dakota: Land of Changing Seasons.* 1977. *South Dakota: Land of Shining Gold.* Flying Diamond Books, Box D301, Hettinger ND 58639, 1982.

Family Favorites Featuring Dutch Recipes. Hills Chapter of Western Christian High. Crescent Publishing Co., Hills, Minnesota. Second printing 1966.

The Greff Eater's Digest. Edited by Kas Greff and Peggy Greff, 1982.

The Greff Family: A History. Edited by Kas Greff and Peggy Greff.

Gulutsan, Lena. *The Mosquito's Wedding.* Kazka Productions Ltd. 1152-78 Ave., Edmonton, Alberta, Canada T6GON5, 1980.

Heritage Review. Edited by Armand Bauer. Germans from Russia Heritage Society, 1008 Central Avenue, Bismarck ND 58501.

In Retrospect: Teaching in North Dakota. Edited by Marie Mynster Feidler. North Dakota Retired Teachers Association, 1976.

Kovash, Emily. *Children of the Prairie.* Printed by Lorraine and George Kovash, New Hradec, North Dakota, 1975.

Nadvornik, Frank. *My Experiences.* Unpublished manuscript by F. Nadvornik of Dickinson, 1936.

North Dakota Horizons. Greater North Dakota Assoc., 107 Roberts St., Fargo ND 58102.

North Dakota Indians: A Time of Transition. Bismarck Tribune, October 23, 1981.

North Dakota REC Magazine. N.D. Association of Rural Electric Cooperatives, Box 727, Mandan ND 58554.

North Dakota: The American Guide Series. Federal Writers' Project, Works Progress Administration. Copyright State Historical Society of North Dakota, 1938.

Pohl, Federick J. *The Viking Settlements of North America.* Clarkson N. Potter, Inc. New York, 1972.

Polzin, Theresita. *The Polish Americans: Whence & Whither.* Franciscan Publishers, Pulaski WI 54162, 1973.

Potter, Edgar R. *Whoa...Yuh Sonsabitches.* Griggs Printing & Publishing. Havre, Montana, 1977.

Prairies Magazine. Edited and published by Warren Overlie, Box 178, Ashley ND 58413, 1977.

Robinson, Elwyn B. *History of North Dakota.* University of Nebraska Press, Lincoln NE 68504, 1966.

Rolfsrud, Erling Nicolai, *The Story of North Dakota.* Lantern Books, Alexandria, Minnesota, 1963.

Rolvaag, O.E. *Giants in the Earth.* Harper & Row, New York, 1927.

St. Olaf Lutheran Church. *75th Anniversary Cookbook.* Turtle Lake, North Dakota, 1977.

Shank, Margarethe Erdahl. *The Coffee Train.* Doubleday & Co., Garden City, New York, 1953.

Sherman, William C. *Prairie Mosaic: An Ethnic Atlas of Rural North Dakota.* ND. Institute for Regional Studies. North Dakota State University, Fargo, 1983.

Songs We Love to Sing. North Dakota Historical Society of Germans from Russia, Box 1671, Bismarck N.D. 58501, 1977.

Spiewniczek Koscielny. St. Stanislaus Church, Warsaw. (Polish songs.) Stan Stanislowski, Rt. 1, Minto ND 58261, 1983.

Stavig, Art. *Grandpa's Troll Stories.* Pine Hill Press, Freeman 57029, 1975.

They Chose Minnesota: A Survey of the State's Ethnic Groups. Edited by June Drenning Holmquist. Minnesota Historical Society Press, St. Paul, Minnesota, 1981.

Thompson, Era Bell. *American Daughter.* University of Chicago Press, 1946, revised 1967.

Time for Trolls. Told by Asbjornsen and Moe. Edited by Joan Roll-Hansen. Tanum, Norli, Oslo, Norway, 1962.

Trolls of District IV. Edited by Valborg Fisher. Sons of Norway, Bismarck ND 58501.

Tryckare, Tre. *The Viking.* Published in Sweden. U.S.A. publisher: Crescent Books, Crown Publishers, 1967.

Tweton, Jerome D. and Jelliff, Theodore B. *North Dakota: the Heritage of a People.* North Dakota Institute for Regional Studies, NDSU, Fargo, 1976.

Ukrainian Cultural Institute Newsletter. Edited by Agnes Palanuk. Ukrainian Cultural Institute, Box 6, Dickinson State College, Dickinson ND 58601.

United Tribes News. Edited by Shirley Bordeaux. United Tribes Educational Technical Center Office of Public Information, 3315 South Airport Road, Bismarck ND 58501.

Viking Magazine. Sons of Norway, 1455 West Lake Street, Minneapolis MN 55408.

Vrooman, Nicholas, Edit. *Iron Spirits.* North Dakota Council of Arts, Fargo.

Walters, Thorstina. *Modern Sagas: the Story of Icelanders in North America.* North Dakota Institute for Regional Studies, NDSU, Fargo, 1953.

We, the People. Bismarck Tribune, February 16, 1982.

Welcome to Assumption Abbey and *Life Together.* Brochures by Assumption Abbey Press, Richardton ND 58652.

Wishek, Nina Farley. *Along the Trails of Yesterday: A Story of McIntosh County.* The Ashley Tribune, 1941. New edition available from Max A. Wishek, Ashley ND 58413.

Wisness, Hilda and Quarve, Levard. *Viking Settlement Days.* Viking Lutheran Church, 1936.

Wold, Frances. *Prairie Scrapbook.* Printed by Borlaug Publishing Company, Washburn ND 58577, 1982.

Photo Credits

Cover photos, clockwise from upper left: North Dakota Travel Department, F. Berg, Bismarck Tribune, William Kosmatka, Ukrainian Cultural Institute, Bismarck Tribune, North Dakota Travel Department, (center) Inger Dahlin.
Assumption Abbey: 66a, 66b

A hallingdal Norwegian spinning wheel.

Attiyeh Foundation: 1
Babinski, Gary: 34e
Berg collection: 6,34b, 34c, 71a, 96, 97, 99a, 150
Berg, F.: 9b, 12, 32, 35b, 38a, 39a, 39b, 39c, 41c, 43d, 43e, 44b, 45c, 45d, 45e, 46c, 49c, 51c, 51d, 65b, 75, 79, 91b, 122, 126b, 158, 162a
Berg, Rolf: 57, 94, 99b, 99c, 171
Bismarck Tribune: 18, 21, 33, 34a, 34d, 35a, 36, 41a, 43a, 43b, 43c, 44a, 45a, 49a, 49b, 49d, 50, 65a, 69, 70b, 71b, 81, 82 83a, 83b, 84b, 85b, 87b, 87f, 90, 91a, 92, 100, 113, 123b, 130a, 134a, 134b, 135, 136, 141, 159b, 161, 165a, 165b
Dickinson Press: 37a, 37b
Ficek, Albert: 19, 55, 133
Friez, Earleen: 51a, 51b
Grant County News, Duane Schatz: 61b, 61f, 110
Hakanson, Odell: 62, 63
Heidt, Ida: 118
Kosmatka, William: 24
LeFebre, Greta: 126a
Minot Daily News: 3, 29, 38b, 61e, 73, 104, 146
Mott Pioneer Press: 27b
Myrdal, Rosemarie: 16, 41b, 107a, 107b, 109
North Dakota Travel Department: 9a, 27a, 27c, 84a, 91c, 103, 123a, 124
Schnabel, Alvina: 17, 30, 45b, 61d, 114a, 114b, 115, 117, 159a
Sigfusson, Ava: 40a, 40b, 46a, 46b, 106, 164
South Dakota Travel Department: 160, 162b
State Historical Society of North Dakota: 22, 74, 76, 89, 116, 121, 139a, 139b, 144, 147, 151, 153, 154, 157
Stubbins Pat: 140a, 140b, 165c
Trolls of District IV, Valborg Fisher: 58
Ukrainian Cultural Institute: 14, 28a, 28b, 52, 54, 70a, 130b, 165d
United States Library of Congress: 148
United Tribes Educational Technical Center: 5, 10, 35c, 61a, 61c, 78, 85a, 87a, 87c, 87d, 87e, 93, 166
University of North Dakota: 108

Letters designate photographs in clockwise order beginning with upper left.

We want to express our gratitude to the many people who contributed to this book. Many have shared their feelings and experiences through interviews and personal writings; they have offered results of extensive research and have loaned photographs from personal collections.

We are particularly indebted to the Rev. William C. Sherman for his willingness to serve as resource person for the editor of this book and the Bismarck Tribune journalists in writing the special edition, "We, the People." We are also grateful to Sherman's team of professors from the University of North Dakota, North Dakota State University and Bismarck Junior College, who are researching ethnic groups in North Dakota for a forthcoming book to be edited by Sherman, for sharing their expertise with the Tribune writers, and to Dr. Kang-tsung Chang for use of his map charting ethnic distribution.

We thank the representatives from North Dakota ethnic groups who gathered photographs and other materials, especially Rosemarie Myrdal, Mountain; Agnes Palanuk, Dickinson; Lillian and Albert Ficek, New Hradec; Alvina Schnabel, Bismarck; Gary Babinski, Minto and also the staff at the United Tribes News and the Minot Daily News.

Again we express our appreciation to the management, writers and photographers of the Bismarck Tribune for making available the two special editions on which this book is based. In addition we are grateful for the opportunity to reprint from writings of the following: George Aberle, Robert Boxrud, Kas Greff, Frank Nadvornik, Era Bell Thompson, Marja Venscha, Nina Farley Wishek and Frances Wold.

about the publisher

Organized by Arab Americans, descendants of Arab immigrants to the prairies and plains, the Attiyeh Foundation was formed as a means of continuing appreciation of a rich cultural heritage in the new world.

The Attiyeh Foundation offers cultural and educational programs all over the United States designed to bridge the knowledge gap between Americans and Arabs, and to help Arab Americans retain their ethnic heritage. With the ever-increasing global importance of the Middle East, the Attiyeh Foundation stresses the importance of greater understanding between Arabs and Americans. National outreach programs provide opportunities for personal contact and direct experience with Arab culture and history through lectures, conferences, film, art and photographic exhibitions, antiquities displays, essay contests, exchange programs and publications.

The foundation offers information and referral services to Americans interested in the Arab world and contemporary Middle East affairs. Through its support of talented individuals working to heighten social and cultural awareness between Americans and Arabs, the Attiyeh Foundation creates links with communities and groups across America, with particular emphasis on the midwest.

The word "Attiyeh," from the root word "to give," means "gift of god" in Arabic. The name comes from a pre-Islamic group of inhabitants of the Arabian peninsula whose descendants today extend throughout the Middle East, Africa and the Americas.

The Attiyeh Foundation was incorporated in 1980 in Colorado by descendants of Arab immigrants to the midwest. It is a non-profit, tax exempt organization based in Washington, D.C. and has received funding from, among others, the National Endowment for the Humanities, Hughes Aircraft and Westinghouse Electric Corporation. The foundation may be reached by contacting Michael Saba, president, or Paula Stinson, director: The Attiyeh Foundation; 1806 T Street Northwest, Suite 201; Washington, D.C. 20009.

about the author

Francie M. Berg from Hettinger, North Dakota, is a teacher, youth leader, historian, regional publisher and author. Born on a family homestead in the Missouri River breaks, she grew up on a ranch near Miles City, Montana. Her ethnic heritage is Swedish and old stock American: Scotch-Irish, English, French and German. Her husband Bert, a Hettinger veterinarian, is Norwegian, and for the first five years of marriage they lived on the Berg family farm near Maddock in a solidly-Norwegian community.

Berg's regional books, *"North Dakota: Land of Changing Seasons"* and *"South Dakota: Land of Shining Gold"* are the first two volumes of her *Old West Region Series* which will span five states. She also writes self-help and is the author of the 1983 book *"How to Be Slimmer, Trimmer & Happier."* She graduated from Montana State University and obtained a master's degree in family social science and anthropology at the University of Minnesota.

The Bergs are active in 4-H and international programs. Both Francie and her husband have been International Farm Youth Exchangees, to Switzerland and England-Wales, and were leaders on a 4-H Labo exchange to Japan. They have four children, Kathy, Rick, Cindy and Michael.

Index

Abdalla, Mike, 140
Aberle, Msgr. George, 117
Anderson, Yvonne, 17
Anglo-Saxon, 70
Arab Americans, 1, 8, 30, 138-141
Arab mosque, 73
Architecture, 157-160
Arikara, 8, 75, 83, 84, 91
Armenian, 143
Assumption Abbey, 66
Azure, George and Elizabeth, 80

Backman, Emily, 65
Baker, Paige and Cora, 91
Baptism, 10, 72
Barkie, Evelyn, 139
Basaraba, Pete, 128
Basketry, 32, 34
Bauer, Armand, 113, 114
Beadwork, 32, 34, 35
Belgian, 8, 143
Bemis, Myrtle, 101
Blacks, 8, 145, 146
Bohemian. See Czech.
Bohemian band, 16
Boutrous, Floyd, 138
Boxrud, Robert, 58
Brauche, 56
Brethren (Dunkards), 67, 151, 156
Bricks, sun-baked, 157-160
Brown, Sara, 68
Brydl, Rev. Ladislaus, 132, 134
Bulgarian, 144
Bullhead, Earl, 26
Burns', Robert, birthday, 60

Cambodia, 143
Canada, 9, 10, 120, 122, 123, 143, 153
Canadian, 8, 9, 13, 125
Case, Jack E., 60, 75
Catholic, 7, 8, 11, 12, 62-65, 70-73, 88, 137
Celebrations, 10, 11, 52-61
Celtic, 8, 120-123
Cemeteries, 74, 75
Chang, Kang-tsung, 13
Chinese, 143, 144
Chippewa, 8, 25, 26, 32, 34, 35, 75, 82, 88, 89
Christianson, Randy, 50
Christmas, 10, 52, 53, 56, 58, 59
Churches, 10, 62-75
Church conflict, 69-72
Congregationalist, 62
Cowboys, 144, 146
Crafts, 10, 11, 32-41
Cree, 8, 25, 26
Cree, Francis and Rose, 32, 34
Crowfeather, Adrian, 81
Cuban, 143
Czech (Bohemian), 7, 8, 11, 16, 19, 22, 43, 47, 53, 55, 69, 132-135, 150

Dancing, 11, 13, 15, 24-31
Danish, 8, 10, 45, 64, 102, 103, 163
Danish mill, 102, 103
Davis, Tom, 88, 89
Dosch, Mike, 16, 18
Duda, Rev. Stanislaus, 19, 53, 136
Dulcimer, 21
Dutch, 8, 45, 67, 126, 127, 144, 162, 163

Earthlodges, 79
Easter eggs (pysanky), 32, 37
Eastman, Oliver, 79
Eichkoff, Rev. Hildebrand, 72
English, 8, 22, 34, 44, 45, 120-123, 144
Episcopalian, 62, 68, 122
Ethnic communities, 8, 10, 15, 77
Ethnic distribution, 13

Farris, Mary, 140, 141
Feickert, Gloria, 36, 50
Feser, Phyllis, 112, 113
Ficek, Albert and Lillian, 53, 55, 132-135
Finnish, 8, 46, 53, 64, 104-106, 151, 161, 163
Fix, Patricia, 16, 134, 137
Folk songs, 16-23
Foods, 9-11, 15, 42-51
Fox, Connie, 80, 81
Freeburg, Don, 49
French, 8, 22, 25, 65, 82, 88, 124, 125, 163
Freytag, Gustav, 17
Friez, Earleen, 51
Fruth, Rev. Glen, 67
Fort Berthold reservation, 83, 84, 91
Fort Totten reservation, 84, 85, 93
Funeral, 10, 74, 75, 99

Geiger, Wilhelmina, 50
German, 8, 13, 22, 37, 42-44, 51, 52, 59, 64, 67, 110-119, 144, 151, 160, 161, 163
German-Hungarian. See Hungarian.
German-Russian, 7-11, 13, 17-19, 22, 23, 40-44, 50, 51, 56, 63, 71, 72, 74, 113-119, 153, 156, 157, 160
Gerszewski, Walter, 136, 137
Gift-giving, 75
Gilbertson, Bishop Roy, 64, 71
Gillette, Vance, 79
Gipp, Louis, 92
Goldade, Linda, 160
Goodhouse, Rev. Innocent, 68
Gray, Leroy, 81
Greek Orthodox, 70, 71, 141
Greff, Kas, 58, 59
Gross, John J., 17
Gudajtes, Ed, 136, 137
Gudajtes, Kathy, 25
Gypsies, 143

Halich, Wasyl, 17
Hardanger embroidery, 33, 36, 41
Hardanger violin, 20
Harju, Otto, 104, 105
Harris, Marcia, 146
Heidt, Ida Greff, 58, 59, 118, 119
Helphrey, Juanita, 81
Hendrickson, Lucille, 65, 73, 80, 86, 90, 92
Henry, Jim, 82
Herigstad, Oman B., 95
Hidatsa, 8, 25, 26, 75, 83, 84
Hjelm-Hansen, Paul, 95
Homesteads, 8, 153-156
Horner, Virgil, 30, 31
Hostetler, John, 75
Hostfest, 60, 61
Houses
sod, 154, 155, 157, 160
sun-baked, brick, 157-160
Howard, Thomas, 125
Hudson, John, 157
Hungarian, 7, 8, 22, 63, 112, 113, 156
Hurinenko, George and Julia, 129
Hutmacher, Alexander, 160
Hutterites, 67, 75

Icelandic, 8, 10, 17, 22, 23, 46, 52, 53, 56, 57, 59, 106-109, 165
Icelandic independence, 59
Immigrants, 148-163
Indian, 8, 10, 11, 17, 21, 24-27, 50, 52, 68, 75, 79-93, 166
Irish, 8, 25, 120, 122, 144
Iron crosses, 7, 12
Italian, 144

Jahner, Joe and Beata, 118, 119
Jansen, Bob, 96, 101, 102, 105, 108, 111, 143, 152, 163
Jelinek, Agnes, 132, 133
Jewish, 8, 47, 50, 69, 142
Johnson, Larry, 82, 89, 110, 115
Johnson, Marlin, 17
Johnsrud, Joanna, 95
Juel, Dick, 48
Juleboks, 57
Juma Sr., Charlie, 138, 139

Kadrmas, Chuck, 16
Kamins, Norman, 142
Katus, Tom, 11, 12
Keogh, Brooks, 147
Kinders, Mark, 26, 54, 129, 131, 135
King, Shirley, 80
Kinnoin, Frithiof, 151
Kinzel, Gabe, 16
Kloberdanz, Tim, 56, 74, 110, 113, 114, 160
Kolar, Joe, 132
Kottsick, Charles, 132, 134
Kraft, Pius, 31
Kuczynski, Judith, 32
Kuylen, John, 126

Language, 10, 11, 13
Laos, 143
Latvian, 143
Lebanese, 12, 44, 47, 138-141, 151, 165
Lima, Ole, 95, 96, 152
Lindbergh, Duane, 74, 75
Link, Arthur, 111
Loynes, Hazel J., 67
Lunday, Berneice, 72, 73
Lutefisk, 48, 49, 58
Lutheran, 8, 11, 62-65, 71, 73, 98, 99, 105
Luxembourg, 143
Lynch, Rosemary, 27, 81, 85, 93

Mandan 8, 75, 83, 84
Markley, Tei-Tei, 48
Matejcek, R. F., 132, 134
Mattern, Leo, 31

McKay, Carl, 84, 85
Melstad, Mrs. Alvin, 17
Mennonites, 67
Methodist, 62, 122
Metis, 8, 26, 88, 89, 125
Mexican, 8, 143, 144
Midsummer Day, 101
Miele, Frank, 97
Miller, Patrick, 49
Mischt ("Russian lignite"), 117
Misialek, Katie, 137
Missouri Synod, 64, 110
Moore, Rex, 85
Moslem, 73, 138-141

Nadvornik, Frank, 17, 55, 150, 151
Newgard, Thomas, 145
North Dakota Federal Writers project, 8, 127
Norwegian, 7, 8, 11, 13, 19, 22, 25, 28, 29, 37-39, 42, 45, 46, 48, 49, 53, 57, 59, 60, 61, 64, 74, 75, 94-99, 161, 163, 165

Ojibwa, 8, 88
Oktoberfest, 59, 61
Old stock American, 9, 144-147
Omafray, Catherine, 69, 70
Ovens, sun-baked brick, 158

Pacifism, 67
Palanuk, Agnes, 20, 75, 128
Paper cutting, 32, 35
Paraskeva, Sandy, 160
Patneaud, Alvina, 81
Peace churches, 67
Peace Gardens, 9
Peace Pipe Indian Center, 80, 81
Pearson, John, 53, 67, 113
Pecka, Myron, 16
Pedeliski, Ted, 20, 115
Peterson, Sig and Marge, 96, 97
Polish, 8, 11, 12, 19, 22, 24, 25, 32, 34, 35, 46, 47, 53, 63, 64, 136, 137, 144
Powwow, 11, 21, 26, 27, 60, 87
Preabt, Dorothy, 17
Prepiora, Stephanie, 137
Presbyterian, 62, 122
Procive, Lana, 24, 25, 54
Prohibition, 11
Protestant, 70-72
Pysanky. See Easter eggs.

Quanrud, Ted, 122, 147
Quilting, 32, 34

Railroad grant lands, 8, 153, 156
Reinke, Rolland, 48
Reiten, Chester, 60
Religious institutions, 62-75
Richardson, Donna, 68
Rockenback, Judy, 34
Rolvaag, Ole, 8
Rosemaling, 35, 60
Rumanian, 8
Runs After, Gordon, 27
Rush, Don, 26
Russell, Vicki, 21

Saba, George, 151
Saba, Michael, 30, 138, 139, 141
Sauerkraut Day, 59, 60
Sauna, 104-106
Schnabel, Edmund, 117, 158
Schneider, Mary Jane, 75
Schweigert, Kurt, 160
Scotch, 8, 22, 60, 120-123, 144
Seventh-day Adventist, 73
Sherman, William, 9, 13, 62, 67, 72, 94, 95, 100-102, 105, 110, 113, 115, 143, 145, 157
Silverman, Sam, 142
Sioux, 8, 32, 35, 75, 84-86, 90, 92
Skaff, George, 140
Skye, Harriet, 87
Smith, Matilda Stagel, 10
Sod houses, 154, 155, 157, 160
Soliders, 144
Sologuk, Nick and Anna, 130, 131
Southeast Asian, 8, 143
Spinning, 36, 40, 41
Spotted Horse, Emerald, 93
Sprynczynatyk, Connie, 34, 36
Standing Rock reservation, 86, 90, 92
Strasburg Blue Room, 30, 31
Stein, Rose, 63
Stelter, Stan, 56, 127
Storlie, Helen, 25
Strand, Serena, 10
Struchynski, John, 128
Sturlaugson, Bill, 59
Stuth, Adolph, 161
Sun Dance, 68
Swedish, 8, 13, 17, 42, 44, 45, 48, 62, 64, 65, 69-71, 100, 101, 161,163, 165
Swift Horse, Harry and Lillian, 32, 90, 91
Swigart, Mary, 85
Swiss, 143, 144
Syrian. See Arab American, Lebanese.

Thailand, 143
Thompson, Era Bell, 138, 145, 146
Thorson, P.V., 74, 94, 96, 101, 102, 107
Thunderhawk, Wallace, 27
Tibor brothers, 18
Tole painting, 34
Trolls, 58
Turosak, Greg, 68, 79, 84, 91, 126, 129
Turtle Mountain reservation, 82

Ukrainian, 7, 8, 10, 11, 15, 17, 20, 23-25, 28, 32, 37, 42, 43, 52-54, 65, 69-71, 75, 128-131, 160, 161, 165
United Tribes, 10, 93

Vallevik, Osmund, 19
Van Boven, Gerritt, 126, 127
Venscha, Marja, 28
Viking community, 98, 99
Vrooman, Nicholas, 75

Walters, Thorstina, 56, 57, 107, 108
Weddings, 10, 54, 55, 98
Wedding dances, 30, 31, 63
Welk, Lawrence, 18
Welsh, 120, 144
Westley, Hans, 157
Wezelman, Sol, 69
Whalen, Kevin, 31
Wheat weaving, 34, 36
White, Matilda, 91
Whitman, Carl, 79
Wilkins, Robert, 122
Wilson, Bob, 27
Winter, Abe, 69, 139, 142
Wishek, Nina Farley, 40, 116, 117, 158
Wold, Frances, 42, 43, 70

Zander, Dominic, 63
Zimmerman, Robert, 60